Jill,

Thank you for everything!
YOU HAVE INNER STRENGTH!

Best wishes,
Brian J. Marinelli

DISCOVER *your* INNER *Strength*

INSIGHT PUBLISHING
SEVIERVILLE, TENNESSEE

Insight Publishing Presents ...

DISCOVER YOUR INNER STRENGTH

Shannon Cassidy

Dr. Ken Blanchard

Yun Li

Dr. Larry J. Linden

Brian J. Marinelli

Mona Pearl

Stephen Covey

Margie Warrell

Sara Canuso

Mike Jay

Brian Tracy

Scott V. Black

Arty Coppes, MA
ACC

Alice Fulton-
Osborne & Patty
Liston

Ann Tardy

Joy Klepac

Contents

INTERVIEWS WITH...

A Message from the Publisher

I've faced many challenges in my life and I know what it means to struggle. I sure wish I'd had this book during those times. We handpicked some of the most successful people we know who have had to learn how to discover their inner strength. The authors I interviewed for this book have the experience and knowledge that will help everyone learn a little more about this vital component for success—inner strength.

This book is custom designed for those who want to increase their skills and knowledge. Self-development is vital to success. One author made this poignant observation: "Self-development tends to fall to the bottom of the priority list for most people and they are not the only ones to suffer for this choice. Their family suffers. Their coworkers suffer. Their employees suffer. All of the crucial relationships in their life suffer because they are not being the absolute best they could truly be."

If you strive for excellence and want valuable information about how some of the most successful people in business today have found their inner strength and achieved success, this book is the resource you need. People who want to hone their skills to cope with life's challenges will learn from what these authors have to say. I know that I did and I believe you will too.

Interviews Conducted by:
David E. Wright, President
Insight Publishing & International Speakers Network

Leverage Leadership Strengths

AN INTERVIEW WITH...

Shannon Cassidy

bridge between, inc.
Two Penn Center, Suite 200
Philadelphia, PA 19102
610-431-2888
Shannon@bridgebetween.org
www.bridgebetween.org

ABOUT THE AUTHOR

Shannon Cassidy is the Executive Director of bridge between inc., www.bridgebetween.org. She helps leaders (particularly VP's and executives) bridge the gap from where they are presently to where they want to be. She and her clients devise strength-based action plans for leading high performance teams, communicating with vision and inspiration, successfully navigating corporate politics, and creating win-win resolutions to conflict. She holds a corporate negotiation training certification from Harvard Law School. A sought-after keynote speaker, she has presented on topics such as "The Power of Questions," "Political Savvy," and "Leading With Strengths" at national conferences, women's events, and corporate retreats. Audiences and meeting planners rave about her speaking. A senior director at *TV Guide* said, "Shannon immediately engages her audience with energy, a sense of humor, and colorful personal stories."

Shannon has authored several articles and has been featured on Forbes.com as one of the Top Five Coaches in Philadelphia. Before starting her own company, Shannon spent years as a corporate leader.

DAVID WRIGHT (WRIGHT)

Today we're talking with Shannon Cassidy. She is the executive director of bridge between inc., www.bridgebetween.org. She coaches and mentors corporate leaders on political savvy, executive presence and emotional intelligence.

Shannon, welcome to *Discover Your Inner Strength.*

SHANNON CASSIDY (CASSIDY)

Thank you, David.

WRIGHT

So many folks define strengths as things that they're good at. How do you define strengths?

CASSIDY

It all comes down to having the answer contain questions, David. When we ask ourselves, "What energizes me and makes me feel good," we connect to our strengths. Regardless of talent and skill, an activity you're naturally attracted to and strengthened by is an inner strength. When engaged with strengthening activities, time disappears—you get lost in the moment because the activity is a vehicle for pleasure.

One of my favorite management thinkers, Peter Drucker, says, "Most Americans do not know what their strengths are. When you ask them, they look at you with a blank stare, or they respond in terms of subject knowledge, which is the wrong answer." It's about passion and energy—not about technical expertise.

WRIGHT

Shannon, what would you say would be the biggest benefit to focusing on strengths?

CASSIDY

It's natural—strengths are the natural DNA of a person's innermost passion and desire. Working and focusing on weaknesses is a drain. Notice that my voice and tone lower just talking about it. It's a downer. There is notable pain associated with fixing what's perceived to be broken. Many of us have bought into this concept of fixing weaknesses so much that we are challenged to think of our strengths in any real way. Remedial development and weakness-based management are what a lot of companies, and some managers, are accustomed to doing either because they're not really focused on strength or not aware of the power of strength development. Focusing on strengths is not only easier, it's more sustainable and far more beneficial.

The results of strength-based leadership validate effectiveness. People are more motivated to focus on their strengths. Once they identify what strengthens them, they become drawn to those activities. Passion and purpose result from team players volunteering their strengths and appreciating the unique value of other team members. No one person is perfectly well-rounded and can do all things. The concept of team, however, is designed so that all of us imperfect people, with unique and specific strengths, combine to make a well-rounded team whose purpose is to make the greatest contribution.

I had the opportunity to facilitate a team-building Lead With Strengths program for one of our clients. We had a lot of fun crafting each person's strength activity statement. One person—an advertising sales rep named Chris—was strengthened by analyzing trends in data, specifically related to sales of churn accounts (accounts that stopped buying, for whatever reason), even more specifically, accounts in his former territory. Kim, another member of the team, was strengthened by client interaction, but loathed the preparation and data analysis necessary for presentations. Once this was discovered, the two teammates combined their strengths. Chris did the research, data-crunching, and presentation development. Kim scheduled and delivered the sales calls and provided personal follow-up. Both were strengthened individually and as a team. The increase of sales and decrease of churn proved the benefits of leading with strengths.

WRIGHT

So, how can the people who are reading this chapter leverage their strengths to manage their weaknesses?

CASSIDY

First, take an inventory of your strengths and weaknesses. Certainly, you need to acknowledge the things you're not good at, especially if you're responsible for getting those tasks done in your job. For example, if you loathe extensive administrative paperwork, but that's part of your job responsibility, think about how your strengths, on a broader scale, can help you manage anxiety and procrastination of tasks like completing paperwork or reports. If you are a high achiever, for instance, it means you are a doer. You achieve all day long, including the weekends and when on vacation. You're one of those people who is just very active and you like to get things done. You wake up with a score of zero each morning and you need to achieve to gain points throughout the day. As an achiever, you can leverage this strength to help you complete expense reports, your paperwork, and your administration. You could create a point value to each thing that you have to do. You could time yourself to see how long it takes you and try to complete it more quickly next time. Use your strengths to manage your weaknesses. You may end up enjoying it.

The strengths guru, Marcus Buckingham, also suggests that we just stop doing the activity we loathe and see if anyone notices. Some tasks originated as great ideas or processes at one time and may have been replaced. They may no longer serve a purpose. So stop doing some of the things you cannot stand and see if it matters. A client of mine tried this. She used to provide a written follow-up to all participants after meetings. She was not an administrator or responsible for scribing, she just did it. It consumed hours of time and subliminally branded her as an assistant to the team. As a leader, she recognized the need to be fully engaged in the meetings and not be consumed with documentation. She shifted her focus to speaking up, sharing her thoughts, and empowering people to note their commitments and agree to their action items and deadlines. Her strength for organization and responsibility were helpful. She now uses those strengths in ways consistent with her career goals.

WRIGHT

What process would someone use to help discover his or her strengths?

CASSIDY

There are several things one can do. Three options come to mind: a workshop, books, and self-discovery. You can take a program through an organization like bridge between that walks participants through a process to discover personal and team strengths. Each person identifies his or her top three strengths and weaknesses; the objective is to find ways to leverage and manage them. Everyone must start with himself or herself before assessing others. It's essential that each of us know our own drivers before we try to help and coach others.

Another resource is the strength-finder assessment that can be found in a book by Tom Rath, *Strength Finder 2.0*. This book is a glossary of thirty-four themes of human strengths. The assessment included provides your top five signature strengths. It gives you a broader sense of where your strengths might originate. For example, one theme is Woo. It stands for Winning Others Over. People strong in Woo don't view anyone as a stranger, only friends they haven't met yet. Woo, as a theme, informs the person about his or her strengths. People strong in Woo may love to win over strangers or be the most popular people in the office or take leadership roles for exposure and recognition.

The specific detail of the strength can be revealed through the third option, self-discovery. Self-discovery includes documentation, reflection, and refinement. Document the activities throughout your day that energize you and deplete you. What do you look forward to and yearn for? What do you loathe and bores you to tears? Be as granular and specific as possible when describing these activities. They are your strengths and weaknesses. Once clear, you can find similar activities to volunteer for or delegate.

Typically, we're not very unique or creative when sharing our strengths. Nine times out of ten people will say something like, "I'm really good with people." It's important to clarify—what kind of people? What are you doing with them? Are you selling to them? Are you negotiating something? Are you trying to build the relationship? Is it a long-term relationship or a one-and-done kind of thing? You want to be as specific as you can when defining what strengthens you.

WRIGHT

Almost everyone down through the years who has applied for jobs with me has always said, "I'm a people person."

CASSIDY

It's common, but I don't think they are clear enough about what they mean. It's a start, but not specific enough for others to know how to help you have more of what you love doing most. We've got to ask powerful questions to help unravel the answers.

WRIGHT

So, is the process different for staff members' strengths?

CASSIDY

It's a similar process. For strengths-based organizations to work, it has to start at the top. Leaders start with their own self-awareness and then use a similar process to help determine the strengths of others. Most simply, strengths can be included as part of the performance review process.

Ask employees to come prepared with a list of powerful questions to inform the conversation—questions like:

- What specific tasks did you really enjoy this week? This month? This year?
- What aspects of your job are you most excited about?
- What activities drain your energy in your role?
- What responsibilities do you wish you could eliminate?

The performance review can provide valuable insights into strengths and weaknesses. The manager providing the review needs some savvy to manage employees' responses. Expectations need to be clear that eliminating weakening activities may not be possible, but it's helpful and changes may result from knowing what employees really want.

Some organizations have taken this to another level and have become strengths-based organizations. Strengths identification and awareness is how they hire, manage people, evaluate performance—everything is strengths-based. It's really powerful but may not be a viable solution for everyone.

What is possible, and less organizationally driven, is acknowledging each employee for his or her two to three gems—the things each one does that are outstanding. As a leader, it's your responsibility to figure out what those things are and maximize them.

Peter Drucker said in his book, *The Effective Executive,* that an effective executive asks about employees, "What can they do uncommonly well?" Effective executives don't go into it trying to figure out, "Where is this person weak, and how do we fix them?" They want to find out what employees can do that other people can't and make the most of their talents.

WRIGHT

How can I reasonably focus on my strengths at work when it seems like performance appraisal is all constructive?

CASSIDY

Often times that is the case. It's a conditioned behavior. The questions most managers ask themselves when preparing for a performance review is, "What should they change?" "What do they need to improve on?" Better questions are:

- What can I maximize about this employee?
- What superior strengths do they offer that are better than anyone else's?
- How can I leverage employees' strengths and empower them to delegate things they don't like?

Have a proactive conversation with the head of human resources or whoever designs your company people systems—systems such as: employment development, the appraisal process, compensation system, selection process, performance management, succession planning, etc. Encourage them to consider adding the discovery and development of strengths to those processes. The systems already in place can be repurposed to develop and manage talent.

Short of an entire culture shift, which may not be possible in your organization, you can do these three things for yourself:

1. Discover your strengths and take responsibility for yourself and your own development.

2. Clearly and simply learn how to discuss your strengths in terms of how it helps the team and organization. People often shy away from that one because they think it's arrogant or not appropriate. In order for people to be unleashed, a shift has to occur from, "I'll do whatever the team needs" to "Here are my strengths and how I can best support this team."

3. Find opportunities to volunteer your strengths. Look for resources or outlets to utilize your strengths. Don't resent your company if it's not a strengths-centered organization. Know that strengths-based organizations are counterintuitive and rare. It's uncommon to focus on strengths over weaknesses. You can be a resource and inform your managers and human capital team about the value of strengths development and the possible performance results when developing what's right about people. Start by being a model. Look for opportunities to volunteer the strengths you have and see what happens.

WRIGHT

As a leadership coach, how do you encourage executive teams to consider strengths-based leadership?

CASSIDY

Primarily, my focus is driving human performance. We all have one main talent; mine is finding out what gets people from where they are now to where they ultimately want to be—and getting them there. Human performance is my passion. I've studied the best of the best in this area and have found that most roads lead to strengths. There is a strong business case for strengths. It's efficient and effective.

Strengths development makes sense because it is a natural motivator and has proven results.

The process I use to encourage executive teams to consider strengths-based leadership is first learn about their current performance appraisal system. Questions I ask are:

- What is the regularity of reviews? (I suggest monthly check-in meetings and quarterly reviews.)
- Who is involved in the review? Line supervisor? Human resources? Other teammates?
- What is the intention behind the review process design? (Sometimes the process is outdated and needs to be analyzed.)
- What are the objectives of the review?
- What is the process for hiring and how do they search for talent?
- Lastly, are they open to suggestions on how to improve the process? We wouldn't make much improvement if they weren't open. If they're open, we can evaluate effectiveness and suggest processes and improvements to help focus on strength development and team synergies.

The goal is to make the most of the people who already exist in the organization. Clearly, it's less expensive than clearing house and hiring new people. Employees often have a lot of untapped value to offer. I hear coaching clients say, "Only a fraction of my abilities are used in my daily work," so they look for outside activities to feed their strengths. If managed properly they channel that power directly to the organization.

WRIGHT

What do you think are the biggest obstacles people face in maximizing their strengths at work?

CASSIDY

The biggest challenge is beliefs. By "beliefs," I mean the rules and boundaries we accept as true. Whatever you believe to be true either is true or the belief in it makes it true, right? Two examples are beliefs that inform the strengths conversation—one is, "what is work?" and another is, "what does it means to be an effective team player?"

Many people have a limiting belief about what work is. Work is often linked with and associated to pain. We use terms like "daily grind" to describe our work. The belief is that work should be hard and burdensome. It's a big challenge to overcome and endure so we can retire. As humans, we do our best to avoid pain and gain pleasure. In a nutshell, that's why we do what we do—avoid pain, gain pleasure, in that order. Now associate pain and work to strength. It doesn't fit. If we're doing something we enjoy at work, it feels wrong.

Progress happens when we become aware of our beliefs and recognize a choice to shift our focus and ask better questions. Once empowered with the awareness that we choose our focus (the quality of questions we ask ourselves), we can ask: "Which activities do I relish?" "How can I offer to do those things and help my team?" "What must I focus on for my work to be a source of pleasure?"

The second belief that often gets in the way of a strengths movement is, "What my team needs most from me is to take things off the list and do whatever the team needs me to do." That simply isn't true. What your team needs from you is for you to know how you contribute most, know what you're most passionate about, and know what you do consistently well, and then volunteer it! You're the one who knows what your strengths are—they're internal drivers behind the scenes that either makes you pumped or pooped.

My client Kim tried this. She agreed to focus on her strength for public speaking. She wasn't particularly skilled but loved the challenge of growth and development. We had many practice sessions. Kim volunteered to speak at meetings, fundraisers, and three professional organizations she's involved with. Over the course of three months, she honed her skills and was recognized for her effectiveness. Kim is currently pursuing a new position, in the same company, that includes presenting quarterly updates to the entire company. It's a win/win.

Your team needs you to be aware and find opportunities to add value. To stay essential (something that people really need to be thinking about), you need to contribute beyond the usual expectations. You're most influential and most willing to raise the bar when working from your strengths. Challenge yourself to think about your beliefs. Be open to these truths: work is a source of pleasure and that pleasure enables me to make the greatest contribution for the longest amount of time.

WRIGHT

What happens when you're drawn to something that you have no skill or talent for?

CASSIDY

That's called a closet dream or hobby. We all have secret wishes that we could do things we'll never be able to do. If you want to be a rock star, go to karaoke night and sing your heart out. Or, for less ego damage, keep your singing to the shower or car. If no one is paying you to do it, and you're not good at it, it's a hobby. If you're being paid to do it and you lack skill, you need coaching, training, and possibly a search for a position more suited to your strengths.

WRIGHT

How do you know when you're using your strengths effectively and when they're overdone?

CASSIDY

Good distinction, David. Any strength overdone is a weakness. It's true for all of us. We can get carried away. For example, one of my strengths is responsibility—I take psychological ownership for anything I commit to. Whether large or small, I feel emotionally bound to follow any commitment I make through to completion. If, for some reason I can't deliver, I automatically start looking for ways to make it up. It's a blessing and a curse. My reputation is based on a combination of my conscientiousness (almost obsession) for doing things right and my strong ethics. I see myself as utterly dependable, so when assigning a new responsibility, people often look to me because they know I'll get it done. It's a useful strength in terms of my integrity and being true to my word. I own my decisions and choices—good or bad.

It becomes a weakness when I can't give myself a break or when I overcommit and still want to be fully responsible. It's also a liability when I take on other people's responsibility. My responsibility strength needs boundaries and limits. So whenever I'm invited to participate in something like speaking at a function, mentoring someone, helping out at church, or at my child's school, I always think, "How could this challenge my responsibility strength?" I don't want to set myself up for failure or "strengths abuse" where I'm overcommitting to too many obligations making it more difficult for effective follow-through.

We all struggle with this boundary around our strengths. When mapping out your strengths, ask yourself, "How does this strength serve me and others?" By this I mean, what is the value of having this uniqueness? And ask, "How might I overdo this strength and create a liability?" Identifying, in advance, how a particular strength may get out of control helps to keep it in check.

WRIGHT

Would you tell our readers a little bit more about your strengths and how they serve you?

CASSIDY

Absolutely. I feel strong when (a good way to open up a strengths statement) I ask clarifying questions to identify patterns with professionals who are ripe for learning. I help them unleash and empower their self-mastery. Whenever I get an opportunity to explore and mine the depths of a person who is searching for power and a way to contribute, I am completely energized and engaged. I like to analyze where people spend their time and help them accomplish what they want most in life.

It serves others and me because I am relentless in getting individual and organizations what they want. I ask dozens of questions and encourage a leap outside the zone of comfort so people can grow. People are deep and massively powerful. We don't lack the desire to be outstanding or have an incredible life. We lack beliefs, values, and rules that support our desire. We make it so difficult to succeed and we keep changing our definition of success. My strengthening activity of provocatively asking questions to get to the core of the issue makes me an effective coach.

I also feel strong engaging in powerful conversations with executives on how to best express themselves clearly and purposefully, especially in a serious situation or crisis. I'm good under pressure. The urgency and importance of the situation pique my interest and put me in the zone. This serves me well personally and professionally. I'm able to think quickly, ask powerful questions, and empower people to collect their thoughts, design a message, and confidently deliver with effectiveness.

One client, Ted, SVP of Media and Communications Strategy, comes to mind. His strengths, according to my assessment, were Strategic and Relator. He saw patterns where others saw confusion. He asked, "What if" questions to test scenarios, thought of several solutions, and definitively selected and executed his approach. As a Relator, he had a few very close colleagues whom he considered friends.

Ted called in a panic from his cell phone at 5:30 PM one Friday. The executive team had just ended an emergency meeting that resulted in a decision to lay off fifteen percent of the workforce. Knowing that line functions—the sales and manufacturing people—were less vulnerable, he feared for his team's security since they were staff positions and less mission critical.

He downloaded the main points they exchanged in the meeting and expressed confusion and concern. He needed to present his headcount reduction by Monday. After changing his state and calming him down, I asked him, "What is your goal? What must you do? What are the best 'what if' scenarios you can think of [strategic thinkers need this one]? Who are you most concerned about?"

Ted answered and processed his thoughts. He was empowered to develop a plan over the weekend that: met his goal, was the best choice from the options he had created, and protected the people he needed most to operate his department.

My Strengths-finder themes, are maximizer, responsibility, activator, arranger, and individualization. Most are made up words that don't make sense out of context. My number one theme is maximizer. It means that excellence—not average—is my measure. Taking something from below average to slightly above average takes a lot of effort and, in my opinion, is not very rewarding. My passion is trying to transform something strong into something superb. It's fun.

Strength, whether mine or somebody else's, fascinates me. Like a diver after a pearl, I watch for the signs of a strength—a glimpse of excellence. Then I try to figure out how to make whatever the person is doing outstanding. My lens of life seeks to bring forth strengths, clarified through questions, and find ways of magnifying them.

WRIGHT

So why are more people not in tune with their strengths if it's so empowering and effective?

CASSIDY

Because we like to be normal, mainstream, and just like everyone else so we can fit in. Seriously, it's much more common to focus on weaknesses and areas for improvement. It's a, "pool's warm, jump in," type of thing. But who wants to be normal, mainstream, and common? I don't. We've got to encourage people to stretch themselves, challenge their beliefs, and open up to the possibility that exists for their own potential. It's an awkward step to take. It's out of the comfort zone. It's not as familiar and certain as weakness-based leadership.

We're more comfortable preparing a performance review to discuss things that need improvement, or more commonly called, "development opportunities." We're not as comfortable talking about our strengths. We don't want to be seen as arrogant or conceited. We don't want to be abnormal. We don't want to change the conversation that most people are expecting to have. We also don't want to be seen as incompetent.

To argue the opposite, we must consider the ways in which we stay essential. We should respect the impression we make when we clearly articulate our value and how we can contribute more to the organization. It's more interesting and productive to have a conversation about what you add versus why you aren't perfect.

WRIGHT

I'm driven or motivated by results, generally speaking. If I'm trying to help people do something, I'm motivated by their results and how well they're getting along. Are you driven by results?

CASSIDY

Yes. That's why I love coaching. I get to work with someone as a complete person, as I believe we all are. For example, Bill is effective, but has a big but. What I mean is, when people describe Bill they say, "Oh, Bill? Yeah, he's great, but—" What comes after the "but" is what I strive to change. I'm driven to help the people I work with figure out what's in the way, leverage their strengths to change the perception or opinion, and recreate their brand image.

On our intake form, each client rates his or her quality of life on a scale from one to ten. One is low and ten is high. The form later asks the client to rate his or her stress level on the same scale. If his or her quality of life is a six and his or her stress level is a nine, I'm motivated to increase the quality and decrease the stress. When that happens, as it almost always does, my rules kick in and tell me that I served this person well. If it doesn't happen, I work hard not to take the blame. Remember, one of my strengths is responsibility—overdone, it's a weakness. When clients don't reach their goals, it's tough for me. I've got to ask myself better questions when that happens. I ask, "What progress did they make?" "What would I have done differently?" "How can I best serve this person, regardless of his or her actions or commitment to the goal?' Honestly, it's a challenge.

WRIGHT

So, how did you begin coaching and why did you choose strengths as a focus area?

CASSIDY

Because the single most important driver of performance on a team is whether or not people feel that their strengths are at play. As a Maximizer, I'm fond of efficiency. When I started bridge, between, inc. in 2000, I researched what makes people most productive, how to increase performance, and create sustainable results. Performance happens best when strengths are at play. Statistics from the

Marcus Buckingham Company state that less than 12 percent of people use their strengths most of the time. That's a huge waste of talent, energy, and resources. I felt compelled to correct that statistic.

The strength-based research says when people are asked, "Do you get high from your job at least once a week?" "Are you so engaged that you lose track of time?" 73 percent respond this happens at least once a week. I'm curious to know how people go from using the strength once a week to most of the time.

The last part of my mission statement says, "*we are created to support each other; and how constant gratitude for our abundant gifts and precious time sets us free to purposefully enjoy vocation and life.*" Being a coach is a purpose-centered career for my strength because I love unearthing what I am certain exists in every person, which is immeasurable wisdom and absolute excellence. It's always been there. Some of us keep it buried deeper than others. As a woman of faith, developing God-given strengths are my purpose and vocation. So my quest—my life goal—is to help people figure out how they can make the greatest contribution for the longest amount of time, and of course, have fun doing it.

WRIGHT

Most successful people can look back and see those folks who have influenced them through their lives. Who are some of the key people who influenced your coaching and awareness of strengths-based leadership?

CASSIDY

Thank you for asking that. That's a great question. Learning is so much fun and I've had phenomenal teachers. I'll begin with the famous and go on to the not-so-famous.

Dr. Maya Angelou is a favorite. She has taught me a lot about personal greatness and power. She spoke, sang, and shared at a Women in Cable Telecommunications event recently. I was awestruck by her wisdom.

As mentioned, Peter Drucker's work is often in my hands as a reference, guidepost or source of insight. What an amazing thinker he is.

Tony Robbins, a valuable coach of mine, has taught me a lot about human needs and behavior and how to really step it up and conquer fear. His energy, wisdom, and commitment to helping others are among the things I admire most about Tony.

I've been a huge Stephen Covey fan for years. He taught me how every person can truly control his or her legacy with profound guidance. He's brilliant. How many degrees does he have?

Ken Blanchard, another contributor to this book, has taught me countless lessons on management and leadership. His teachings are logical and applicable.

Then, there's no greater strengths teacher than Markus Buckingham. He has mastered the art and science of strengths and does so with professionalism, passion, and humility. Marcus' work with the Gallup organization, his research, and relentless ambition have resulted in a revolutionary movement toward strengths. I've learned so much from him.

My personal and professional coaches have each given me valuable insights into my strengths and how to find and leverage other peoples' gifts.

Then lastly, in a personal sphere, is my family. My husband made a really bold move several years ago when he found himself truly unhappy in his sales career. He quit his job and went back to school full-time to become a teacher. He's now a seventh grade science teacher. He is so wonderfully aligned with his true passion. His career is a daily reminder to me of the power you can achieve by discovering your inner strengths.

My parents and sister are amazing. They have always encouraged me to do what I love. They don't always get my Maximizer, Activator, seize-the-opportunity view of life, but they support me anyway!

Oh, one last key person. Strengths-based leadership goes way back. One of my favorite quotes is from Benjamin Franklin. He said, "Hide not your talents. They for use were made. What's a sundial in the shade?" Don't you love that?

WRIGHT

Yes, that's excellent.

Well, what a great conversation. I've certainly learned a lot here today and you've given me a lot more to think about. I'm sure our readers are really going to enjoy this conversation on strengths.

CASSIDY

Thank you. I appreciate the conversation.

WRIGHT

Today we've been talking with Shannon Cassidy from bridge between, inc., a national organization based in Philadelphia, Pennsylvania. She helps leaders create strengths-based action plans for leading high performing teams, navigating corporate politics, and creating win-win resolutions to conflict. She holds a corporate negotiation training certificate from Harvard Law School.

Shannon, thank you so much for being with us today on *Discover Your Inner Strength*.

CASSIDY

Thank you for inviting me, David. It was a pleasure to share this time with you. It was... strengthening!

CHAPTER Two

Attitude is Everything

AN INTERVIEW WITH...

Dr. Kenneth Blanchard

800.728.6000
www.kenblanchard.com

ABOUT THE AUTHOR

Few people have created more of a positive impact on the day-to-day management of people and companies than Dr. Kenneth Blanchard, who is known around the world simply as "Ken."

When Ken speaks, he speaks from the heart with warmth and humor. His unique gift is to speak to an audience and communicate with each individual as if they were alone and talking one-on-one. He is a polished storyteller with a knack for making the seemingly complex easy to understand.

Ken has been a guest on a number of national television programs, including *Good Morning America* and *The Today Show*. He has been featured in *Time, People, U.S. News & World Report*, and a host of other popular publications.

He earned his bachelor's degree in Government and Philosophy from Cornell University, his master's degree in Sociology and Counseling from Colgate University, and his PhD in Educational Administration and Leadership from Cornell University.

DAVID WRIGHT (WRIGHT)

Few people have created a positive impact on the day-to-day management of people and companies more than Dr. Kenneth Blanchard. He is known around the world simply as Ken, a prominent, gregarious, sought-after author, speaker, and business consultant. Ken is universally characterized by friends, colleagues, and clients as one of the most insightful, powerful, and compassionate men in business today. Ken's impact as a writer is far-reaching. His phenomenal best-selling book, *The One Minute Manager®*, coauthored with Spencer Johnson, has sold more than thirteen million copies worldwide and has been translated into more than twenty-five languages. Ken is Chairman and "Chief Spiritual Officer" of the Ken Blanchard Companies. The organization's focus is to energize organizations around the world with customized training in bottom-line business strategies based on the simple, yet powerful principles inspired by Ken's best-selling books.

Dr. Blanchard, welcome to *Discover Your Inner Strength*.

DR. KEN BLANCHARD (BLANCHARD)

Well, it's nice to talk with you, David. It's good to be here.

DAVID WRIGHT (WRIGHT)

I must tell you that preparing for your interview took quite a bit more time than usual. The scope of your life's work and your business, the Ken Blanchard Companies, would make for a dozen fascinating interviews.

Before we dive into the specifics of some of your projects and strategies, will you give our readers a brief synopsis of your life—how you came to be the Ken Blanchard we all know and respect?

BLANCHARD

Well, I'll tell you, David, I think life is what you do when you are planning on doing something else. I think that was John Lennon's line. I never intended to do what I have been doing. In fact, all my professors in college told me that I couldn't write. I wanted to do college work, which I did, and they said, "You had better be an administrator." So I decided I was going to be a Dean of Students. I got provisionally accepted into my master's degree program and then provisionally accepted at Cornell because I never could take any of those standardized tests.

I took the college boards four times and finally got 502 in English. I don't have a test-taking mind. I ended up in a university in Athens, Ohio, in 1966 as an

Administrative Assistant to the Dean of the Business School. When I got there he said, "Ken, I want you to teach a course. I want all my deans to teach." I had never thought about teaching because they said I couldn't write, and teachers had to publish. He put me in the manager's department.

I've taken enough bad courses in my day and I wasn't going to teach one. I really prepared and had a wonderful time with the students. I was chosen as one of the top ten teachers on the campus coming out of the chute!

I just had a marvelous time. A colleague by the name of Paul Hersey was chairman of the Management Department. He wasn't very friendly to me initially because the Dean had led me to his department, but I heard he was a great teacher. He taught Organizational Behavior and Leadership. So I said, "Can I sit in on your course next semester?"

"Nobody audits my courses," he said. "If you want to take it for credit, you're welcome."

I couldn't believe it. I had a doctoral degree and he wanted me to take his course for credit—so I signed up.

The registrar didn't know what to do with me because I already had a doctorate, but I wrote the papers and took the course, and it was great.

In June 1967, Hersey came into my office and said, "Ken, I've been teaching in this field for ten years. I think I'm better than anybody, but I can't write. I'm a nervous wreck, and I'd love to write a textbook with somebody. Would you write one with me?"

I said, "We ought to be a great team. You can't write and I'm not supposed to be able to, so let's do it!"

Thus began this great career of writing and teaching. We wrote a textbook called *Management of Organizational Behavior: Utilizing Human Resources*. It came out in its eighth edition October 3, 2000, and the ninth edition was published September 3, 2007. It has sold more than any other textbook in that area over the years. It's been over forty years since that book first came out.

I quit my administrative job, became a professor, and ended up working my way up the ranks. I got a sabbatical leave and went to California for one year twenty-five years ago. I ended up meeting Spencer Johnson at a cocktail party. He wrote children's books—a wonderful series called *Value Tales*® *for Kids*. He also wrote *The Value of Courage: The Story of Jackie Robinson* and *The Value of Believing In Yourself: The Story of Louis Pasteur*.

My wife, Margie, met him first and said, "You guys ought to write a children's book for managers because they won't read anything else." That was my introduction to Spencer. So, *The One Minute Manager* was really a kid's book for big people. That is a long way from saying that my career was well planned.

WRIGHT

Ken, what and/or who were your early influences in the areas of business, leadership, and success? In other words, who shaped you in your early years?

BLANCHARD

My father had a great impact on me. He was retired as an admiral in the Navy and had a wonderful philosophy. I remember when I was elected as president of the seventh grade, and I came home all pumped up. My father said, "Son, it's great that you're the president of the seventh grade, but now that you have that leadership position, don't ever use it." He said, "Great leaders are followed because people respect them and like them, not because they have power." That was a wonderful lesson for me early on. He was just a great model for me. I got a lot from him.

Then I had this wonderful opportunity in the mid-1980s to write a book with Norman Vincent Peale. He wrote *The Power of Positive Thinking*. I met him when he was eighty-six years old; we were asked to write a book on ethics together, *The Power of Ethical Management: Integrity Pays, You Don't Have to Cheat to Win*. It didn't matter what we were writing together; I learned so much from him. He just built from the positive things I learned from my mother.

My mother said that when I was born I laughed before I cried, I danced before I walked, and I smiled before I frowned. So that, as well as Norman Vincent Peale, really impacted me as I focused on what I could do to train leaders. How do you make them positive? How do you make them realize that it's not about them, it's about who they are serving? It's not about their position—it's about what they can do to help other people win.

So, I'd say my mother and father, then Norman Vincent Peale. All had a tremendous impact on me.

WRIGHT

I can imagine. I read a summary of your undergraduate and graduate degrees. I assumed you studied Business Administration, marketing management, and related courses. Instead, at Cornell you studied Government and Philosophy. You received your master's from Colgate in Sociology and Counseling and your PhD from Cornell in Educational Administration and Leadership. Why did you choose this course of study? How has it affected your writing and consulting?

BLANCHARD

Well, again, it wasn't really well planned out. I originally went to Colgate to get a master's degree in Education because I was going to be a Dean of Students over men. I had been a Government major, and I was a Government major because it was the best department at Cornell in the Liberal Arts School. It was exciting. We would study what the people were doing at the league of governments. And then, the Philosophy Department was great. I just loved the philosophical arguments. I wasn't a great student in terms of getting grades, but I'm a total learner. I would sit there and listen, and I would really soak it in.

When I went over to Colgate and got into the education courses, they were awful. They were boring. The second week, I was sitting at the bar at the Colgate Inn saying, "I can't believe I've been here two years for this." This is just the way the Lord works: Sitting next to me in the bar was a young sociology professor who had just gotten his PhD at Illinois. He was staying at the Inn. I was moaning and groaning about what I was doing, and he said, "Why don't you come and major with me in sociology? It's really exciting."

"I can do that?" I asked.

He said, "Yes."

I knew they would probably let me do whatever I wanted the first week. Suddenly, I switched out of Education and went with Warren Ramshaw. He had a tremendous impact on me. He retired some years ago as the leading professor at Colgate in the Arts and Sciences, and got me interested in leadership and organizations. That's why I got a master's in Sociology.

The reason I went into educational administration and leadership? It was a doctoral program I could get into because I knew the guy heading up the program. He said, "The greatest thing about Cornell is that you will be in the School of Education. It's not very big, so you don't have to take many education courses, and you can take stuff all over the place."

There was a marvelous man by the name of Don McCarty who eventually became the Dean of the School of Education, Wisconsin. He had an impact on my life; but I was always just searching around.

My mission statement is: to be a loving teacher and example of simple truths that help myself and others to awaken the presence of God in our lives. The reason I mention "God" is that I believe the biggest addiction in the world is the human ego; but I'm really into simple truth. I used to tell people I was trying to get the B.S. out of the behavioral sciences.

WRIGHT

I can't help but think, when you mentioned your father, that he just bottom-lined it for you about leadership.

BLANCHARD

Yes.

WRIGHT

A man named Paul Myers, in Texas, years and years ago when I went to a conference down there, said, "David, if you think you're a leader and you look around, and no one is following you, you're just out for a walk."

BLANCHARD

Well, you'd get a kick out of this—I'm just reaching over to pick up a picture of Paul Myers on my desk. He's a good friend, and he's a part of our Center for FaithWalk Leadership where we're trying to challenge and equip people to lead like Jesus. It's non-profit. I tell people I'm not an evangelist because we've got enough trouble with the Christians we have. We don't need any more new ones. But, this is a picture of Paul on top of a mountain. Then there's another picture below that of him under the sea with stingrays. It says, "Attitude is everything. Whether you're on the top of the mountain or the bottom of the sea, true happiness is achieved by accepting God's promises, and by having a biblically positive frame of mind. Your attitude is everything." Isn't that something?

WRIGHT

He's a fine, fine man. He helped me tremendously. I wanted to get a sense from you about your own success journey. Many people know you best from *The One Minute Manager* books you coauthored with Spencer Johnson. Would you consider these books as a high water mark for you or have you defined success for yourself in different terms?

BLANCHARD

Well, you know, *The One Minute Manager* was an absurdly successful book so quickly that I found I couldn't take credit for it. That was when I really got on my own spiritual journey and started to try to find out what the real meaning of life and success was.

That's been a wonderful journey for me because I think, David, the problem with most people is they think their self-worth is a function of their performance plus the opinion of others. The minute you think that is what your self-worth is, every day your self-worth is up for grabs because your performance is going to fluctuate on a day-to-day basis. People are fickle. Their opinions are going to go up and down. You need to ground your self-worth in the unconditional love that God has ready for us, and that really grew out of the unbelievable success of *The One Minute Manager.*

When I started to realize where all that came from, that's how I got involved in this ministry that I mentioned. Paul Myers is a part of it. As I started to read the Bible, I realized that everything I've ever written about, or taught, Jesus did. You know, He did it with the twelve incompetent guys He "hired." The only guy with much education was Judas, and he was His only turnover problem.

WRIGHT

Right.

BLANCHARD

This is a really interesting thing. What I see in people is not only do they think their self-worth is a function of their performance plus the opinion of others, but they measure their success on the amount of accumulation of wealth, on recognition, power, and status. I think those are nice success items. There's nothing wrong with those, as long as you don't define your life by that.

What I think you need to focus on rather than success is what Bob Buford, in his book *Halftime,* calls "significance"—moving from success to significance. I think the opposite of accumulation of wealth is generosity.

I wrote a book called *The Generosity Factor* with Truett Cathy, who is the founder of Chick-fil-A. He is one of the most generous men I've ever met in my life. I thought we needed to have a model of generosity. It's not only your *treasure,* but it's your *time* and *talent.* Truett and I added *touch* as a fourth one.

The opposite of recognition is service. I think you become an adult when you realize you're here to serve rather than to be served.

Finally, the opposite of power and status is loving relationships. Take Mother Teresa as an example—she couldn't have cared less about recognition, power, and status because she was focused on generosity, service, and loving relationships; but she got all of that earthly stuff. If you focus on the earthly, such as money, recognition, and power, you're never going to get to significance. But if you focus on significance, you'll be amazed at how much success can come your way.

WRIGHT

I spoke with Truett Cathy recently and was impressed by what a down-to-earth, good man he seems to be. When you start talking about him closing his restaurants on Sunday, all of my friends—when they found out I had talked to him—said, "Boy, he must be a great Christian man, but he's rich." I told them, "Well, to put his faith into perspective, by closing on Sunday it costs him $500 million a year."

He lives his faith, doesn't he?

BLANCHARD

Absolutely, but he still outsells everybody else.

WRIGHT

That's right.

BLANCHARD

According to their January 25, 2007, press release, Chick-fil-A was the nation's second-largest quick-service chicken restaurant chain in sales at that time. Its business performance marks the thirty-ninth consecutive year the chain has enjoyed a system-wide sales gain—a streak the company has sustained since opening its first chain restaurant in 1967.

WRIGHT

The simplest market scheme, I told him, tripped me up. I walked by his first Chick-fil-A I had ever seen, and some girl came out with chicken stuck on toothpicks and handed me one; I just grabbed it and ate it; it's history from there on.

BLANCHARD

Yes, I think so. It's really special. It is so important that people understand generosity, service, and loving relationships because too many people are running around like a bunch of peacocks. You even see pastors who measure their success by how many are in their congregation; authors by how many books they have sold; businesspeople by what their profit margin is—how good sales are. The reality is, that's all well and good, but I think what you need to focus on is the other. I think if business did that more and we got Wall Street off our backs with all the short-term evaluation, we'd be a lot better off.

WRIGHT

Absolutely. There seems to be a clear theme that winds through many of your books that has to do with success in business and organizations—how people are treated by management and how they feel about their value to a company. Is this an accurate observation? If so, can you elaborate on it?

BLANCHARD

Yes, it's a very accurate observation. See, I think the profit is the applause you get for taking care of your customers and creating a motivating environment for your people. Very often people think that business is only about the bottom line. But no, that happens to be the result of creating raving fan customers, which I've described with Sheldon Bowles in our book, *Raving Fans*. Customers want to brag about you, if you create an environment where people can be gung-ho and committed. You've got to take care of your customers and your people, and then your cash register is going to go ka-ching, and you can make some big bucks.

WRIGHT

I noticed that your professional title with the Ken Blanchard Companies is somewhat unique—"Chairman and Chief Spiritual Officer." What does your title mean to you personally and to your company? How does it affect the books you choose to write?

BLANCHARD

I remember having lunch with Max DuPree one time. The legendary Chairman of Herman Miller, Max wrote a wonderful book called *Leadership Is an Art*.

"What's your job?" I asked him.

He said, "I basically work in the vision area."

"Well, what do you do?" I asked.

"I'm like a third-grade teacher," he replied. "I say our vision and values over, and over, and over again until people get it right, right, right."

I decided from that, I was going to become the Chief Spiritual Officer, which means I would be working in the vision, values, and energy part of our business. I ended up leaving a morning message every day for everybody in our company. We have twenty-eight international offices around the world.

I leave a voice mail every morning, and I do three things on that as Chief Spiritual Officer: One, people tell me who we need to pray for. Two, people tell me who we need to praise—our unsung heroes and people like that. And then three, I leave an inspirational morning message. I really am the cheerleader—the Energizer

Bunny—in our company. I'm the reminder of why we're here and what we're trying to do.

We think that our business in the Ken Blanchard Companies is to help people lead at a higher level, and to help individuals and organizations. Our mission statement is to unleash the power and potential of people and organizations for the common good. So if we are going to do that, we've really got to believe in that.

I'm working on getting more Chief Spiritual Officers around the country. I think it's a great title and we should get more of them.

WRIGHT

So those people for whom you pray, where do you get the names?

BLANCHARD

The people in the company tell me who needs help, whether it's a spouse who is sick or kids who are sick or if they are worried about something. We've got over five years of data about the power of prayer, which is pretty important.

One morning, my inspirational message was about my wife and five members of our company who walked sixty miles one weekend—twenty miles a day for three days—to raise money for breast cancer research.

It was amazing. I went down and waved them all in as they came. They had a ceremony; they had raised $7.6 million. There were over three thousand people walking. A lot of the walkers were dressed in pink—they were cancer victors—people who had overcome it. There were even men walking with pictures of their wives who had died from breast cancer. I thought it was incredible.

There wasn't one mention about it in the major San Diego papers. I said, "Isn't that just something." We have to be an island of positive influence because all you see in the paper today is about celebrities and their bad behavior. Here you have all these thousands of people out there walking and trying to make a difference, and nobody thinks it's news.

So every morning I pump people up about what life's about, about what's going on. That's what my Chief Spiritual Officer job is about.

WRIGHT

I had the pleasure of reading one of your releases, *The Leadership Pill*.

BLANCHARD

Yes.

WRIGHT

I must admit that my first thought was how short the book was. I wondered if I was going to get my money's worth, which by the way, I most certainly did. Many of your books are brief and based on a fictitious story. Most business books in the market today are hundreds of pages in length and are read almost like a textbook.

Will you talk a little bit about why you write these short books, and about the premise of *The Leadership Pill?*

BLANCHARD

I really developed my relationship with Spencer Johnson when we wrote *The One Minute Manager.* As you know, he wrote, *Who Moved My Cheese*, which was a phenomenal success. He wrote children's books and is quite a storyteller.

Jesus taught by parables, which were short stories.

My favorite books are *Jonathan Livingston Seagull* and *The Little Prince.* Og Mandino, author of seventeen books, was the greatest of them all.

I started writing parables because people can get into the story and learn the contents of the story, and they don't bring their judgmental hats into reading. You write a regular book and they'll say, "Well, where did you get the research?" They get into that judgmental side. Our books get them emotionally involved and they learn.

The Leadership Pill is a fun story about a pharmaceutical company that thinks they have discovered the secret to leadership, and they can put the ingredients in a pill. When they announce it, the country goes crazy because everybody knows we need more effective leaders. When they release it, it outsells Viagra.

The founders of the company start selling off stock and they call them Pillionaires. But along comes this guy who calls himself "the effective manager," and he challenges them to a no-pill challenge. If they identify two non-performing groups, he'll take on one and let somebody on the pill take another one, and he guarantees he will outperform that person by the end of the year. They agree, but of course they give him a drug test every week to make sure he's not sneaking pills on the side.

I wrote the book with Marc Muchnick, who is a young guy in his early thirties. We did a major study of what this interesting "Y" generation—the young people of today—want from leaders, and this is a secret blend that this effective manager uses. When you think about it, David, it is really powerful in terms of what people want from a leader.

Number one, they want integrity. A lot of people have talked about that in the past, but these young people will walk if they see people say one thing and do another. A lot of us walk to the bathroom and out into the halls to talk about it. But these people will quit. They don't want somebody to say something and not do it.

The second thing they want is a partnership relationship. They hate superior/subordinate. I mean, what awful terms those are. You know, the "head" of the department and the hired "hands"—you don't even give them a head. "What do I do? I'm in supervision. I see things a lot clearer than these stupid idiots." They want to be treated as partners; if they can get a financial partnership, great. If they can't, they really want a minimum of a psychological partnership where they can bring their brains to work and make decisions.

Then finally, they want affirmation. They not only want to be caught doing things right, but they want to be affirmed for who they are. They want to be known as individual people, not as numbers.

So those are the three ingredients that this effective manager uses. They are wonderful values when you think about them.

Rank-order values for any organization is number one, integrity. In our company we call it ethics. It is our number one value. The number two value is partnership. In our company we call it relationships. Number three is affirmation—being affirmed as a human being. I think that ties into relationships, too. They are wonderful values that can drive behavior in a great way.

WRIGHT

I believe most people in today's business culture would agree that success in business has everything to do with successful leadership. In *The Leadership Pill*, you present a simple but profound premise; that leadership is not something you do to people; it's something you do *with* them. At face value, that seems incredibly obvious. But you must have found in your research and observations that leaders in today's culture do not get this. Would you speak to that issue?

BLANCHARD

Yes. I think what often happens in this is the human ego. There are too many leaders out there who are self-serving. They're not leaders who have service in mind. They think the sheep are there for the benefit of the shepherd. All the power, money, fame, and recognition move up the hierarchy. They forget that the real action in business is not up the hierarchy—it's in the one-to-one, moment-to-moment interactions that your frontline people have with your customers. It's how the phone is answered. It's how problems are dealt with and those kinds of things. If you don't think that you're doing leadership *with* them—rather, you're doing it *to* them—after a while they won't take care of your customers.

I was at a store once (not Nordstrom's, where I normally would go) and I thought of something I had to share with my wife, Margie. I asked the guy behind the counter in Men's Wear, "May I use your phone?"

He said, "No!"

"You're kidding me," I said. "I can always use the phone at Nordstrom's."

"Look, buddy," he said, "they won't let *me* use the phone here. Why should I let you use the phone?"

That is an example of leadership that's done *to* employees, not *with* them. People want a partnership. People want to be involved in a way that really makes a difference.

WRIGHT

Dr. Blanchard, the time has flown by and there are so many more questions I'd like to ask you. In closing, would you mind sharing with our readers some thoughts on success? If you were mentoring a small group of men and women, and one of their central goals was to become successful, what kind of advice would you give them?

BLANCHARD

Well, I would first of all say, "What are you focused on?" If you are focused on success as being, as I said earlier, accumulation of money, recognition, power, or status, I think you've got the wrong target. What you need to really be focused on is how you can be generous in the use of your time and your talent and your treasure and touch. How can you serve people rather than be served? How can you develop caring, loving relationships with people? My sense is if you will focus on those things, success in the traditional sense will come to you. But if you go out and say, "Man, I'm going to make a fortune, and I'm going to do this," and have that kind of attitude, you might get some of those numbers. I think you become an adult, however, when you realize you are here to give rather than to get. You're here to serve, not to be served. I would just say to people, "Life is such a very special occasion. Don't miss it by aiming at a target that bypasses other people, because we're really here to serve each other."

WRIGHT

Well, what an enlightening conversation, Dr. Blanchard. I really want you to know how much I appreciate all the time you've taken with me for this interview. I know that our readers will learn from this, and I really appreciate your being with us today.

BLANCHARD

Well, thank you so much, David. I really enjoyed my time with you. You've asked some great questions that made me think, and I hope my answers are helpful to other people because as I say, life is a special occasion.

WRIGHT

Today we have been talking with Dr. Ken Blanchard. He is coauthor of the phenomenal best-selling book, *The One Minute Manager*. The fact that he's the Chief Spiritual Officer of his company should make us all think about how we are leading our companies and leading our families and leading anything, whether it is in church or civic organizations. I know I will.

Thank you so much, Dr. Blanchard, for being with us today.

BLANCHARD

Good to be with you, David.

CHAPTER *Three*

A Journey of a Thousand Miles Starts Within

AN INTERVIEW WITH...

Yun Li

Albuquerque, NM
877.381.8740 or 505.323.1095
yunli@yunexus.com
www.yunexus.com

ABOUT THE AUTHOR

Dr. Yun Li is the owner of Yu*nexus. She is also the co-founder of Holistic Human Performance Alliance, LLC. She grew up in China and came to the US in 1989 to pursue a Doctorate degree in Physics. She served in the high tech field for years before giving in to her inner calling. Currently, Yun Li is working as a coach, facilitator, speaker, and mediator. She works with both hemispheres of the brain— the left brain, the center of analysis and logical thinking, and the right brain that contains the qualities of creativity and empathy. This comes naturally to her. Yun Li says, "Like any good coach and trainer, I must bring all of me into my work, not just my skills and knowledge."

Yun Li is passionate about living with personal inner peace, freedom, and self-empowerment. She believes that peaceful people are happy, productive, and creative people. Working with her clients, she focuses on cultivating individual inner strength and wellness, along with mastering the skills of teamwork, leadership, and relationship. She is an advocate for practicing and taking action to transfer knowledge into behaviors in living and working collaboratively and productively.

Besides running her business, she has been taking graduate classes in the area of human and family development. She serves as the Board Examiner of Quality New Mexico and the Board of Advisors of Technical Venture Corporation. She mediates workplace conflict for government agencies. She is an instructor at the University of New Mexico Continuing Education and at the Central New Mexico Community College Work Force Training Center.

She works with her clients to transform relationships from confusion to clarity, from confrontation to collaboration. Her clients include corporations, small businesses, organizations, and individuals. "I feel blessed because I love what I do." She enjoys being with her friends, nature, books, and music. Tai Chi, yoga, meditation, and cycling are her favorite things to do to quiet her mind. She was a competitive sprinter in college, and now she is enjoying endurance long-distance cycling.

THE INTERVIEW

DAVID WRIGHT (WRIGHT)

Today we're talking with Yun Li, founder of Yu*nexus, a training and coaching firm for team, leadership and personal development. Yun Li grew up in China during the Culture Revolution. At a very young age, she was deeply disturbed by the suffering that many people had to endure as she witnessed the poverty and starvation. At age sixteen, she was admitted into the prestigious TsingHua University in Beijing. She holds a PhD in Physics from Arizona State University. She calls herself a "recovery physicist" who loves the discipline and rigor of science. However, her passion lies in cultivating humanity's emotional and consciousness capacity that allows people to engage life and work productively, powerfully and peacefully from the force within. Her life took an unexpected turn and accelerated her journey in 2005. Ever since then she has been on a path of her own, going to places few have known. However, she says, "Walking through the darkness of pain and confusion, more of me emerges each day. I am grateful for the abundant inner strength god gives to each one of us."

Yun Li, welcome to Discover Your Inner Strength.

YUN LI (LI)

Good to be here. Thank you, David.

WRIGHT

Why is inner strength something that you are interested in and have devoted your life's work to?

LI

This has to go back to my own life experiences and to those I have had the privilege to know through my work. When I came to the United States, I was twenty-five. I felt like an awkward twenty-five-year-old infant who must quickly learn everything—a new language, a new way of interacting, a new culture, a new way of living. I was frightened. With two suitcases containing all my belongings and a little money my father saved up for me, I was facing a world I knew little about. In a situation like this, we naturally go within, often unconsciously, to find the strength to cope with the unknown. I know that I did.

The first night, I moved into a small room in a big apartment complex. I felt as though I was walking into a self-imposed prison. A mattress, a desk, and a chair, together with my two suitcases and me were sitting quietly in darkness. That was the first time I had a room of my own—something I had wanted for many years. All I felt then, however, was loneliness, fear, confusion.. Twenty-five years of having the devoted unconditional love of my parents and the disciplined education my country gave me had not prepared me this new life, not only the outer challenges, but more so the inner struggle, facing the new world. Everything I knew about how to thrive was stripped to the bare bone. It was just me with the two suitcases and the unknown.

For the longest time that night, I just sat and tears streamed down my face. What got me through that dark night, and many others that followed, was the primitive inner force we all have—the sheer willpower to survive the outer challenges.

However, staying in that instinctual level of survival mode takes away our opportunity to discover the enormous potential we all have within. I learned later on in life, through the hard way, that very often it is this unrealized potential that allows us not only to face challenges with courage and clarity, but also to enjoy and to learn about ourselves from the experiences and processes.

That primitive inner power did get me up the next day and the days after. I had school to attend and a goal to achieve. I knew I would do whatever it took to get my PhD and I did. For six years I "suffered" through graduate school. Soon after that dire night, my goal turned into an automatic machine that drove me toward it. I worked insane hours and swallowed my pride, faced what I perceived as "unfairness," and endured two years of depression silently. It was a blind and mad pursuit driven by a goal that meant little after attaining it.

Life became a series of knee-jerk reactions to the outer world. The traits I had of being a hard-working person with focus, and of being analytical and being persistent, got me through many challenges life presented to me. However, I found the experiences neither fulfilling nor enjoyable. It seemed to me that, while the goal was achieved, my life was lost in the rat-race process.

History definitely repeats itself if we do not consciously question and change our course of actions and our way of thinking. In other words, if we do not learn from and take care of our inner struggle, we'll have to face it at another time in our life.

As life went on, I experienced more and more unfulfilling life experiences, and I started to wonder if there was a better way to live—a way where achieving aspirations and goals actually goes hand-in-hand with peace and joy, and with a sense of freedom and power.

Apparently, there is. After stepping out into the territory of inner life and living, I have found that all it required was to consciously engage my awareness and inner power. That is the inner strength I am talking about here. I believe that discovery and development of our inner strength is imperative, not only to achieve goals but also to live in fulfillment. My definition of fulfillment is the state that we experience life with the joy and confidence of being who we are; with the freedom of becoming all we can be; and with the sense of empowerment in achieving what we really want. It is the life energy radiating from inside out. This definition of fulfillment is not a simple act of filling up our days and hours with activities for the sake of staying active and busy.

WRIGHT

So what is your view of inner strength and how does it come about? Is it innate or nurtured?

LI

Well, both innate and nurtured. Everyone has the seeds of inner strength—our primitive inner energy—but we must nurture them and allow them to grow into a nuclear powerhouse for us. Rumi's poem said it well. A grain has its inherent quality to grow into a plant, but only grains that are nurtured will thrive:

A grain of wheat was buried in soil
Even in death, for life it would toil.
Eventually its thirst by water quenched
It sprouted roots which to soil clenched.
And then a stem that upward grew
Its way out of soil, it somehow knew.
Until finally it burst through the ground
And gladly found light all around;
And in the light it grew tall . . .

When I started to work with a personal trainer, the assessment session was an eye-opener for me. After asking me all sorts of questions, he handed me a piece of paper with exercises like "roll on a tube," "stand on a ball." I was agitated because I wanted to know how to build my muscles! He explained, "The physical training regimen focuses on the integrated parts of physical strength—balance, muscle strength, and cardiovascular endurance. You must strengthen all three in the training!"

I venture to say that the same principle applies to our inner strength as well. Our inner balance is our centeredness. It allows us the clarity to see and appreciate different realities—ours and that of others. The inner power includes our character traits that enable us to take action and engage life fully, which we build through life's challenges. Inner endurance is the ability to sustain action through ups and downs. The integration of all three is what I think our inner strength is, and it is the fuel for self-awareness, self-enabling, and self-determination.

Inner balance gives us the ability to see clearly and truthfully, and gives us what Buddha called the "right view," even in our foggy days. It is like a compass that keeps us from going astray. It gives vision, provides purpose, and offers healthy and larger perspectives. When facing the unknown, it enables us to remain centered on ourselves and it grounds us to what is important.

Inner balance is a dynamic process—it is a constant, quick, and subtle shift between losing and regaining emotional balance, losing and regaining clarity. We need clarity to see the realities as well as possibilities. It allows us to exercise our freedom to choose and create in any life situation. Inner balance is also the source of our centered identity during a constantly shifting outer world, and is the source of peace and power, confidence and compassion.

The faster we want to go in life, the more inner balance and centeredness are required of us. The faster I want to ride my bicycle, the more important it is to make sure that the wheels are exactly centered on its axle nuts and the tension in the spokes is carefully balanced.

In our world today, we are required to do more and do it faster. It is vital for our wellbeing that we have centeredness, stability, and balance that originate from within.

Inner powers are like our physical muscles. To build our muscles we must lift weights. Life's challenges are the weights we lift in life to build our inner power for action. Without challenges, our inner power withers. Each of life's situation calls for specific character traits. Sometimes life asks us to be brave and courageous; sometimes, life asks us to be open and adaptable. Sometimes, life calls for both and more. Each character trait needs to be cultivated and nurtured as in weight training. Look at life's challenges with an attitude of "what muscle can I flex and strengthen?" You will find abundant opportunities to build powerful character traits. This will exercise the muscles of self-enabling intentionally and mindfully.

So, what are the big muscle groups that I think are most useful? I am an advocate of taking action and changing behaviors, so I think exercising the following three "muscle groups" can greatly enhance our ability to carry out actions and live the life we desire.

The first one is integrity—consistency between one's words and one's actions. It is about making and keeping a commitment. We must be mindful of what we say to ourselves and others, and pay close attention to following-through with our words. If you tell yourself "I want to eat healthy," then practice eating healthy.

The second one is accountability—the ability to take personal responsibility for one's own life. It is the opposite of being a victim. We accept "what is" instead of dwell on "what should be." We ask, "What do I want it to be and how do I respond?" rather than, "Why they are so stupid or mean or not understanding?" It is the difference between being a victim of external events and being a master of your own life experience.

The third one is courage—the ability to act and behave consciously in the unknown when things are not happening as expected or desired. It is the ability to declare, "I don't know," and to be with the fear. Learning from the unfamiliar, taking risks, having faith, and exercising detachment are part of this muscle group. We must trust ourselves enough to be open to new experiences and perspectives. It is in contrast to our desire to stay with the familiar and believe we have answers to everything.

It is one thing to be brave and courageous when we quickly "win" in life. It is totally another when we keep on "failing" and falling short of our expectations. Overcoming defeat and persevering require more of us. Endurance, persistence, and self-determination are required. We are required to give all we have and go beyond what we think our best effort is.

In endurance training, the tangible goal itself may not be what matters the most. What matters most is to push your limits when you think you can no longer do so. Possibility lies beyond the limitations we set for ourselves. The only way to build physical endurance is through endurance training such as long-distance running, cycling, etc. The only way to build our inner endurance is through practicing persistence and faith through life's good moments as well as during the challenging times. We must embrace our fears and worries so we can stay in the process just a little longer to find more about ourselves.

Inner endurance is the vehicle and path to build desired habits and character traits and to become the person we want to be.

WRIGHT

How does a person's life relate to the discovery of inner strength? Would you give me a picture of what it was like for you to go on this journey?

LI

We discover and develop inner strength through actively participating and mindfully engaging in life, especially during the times we perceive as challenging.

Looking back on my years of living in this country, I can see clearly that many troubling signs were beckoning me to engage life in a different way; but I ignored one after another—from my unhappy pursuit in Tempe, Arizona, to stifled creativity and suffocated self-expression in corporations, to my troubled marriage and stressful motherhood. Lacking the clarity and courage to question my life, I dragged my feet, hoping things would get better and be different. My goal-oriented strategy and exceptional ability of "toughing it out" only helped me dig a deeper and bigger hole for myself to climb out of when I finally woke up one day when my world was turned upside down.

I was mortified. How did I get here with my best intention, kindest heart, and hardest effort? I was heartbroken—not only because of my broken family and my children's heartache, but also for the loss of myself. Facing the "mess" that was beyond my wildest imagination, I realized I was running out of my innate steam of "toughing it out." All my willpower had evaporated.

I highly suggest that people do not blindly "tough it out." There is a reason when life presents a challenge or throws a curve ball. It might be a new lesson for you to learn, a new territory for you to explore, or a new you who wants to emerge and grow.

As I watched the forty years of life that I worked so hard to build and had suffered so much for disappear overnight, I knew intuitively that I could no longer live pretending life is all about solving one outer problem after another. If I want to be alive, I must shed the old skin to find the "me" who hides fearfully behind. I had to do something I had not dared to do before. It was a painful, fearful, and exciting journey to know myself for the first time. It was like going through the "dark tunnel" many talk refer to when they talk about being reborn. I confronted many beliefs I had held so dearly and held so tightly all my life. I had to let go many beliefs on which my identity had been blindly built. It felt like walking into a swamp in the darkness. It was a scary feeling—I had neither control of my life nor me. My best chance of walking out of there alive was to keep on walking with faith and eyes and ears wide open, while at the same time, totally surrendering to the process and outcome. Here is the second part of Rumi's poem:

> "To be truly alive,
> we must first die.
> Buried in our soil,
> trusting we lie."

Surrendering and stepping into the unknown, giving up part or all of our identity is literally a process of letting part of our self die. We must lie in that dark, ugly, terrifying, and painful place ("the belly of the whale" in Joseph Campbell's words) with nothing to confirm our existence and identity but only the faith of renewal or rebirth. However, if we can mindfully stay in that daunting place, we will discover what we really have within is the God-given power and the dormant seeds of inner strength that are waiting desperately to grow. Now you start to have a glimpse of your true self and a life you might call your own, as well as the infinite possibilities life grants to everyone. With that revelation, it is remarkable how everything starts to look so different.

However, if we are mindful and disciplined in our daily life, we don't have to be in a dark and fierce place to discover our inner strength. One of the inner power muscles that I believe is vital is our ability to notice and take advantage of the small disturbances and dissatisfactions in life and employ them to discover and grow the seeds of inner strength.

However, both paths require us loosening up and giving up what we have known (our beliefs of who we should be, what we should do, what life should be like, and so on) and exploring the unknown. It goes against the grain when we face something we have never faced before. We naturally react in our old way to handle and to cope; however, new situations always require new ways of being and doing. Life comes with no manual, but being human, within ourselves we have the generative power to create a new manual each time we come to face-to-face with something we have never faced before. This generative power originates from within. Consciously using this ability is the path to inner strength development.

WRIGHT

You said that a challenge is a gateway to inner strength development. So how do you know you're at the gateway and how do you spot the opportunities?

LI

As I said earlier, a challenge does not have to be a dramatic life event. Life is gentle when it comes to this—at least at the beginning. All we need to do is to notice where the suffocating smoke comes from and set the fire within free by understanding that the smoke is the sign of "what's missing," "what's important," and "what beliefs are driving me." You set yourself free in that sense. I am not talking about quick problem-fixing or making things we do not like go away, although that will be the outcome. It is more about using such opportunities to learn about ourselves.

Naturally, we are unique and different, so our challenges in life will be different as well. We must pay attention and not fool ourselves when there is smoke in the room, no matter how insignificant it might seem. Here are a few examples of the potentially suffocating smoke we more or less experience in life:

- Dissatisfaction of some kind—life, work, career, relationships, personal aspirations
- A suspicion of missing something or some purpose in life
- A feeling of being stuck—trying to be somewhere in life but unable to move
- A feeling of being weighed down by life
- A feeling of living in a rat race to satisfy the needs of external approval
- Our hot buttons that others cannot push
- Needing constant distraction of some kind in order to be happy
- A feeling of being disconnected from life
- A feeling of lacking passion or being bored
- Certain hot buttons we have that cannot be pushed
- A feeling of uneasiness when life calls for certain things such as self-expression, confrontation, being alone
- Repeated unpleasant and undesirable experiences

I often think life is really generous. It provides us with numerous opportunities to discover more of ourselves and for our innate seeds of inner strength, but we must pay attention to the calls of life. The opportunities are almost always disguised as challenges and discomfort. Unfortunately, many of us either see challenges in one of two ways; both are unproductive. One is to have a victim mentality. We run away from challenges or complain about unfair circumstances. Another is to have a persecution mentality. We treat challenges as problems to get rid of and as situations to bring under control as quickly as possible. By taking these kinds of views, we miss the boat for opportunity and growth. Next time the boat comes around, it is likely to ride on fiercer and more intimidating waves.

I propose a different view—the view of an artist. We see challenges as opportunities for greater creativity and as potential for deeper and broader growth. We allow challenges to guide our imagination to create something that is uniquely ours.

Root sculpture is a Chinese art that is a few thousand years old. The artists use their imagination to appreciate an ordinary root's beauty. They unfold charm and inner power to carve the root based on its shape and nature. Therefore, every piece of artwork is unique.

In my hometown in China, I used to know a root sculpture artist. He'd go to the countryside to collect tree roots every so often that the peasants had dug out of the ground. He said that each root has its uniqueness that calls him, even the ones with ugly worm marks. He turns most ordinary or ugly looking roots into genuine and beautiful works of art.

Our life challenge calls us just as the root calls the artist. Each one of us could choose to artfully carve the challenge into a sculpture of our life and make the most of it.

It helps if we do not take everything for granted and as an accident. Everything happens for a reason. Our job is to find out what it is and make the most out of it by discovering and releasing a wonderful aspect of ourselves. This way we can enjoy the journey as well as the final outcome.

WRIGHT

We all have the inner seed that wants to grow, but what stops us? What suffocates inner strength development?

LI

The short answer is unconsciousness and laziness of mind. I will mention a few specific automatic views that I think can sabotage our life.

The first one is that we tend to live mechanically. In other words, we are on autopilot all the time and we react to life's situations automatically and mindlessly. This is a very deep topic when it comes to how our unconscious mind drives our life and I do not want to get into that here. The automatic way of living deprives us of seeing opportunity when life presents challenges. Some people deliberately choose to live in busyness to avoid the uncomfortable and uneasy feeling of silence—in the nakedness of their mind and idleness of their body. Some people live sometimes like a chicken with its head cut off.

When I was a child, we lived a very rudimentary life. We raised chickens for food. The way my dear father slaughtered a chicken was to cut its head off. When a chicken's head is cut off, it runs very fast around and around automatically until the blood drains out. It is a very disturbing image. There is a similarity to this when we live automatically. Our life's energy of consciousness is cut off from us.

Fragile identity is another one. We solely depend on others and an outer condition to relate to who we are and how we feel. Our sense of wellness relies exclusively on external events or people—of what others say or do—not choosing for ourselves. Lack of choice hinders self-empowerment and it puts us in a vulnerable position. The opposite is centered identity, where we take responsibly for how we feel and how we act in any given moment. This fragile identity often leads to developing a victim mentality, one of the killers of our inner strength discovery and development.

Many of us are living in emotional poverty, which is the root of emotional suffering. Lack of the knowledge of emotions generates either suppressing emotions or dramatizing emotions. However, behind the scene, emotions underline what we think and what we do. Being ignorant about our emotions greatly damages our ability to discover what matters to us and who sits on the driver seat of our life. Being ignorant about our emotions robs us of our chances to develop the inner balance and clarity that is the core of inner strength.

We tend to seek simplicity and generalization over real meaning when we are in conversation (both internal and external). We sort our interpretation of the events in life into "good" and "bad" or "safe" and "danger." I believe the binary way we "code" things is coded into our unconscious through our own relation with language and our past experiences. For example, when someone says, "you are fearful," you might automatically take it as an insult if you code "fearful" as bad. However, the word "fearful" merely describes an emotional state. The meaning of "bad" is imposed by you. After assigning the meaning of "bad" to the word "fearful," you are less likely to remain open for new learning. The binary code talk used in self-talk or in conversation with others, inhibits our ability to openly inquire into the richer world of thoughts and emotions, which is critical to inner strength discovery and development.

Victim mentality is another one. When we have a victim mentality, we can only see how the world wrongs us. There are only two actions available to us when we have a victim mentality. One is complaining and whining, another is acting through the emotion of resentment and resignation. Although the actions can appear brave driven by the victim mentality, they are a knee-jerk reaction fueled by unbalanced emotions, not conscious consideration.

We live in a tangible world; we only believe in what is tangible. Because of our tangible mentality, we prioritize our time and energy for only the activities that can gain us the approval of others and society in the form of money, material possessions, and popularity. Living with a tangible mentality deprives us of the aliveness of dimensions and colors. It deprives us of seeing the possibilities beyond what can be measured, and in my view, it deprives us of the fuel for our consciousness development.

WRIGHT

You've mentioned consciousness several times. What does our consciousness development have to do with inner strength development?

LI

Everything! Consciousness development is the foundation for human development, which includes inner strength development. I am not talking about spirituality. My definition of consciousness is the ability to discern and bring to the surface the conflicted emotions, thoughts, beliefs of needs, and demands that are often hidden in deep unconsciousness, and to deliberately make a choice for action moment by moment.

It is a myth that becoming more conscious means to create new emotions and thoughts. Our emotions and thoughts are driving our life regardless of whether we know it or not, much like gravity was at work long before Newton understood and defined it. The discovery of gravity allows scientists to employ gravity to serve humanity. Becoming more conscious can enable us to deliberately use the forces of emotions and thoughts that are driving our life to serve our wellness and growth. Not knowing, hence automatic reaction, is the root of many problems we face—personal problems, professional problems, societal problems, and world problems.

Intentionally developing our inner balance and clarity goes hand-in-hand with the development of our consciousness. Our inner balance and clarity is dependent on our acute awareness. To maintain a certain level of balance and clarity, we must cultivate an ability to mindfully observe, generate, discern, and integrate perspectives through ours and others' behaviors, emotions, needs, and demands. We must be aware of not only our own state of mind, but also that of others, as well as how the two interplay. Without consciousness, the best we can do is automatically and mechanically cope in the world, which often results in dreadful struggle.

Heightened consciousness enables us to have expanded perspectives on a life event, not only on the outcome. Heightened consciousness also gives expanded perspectives on the actions that lead to the outcome and on the underlying driving forces (guiding principles, values, goals, and habits) of our actions and how these driving forces are formed and how they are in play. Heightened consciousness provides more choices of possible actions, which can lead to more growth and expansion of our inner power.

As we intentionally build our physical muscle power and endurance by weightlifting or endurance training, we must consciously build character traits or habits through deliberate actions with discipline and persistence. Being purposeful requires consciousness. If you are mindful, you are more likely to achieve what you want.

WRIGHT

What's your view of inner strength as it relates to leadership development and teamwork?

LI

In my view, personal inner strength discovery and development is the inseparable part of leadership development and teamwork.

Most of us know the maxim of "give a man a fish, you have fed him for today. Teach a man to fish and you have fed him for a lifetime." The moral here is that it is much better to teach a person how to use a tool rather than do the task for him or her, or tell the person what to do. However, that kind of approach in leadership and human development does not provide a complete picture. It undermines people's incredible creative and generative potential and it oversimplifies life's uncertainties. What if the river runs dry? What if he is tired of eating fish?

In facing the complexity of life at home or at work, giving a tool or teaching a skill is not enough. We must cultivate people's inner capacity to learn, to inquire into the unknown, and to acquire the skills and tools necessary for unknown and complex situations. When that level of capacity is reached, people can really lead (feed themselves) no matter where or what the circumstances are.

The capacity to learn and create can only be cultivated from within—the inner strength of clarity, self-awareness, power, and self-enabling, including the inner strength of endurance and self-determination.

It is very encouraging to see that recent leadership study points to the fact that a higher consciousness is associated with being a great leader today. In his book, *From Good to Great,* Jim Collins uses the phase "paradoxical blend of personal humility and professional will" to describe the level five leadership. The ability to blend personal humility and professional will is the ability to operate from "both" perspectives with clarity and balance. It is the result of conscious clarity and balance in chaos.

In *Action Inquiry*, Bill Torbert describes the highest level of leadership—he calls it the "strategist/alchemist." Strategists/alchemists are leaders who are able to "navigate increasing levels of complexity and paradox, see the interdependent nature of system, dis-identify with ego [be], aware of meaning as a construct, etc." Great leaders have great capacity for clarity and balance and they are able to lead in complexity. They have the broadened and flexible character traits that are not identity based. They have a passion for ongoing learning and sustainable actions.

Teamwork means collaboration. My experience has been that one of the biggest barriers in teamwork is the clash of human difference and personal ego with its unconscious fears. To build a good team, we must first individually uncover unconscious fears that manifest in behaviors that negatively affect teamwork. So we must focus on our personal capacity for self-discovery and inner strength development. Only confident people can be productive team players. Inner strength discovery and development will go beyond the different "types" and "styles" to shed light on the origin and roots of those differences so that we can face them with great compassion, confidence, and courage.

Having said this, I want to add that skills development is also a very important part of human development. Skills development, however, must be built on inner strength development. Skills only serve well if used by those who have the right purpose, views, and actions.

WRIGHT

I understand that you approach leadership and people development differently from many training and motivational professionals, and your workshops are received as highly effective by your clients. So what do you think of the people/leadership development and training methods used today?

LI

Most training dispenses a lot of information and knowledge but engages little power for action and change. That's the primary problem with most training methods today. We gather knowledge like a starved dog digging for a hidden bone, but we apply knowledge like a deer in the headlight.

Most training is heavily focused on "how to" rather than building capacity to move from "how to" to "do." To move from "how to" to "do," we must engage the power from within to take action. Since inner strength and power are not knowledge and information to acquire, but involve muscles to exercise repeatedly, the process can be painfully tedious and disappointingly slow. I think that's why many training and development efforts tend to leave this part out.

Because of that, most of the leadership and teamwork training methods are very mechanical and are only about "how to." They can produce some limited incremental productivity, but they will not necessarily produce the most productive, innovative, and creative leaders. These are the people that today's corporations, organizations, countries, and the world want. If we develop people as we program machines, we only develop them into machines. What a machine can produce is limited by the design of its engineers. The potential of people is boundless. I believe that training in leadership and teamwork must include deep self-discovery and inner strength.

The other problem I see is that companies or people budget money and time disproportionately. They tend to budget too much money for workshops and retreats and allow too little time for real development. The journey inward to discover and acquire unlimited inner power requires time. I always warn my workshop participants about the pitfall of training when there is no practice, and patience. Individuals and companies must allocate sufficient time to allow new behaviors to form through practice. And practice must go beyond the classroom.

Practice implies failing. People must feel safe enough to fail without losing dignity or their sense of identity. The current human development culture is to "fix" people and get rid of weakness as fast as possible. There is little concern to preserve dignity. Providing a safe place for people to develop is hardly a reality. In my view, coaching relationships are the safest place for teams and individuals to develop. The essence of coaching is to create and maintain a safe place for the uncompromised legitimacy of all people and views—the ultimate respect and trust in people.

Last but not least, overly simplified skill training can be counterproductive. For example, you are taught the simple three steps of "how to" manage conflict in a team by "focusing on the team's goals, being objective, and conducting open communication." For some reason, you seem unable to resolve conflict because your emotions get in the way of "being objective" and your concerns and worries get in the way of "open communication." You might be discouraged and think, "Forget it. I will do it my way," and give up trying. People are not machines. There is much more to human development than fine-tuning a machine, and that is what this book is all about.

WRIGHT

Besides professional development, I can see what our inner strength has to do with our life wellness, fulfillment, or achievement. Would you like to elaborate on that?

LI

Our sense of enjoyment, fulfillment, and achievement about life is in direct proportion to our confidence and faith in life's roller coaster ride. Many of us enjoy roller coaster rides with immense anxiety and intense fear, but can hardly accept any anxiety and fear in real life. The difference is whether or not we have a big perspective. In the roller coaster, we accept the ups and downs as a given, and we see with clarity that the ups and down are transient and temporary. We have the confidence and faith that everything is okay. Because of that, the anxiety, anticipation, and fear of falling transforms into fun and enjoyment. If we apply the same principle to life, in order to live well and enjoy fully we must hold a bigger perspective about life. The bigger perspectives constantly demand clarity and awareness.

A sense of fulfillment in life depends on our sense of personal purpose about our life and our identity. Discovery of inner strength and developing it is also the journey to find one's life purpose and to discover and develop the self-identity that is grounded within.

Newton's Law of physics—"an object will remain in its original state until a force is applied to it"—can be applied to life's situations. Our inner power is the force of making life happen. My life experience has everything to do with how and if I apply the force to engage life. Without consciously engaging my inner force, life becomes stale and dormant no matter how busy I am. Vision and intention creates nothing if there are no conscious effort and deliberate action to apply my inner force to move toward them.

Consciously seeking and engaging clarity, inner power, and persistence in daily life is the door opens to fulfillment and happiness; I am convinced of it. My motherhood experience is a perfect reminder for me. I used to be an anxious and stressful mother. I often struggled with the many roles I played. I mistook my roles for my identity, so I did not have the ability to choose what role to play at what time. My different roles were all demanding attention from me at the same time. The struggle that held the most heartache for me was being a mother of two toddlers and being a professional in a large corporation. I was often anxious about getting to work and the things that needed to be done before meetings in the morning when I was feeding my kids breakfast. When I dropped them off at day care, I was sad as I pried open their small fingers clinging onto mine so tightly—"I want my mommy just for five more minutes!" In the mid morning, during an international conference call, I would feel guilty and missed my kids terribly. I was torn apart inside and felt completely lost. When I "woke up" one day from this madness, my sons were already four and five. I was deeply saddened. I wanted so much to enjoy my motherhood and be a happy mother and a successful professional.

To change things around, I started by paying attention to my thoughts while I was with my kids or working, and noticing how my thoughts affected my behavior and mood. Slowly, I started to notice when I felt anxious and worried about work when I was with my kids. The ability to "simply see" myself allowed me to step back. I wanted to spend unhurried quality time with my children, so I knew I must cultivate my patience.

I now make sure I am constantly aware that my purpose is to enjoy the moment with my kids, no matter how long my to-do-list is. By doing so, I give myself permission to be within my children's time schedule rather than be on my timetable. When I am able to really be present and enjoy my time with my kids, I find myself much more focused and productive while I am working and I can appreciate myself when I am playing the role a professional. Although the journey of motherhood has had its ups and downs, I continue to stick to "I am the one to choose" no matter what, and I choose to be the mother I want to be when I am with my kids. I also choose to be the professional when I work.

Now, my sense of wellness when I am with my kids or at work is beyond words. I experience deep love and joy overflows inside of me, along with the stillness of peace and gratitude when I am with them, although my life is busier and more demanding than it has ever been in my entire life. I also thoroughly enjoy my work and the creativity that flows through me. It is miraculous what conscious choice and deliberate action can generate in the long run. Most amazing is that my kids seem ever so fabulous, once now that I am able to enjoy my motherhood.

That's the inner strength discovery and development I am talking about. It's the only road that leads to happiness! If we feel we have no choice but to fight through life stressfully and madly, it's a sign that we are not engaged in the endless life energy that is our inner strength.

WRIGHT

What are the most challenging things that our readers must be aware of or to overcome on this journey of discovering and cultivating inner strength?

LI

First is to overcome the uneasiness of facing yourself alone and being with yourself. Many of us are uncomfortable with being alone—with silence and stillness. But it is when we are alone in silence and in stillness that we can find the pathway to knowing ourselves, to understanding our mind, and to cultivating balance and clarity. We are more comfortable with busyness and distraction, while complaining about how fast time goes by. It is paradoxical. The distraction can be in any form of entertainment—socializing, watching television, mindless reading—anything that distracts us from facing the stripped down self. Reflection is common sense but hardly a common practice.

Second, practice taking conscious action with integrity, accountability, and courage. Taking conscious action can be hard, tedious, and maybe even painful for some people. It is easier to be a bold reactive fighter, using the automatic approach of "toughing it out" to engage life. It is also easier to sit around contemplating life without actually having to personally engage in it.

To have strong muscles, you must lift weight. Trying to build bicep muscles without weightlifting is not going to get you the biceps you want. Understanding how to discover and develop inner strength does not go very far without the daily practice of building inner strength and consciousness, and actively engaging the world. Practice must take up a majority of the time in our personal development. Having said that, slowing down and taking time to ask questions and explore the rich interior terrain is the very first step of the long march.

Third, we must allow ourselves time to pursue something society defines as "intangible" and "esoteric." We want instant gratification of things or success. We don't have the patience to practice as a form of waiting. In the modern culture of more and faster, we do not have time and do not want to take the time to devote to the discipline of self-discovery and development—to "practice for the sake of practice" as succinctly said by George Leonard in his book, *Mastery: The Keys to Success and Long-Term Fulfillment.* If we don't like something about ourselves, we want change right now. We forget how long it took to get where we are now.

WRIGHT

So what practices would you recommend to help us discover our inner strength and start doing what you're talking about?

LI

The answer to this question depends on what your current condition is and where you want to go. But in general, there are practices we all can do. Remember, a healthy balance of reflecting and taking action is the key!

First, give time to reflect and to expand the consciousness of our mind. When the mind is quiet, we can see more and hear more, hence gain clarity. Examples of this type of activity are:

- Meditation
- Yoga, Tai Chi
- Keep a journal that is focused on your thought process—your assumptions, your interpretation, your speculations, your feelings.
- Practice endurance events such as walking, jogging, swimming, hiking, and cycling in silence (without talking or listening to music).
- Explore the paradoxical approaches, ideas, and perspectives in life. Keep a journal of your contradictory thoughts and values, and observe how they play in your life.
- Practice noticing your negative judgments and feelings, while seeing the positive aspects of all things.
- Practice the moment of awareness through self-inquiry. For example, "What do I feel right now and why?" "Right now, are my thoughts, actions, and emotions in alignment?"
- Create a theme for a journal for a few months focusing on one area of the development. I just started a journal to cultivate my capacity of authentic self-expression: "Are you being authentic?"—the daily reflection of my words and deeds. It is incredible how much I have learned about myself and how much strength I have gained from journaling.

Second, take action. Once you decide to do something, take immediate action on "what is the right thing to do now." What action to take/practice is personal—we want different things in life, so we must take different actions. However, "just do it" is something we all can practice more.

- Practice new approaches in life that give you want you want. For example, I like my house to be tidy. After acknowledging to myself that a tidy house is important to me, I began to practice taking care of the little things immediately, such as keeping the desk clean and the sink free of dishes at all times. However, I know people who are the opposite. The many little things in life can tangle them up and they never get around to doing the things they really want, for example, finishing school. In their case, they might need to practice giving themselves permission to allow dishes to pile up now and then in order to focus on the schoolwork. It is about expanding our ability rather than changing or switching from one to another.

- Practice keeping your commitments/promises at all times, especially the ones to yourself.
- Practice making promises only for the right reason. I do not recommend that anyone use external approval or gratification as a motive.
- Practice never blaming others or yourself, but taking responsibility to make things better. When things do not go your way, always ask yourself, "What do I need to do differently?"
- Practice letting go of control and attachment sometimes. Flow a little at times with the rhythm of life and enjoy the process of things becoming and unfolding.

WRIGHT

Before we close this conversation, is there anything you would like to add to this topic?

LI

Remember to use your gift of questioning your own thoughts, feelings, words, actions, sensations, etc. In other words, you've been given a gift of being able to be highly conscious. If you pay attention, you will know a lot about yourself—what you want, what you need to do and to be, and even how to do. It might all just start with learning to listen to your inner nag and pursue the nag to get to the bottom of it. That's a key for self-discovery and development. We have such incredible capabilities and we must use them. I do not recommend that people wait until some dramatic life event; that approach is too painful and too scary.

Be patient, persistent, and enjoy the journey and process. Our inner strength discovery and development is a lifelong journey, so enjoy the process and journey itself with ease, gratitude, and compassion. Some spiritual faith will help ease the anxiety of wanting to reach your destiny on this endless, grand journey.

Poet Ranier Maria Rilke said, "What we choose to fight is so tiny! What fights within us is so great!" The journey inward to our inner strength is a grand journey as well as a tough battle, but the outcome is immensely rewarding from the very beginning.

WRIGHT

Well, what great conversation. I've really learned a lot here today. This is something to think about over time, and I agree with you—just get it done by doing it. This has been a very interesting chapter and I know our readers are going to enjoy it. I appreciate the time you've taken with me today to answer all these questions.

LI

It's truly a pleasure.

WRIGHT

Today we've been talking with Yun Li. She is founder of Yu*nexus. She's a certified coach, a workshop facilitator, and mediator. After listening to her today I'm inclined to think she knows what she's talking about, and I'm sure readers will get a lot out of this chapter.

Yun, thank you so much for being with us today on *Discover Your Inner Strength*.

LI

David, thank you.

AN INTERVIEW WITH...

Dr. Larry J. Linden

402 Deerfield Court
Hendersonville, NC 28792
888.988.4360
LLinden@CareerGameChampionships.com
www.CareerGameChampionships.com

ABOUT THE AUTHOR

Dr. Linden has over twenty years of independent and corporate experience in international career management coaching. He has worked with leading outplacement organizations as a Division Manager, Senior Consultant, Job Developer, and is a Master Trainer of Career Consultants. He has consulted to individual career changers across the United States and in 16 foreign countries including those from Africa, Europe, and the Pacific rim.

Dr. Linden has published articles on career portfolios and effective résumé design. He has conducted workshops and courses on portfolio development, career transition, résumé writing, answering tough interview questions, networking, job search strategies, and self-marketing for success.

Larry has provided career management services to individuals, students, small business owners and Fortune 100 companies. He has consulted to companies with outplacement services, candidate analysis, performance and organizational synergy.

DAVID WRIGHT (WRIGHT)

Today we're talking with Larry J. Linden PhD. Dr. Linden has over twenty years of independent and corporate experience in international career management consulting. He has consulted to all levels of individuals and students across the United States and in sixteen countries. His projects have included development and facilitation of unemployment support groups. He has designed and/or delivered diversified training programs with emphasis on personal development for corporations and curriculum for colleges. Dr. Linden received his master's degree in Education from Cambridge College in Massachusetts and earned his PhD in Sociology from the Union Institute and University in Cincinnati, Ohio. He is a member of the Career Management Alliance and The International Speakers Network.

Dr. Linden, welcome to *Discover Your Inner Strength*.

LARRY LINDEN (LINDEN)

Thank you very much.

By way of introduction, I think the journey to discover inner strength is one that I've been fortunate to observe in people who have sought personal growth and self-empowerment in an area that nearly every American engages at one time or another—getting a job. That may seem a bit trite, but as a Career Consultant I have become keenly aware that people's identities are tightly interwoven with what they do for a living. When that has been taken away from them through layoffs, downsizing, or any of the other industry buzzwords to describe being fired, self-esteem and confidence usually take a hit. At that point, some feel they are between a rock and a hard place.

Not surprisingly, people are typically very good at a number of things, but job searching is not usually one of them. Helping people develop themselves in this area has provided me with the very rewarding experience of watching them regain their sense of self and enhanced inner strength.

WRIGHT

What is it that you have observed in helping people develop themselves and discover their inner strength?

LINDEN

People know what they know. However, the danger is that they don't know what they don't know. Specifically, when it comes to changing careers or getting jobs, people believe they know how to be effective in regaining employment. "Effective" is the operative word there, but the information most people have is overly simplified and the task itself is one that few have ever become skilled at.

To complicate the situation, there is a cornucopia of available information about the topic—too much information. The question immediately becomes what information will best work for them and their individual situation? Many people simply aren't aware of any different or better way. This puts the American worker in a most uncomfortable position of being what I call, "a victim of the system."

One of my favorite stories about this very situation was a software engineer who came to me after over a year of unemployment without having had a single interview. As a techie, he was very good at researching the volumes of available job search tools and processes, all to no avail, however. I coached him though my materials and in a short time he was ready to go out and try it again. Using his newfound knowledge he was able to get a job offer in just forty-eight hours. He enthusiastically accepted the position and his confidence soared. A sense of inner strength that he'd not felt in a long time was rekindled. Observing this happen was extraordinary.

The information was there. What I did was present it to him in a way that allowed him to develop his skill and use it much more effectively. When shown the door, most people are able to walk through. For most job searchers, the door just isn't easily visible and that has been the typical condition with roots that go back more than a hundred years.

At the advent of the industrial revolution many companies took on a strong paternal role in the lives of American workers. This relationship worked well for more than half a century with companies rewarding worker's commitment, loyalty, and good behavior with job security, health and medical plans, pay increases, promotions, and attractive retirement benefits.

Advanced technology, global markets, and the competitive nature of business ultimately brought about a dynamic shift in the original relationship between worker and employer. An exploding population, in conjunction with technological efficiency, has brought about a social anomaly between supply and demand of humans. Along with that came a significant change in workforce function requirements and the skills needed to perform those functions. Service industries are booming while goods manufacturing is in decline and/or being transferred to low cost labor populations in other parts of the world.

These same advancements and significant numbers of unemployed individuals have driven the need for a rapid evolution in the skills required to become re-employed, and the need for people to teach those skills.

I wanted to close the knowledge gap and help eliminate an unknown about something that is near and dear to the America worker—staying employed amid a volatile and shifting business world. To accomplish this I became a Career Consultant.

WRIGHT

So just what is a Career Consultant?

LINDEN

Well, that is an interesting question. It's traditionally been a rather obscure industry, and there are only a few people who really know what we do. By and large, the greater public thinks that we are recruiters. There are some similarities and that's why people get them confused. Recruiters work for companies that look for talented people with very specific skills, and most recruiting offices specialize in particular functions like technology or engineering. So recruiters are paid by the companies that are looking to fill jobs with the right candidate.

Career consultants, on the other hand, are professionals who train and coach people who have paid them to show them how to effectively compete for jobs. They often provide job leads and the specific positions in a targeted geographic area, but for the most part the consultant trains their clients in how to market themselves. This will usually involve one or more résumé types for different scenarios, including coaching. They'll get some help with network coaching and negotiating, for instance. More importantly, consultants will generally build client confidence and self-empowerment, which is key these days. I find that this often translates to inner strength. I've also found that this effort helps the unemployed person feel that he or she knows how to become re-employed.

WRIGHT

Are there different kinds of career counselors or consultants?

LINDEN

Yes, and services can vary from consultant to consultant, but the core ingredients are the ones I mentioned. There are outplacement firms that provide consulting services to corporations that are displacing a large number of employees.

The distinction between counselor and consultant (and I use those two words synonymously here) is a little bit blurred, but there are some differences. So, let me explain. Many people who find themselves in the need of an expert to provide specific tools and action plans that they can implement, already know where they're going. They simply haven't been in the market for many years. Some of them never have, as they came right into a position out of college. They're looking for a consultant to arm them with the tactical tools to avoid making needless mistakes. Executive coaching fits into that same category as well.

Others are looking for direction—in many cases, any direction. So many are looking for the best track that is available to them with their background. This activity usually requires a short period of analysis, some counseling, and discussion before laying any groundwork regarding the tools and the approaches needed to get them into something different. Once they've determined a new direction, both types of career professionals will provide job leads for specific positions and train the clients on how to market themselves.

A great example of career counseling was a lawyer who came to me for assistance. She had been a trial lawyer for some time and was making very good money, but wanted to do something else and had been unable to determine a clear direction. After some diagnostic work and analysis, we focused on her passion for dispute resolution and negotiation. Her job was very demanding and most of our consultations were by way of cell phone while she was driving to or from an appointment. This was all going well except that I found myself strongly urging her to pull over before she had an accident! She was trying hard to concentrate on what I was saying to her and at the same time pay attention to traffic. After several close calls and tense moments she finally gave in and would pull over while we had our discussions, to the delight of other drivers, I'm sure. Very soon, she networked her way to a CEO of a chain that had numerous franchisees who were always bickering. She was excellent at defusing such situations and landed the high paying position very soon after.

It really doesn't matter too much what the professionals call themselves. It's much more about what the client needs that determines the role that the career professional will play. In addition, consultants and counselors generally build client confidence and self-empowerment, which usually translates into an inner strength on the part of their clients.

There are also private consulting firms that offer services to individuals who are willing to pay for that help. These services can include career evaluation and consultation, all the way through to getting a job, but these firms charge anywhere from a couple of thousand dollars to $12,000 and more, so it can get rather expensive.

Colleges, of course, have almost always had career advisors who help students get their heads wrapped around employment. These advisors usually have a pulse on the local employment market and usually have numerous job fairs where students can have direct access to companies that are looking for up and coming talent.

WRIGHT

So how did you become a career consultant?

LINDEN

Actually, it's interesting how that started. In the mid 1980s I was working for a company called Digital Equipment Corporation, which at one point had been at the top of the computer world. Then, in the 1980s, they were beginning to make massive layoffs. At that time I was working in the planning department. The HR manager came by my cubicle and asked if I would be interested in working for him as a trainer because he had noticed my rather extensive training background. Within a couple of weeks I was helping in that department. The training program soon evolved into an outplacement arm, helping employees find new niches in a technology world. We worked and watched as facility after facility was closed with hundreds upon hundreds of employees being dumped into the street every month. And at one point I became one of them.

During that time period, national unemployment numbers were on a dramatic incline all across America. Interestingly enough it was my wife, Margie, who came to me with the notion that since I was so good at changing jobs and careers why shouldn't I show other people how to do it. I thought that was a pretty good idea, so I began putting together some workshops and seminars and so on, in the local and surrounding communities.

As I worked with these people, I became painfully aware that a crucial element was missing for many of these unemployed individuals. Over the previous ten to fifteen years, there had been a deep sociological division in America. Specifically, those individuals who had kept up with technological trends and those that had not. Every day I was meeting people who did not have a home computer or the knowledge of how to use one, and didn't even have an e-mail address. This deficit, in a technological world, is a tremendous handicap for anybody trying to get a job, especially when the market is tough. Even today, in a market where there are as many as three people for every one job, that's available, we see many people who have not kept up. That's a tough situation to face, since most jobs today require some type of computer skills.

Most people are skilled at their particular area of expertise, such as engineers or nurses or something like that. That's great, but very few people are skilled at what it takes to get re-employed. They think they can throw a résumé out there and it will happen, but in this day and age, because of technological changes, it's getting much more challenging. Job searchers need to know more about that skill. Without a doubt, falling behind in the technical world makes things very difficult for individuals who are looking for work today.

WRIGHT

Have you made career changes yourself?

LINDEN

Yes I have, definitely. In my early adult years, I had discovered that my interests were broad and varied. I was the quintessential jack-of-all-trades, master of none. I kept looking and looking for something that would hold my interest, but that didn't happen for many years.

The major careers I experienced included military intelligence, quality assurance, retail management, inventory control, manufacturing, high tech manufacturing, systems planning, training and development, entrepreneur, college instructor, and finally career counseling. Essentially, what I found was that these varied careers were what prepared me and helped me to be a career counselor. I could identify with people at all levels and from many professions because most of them were directly or indirectly related to something I'd done in the past.

WRIGHT

So why do you think this one held your interest more than the others?

LINDEN

The core transferable skills and attributes materialized and evolved from my youth and in my early adulthood. Training and development, teaching, counseling, empathy, and motivation were things that I was most passionate about. Discovering that helping others develop themselves was crucial to the future I was creating. I was following my intuitive inclination without yet putting a name to what the universe was unfolding for me. Later it would become my mission in life to help others find some ground to stand upon amid the rough seas of the world of work.

WRIGHT

How did you find your inner strength to become a success?

LINDEN

I grew up in a highly volatile and dysfunctional alcoholic family. In my formative years the only difference between myself and those who were behind bars were the bars. I had already begun my journey to the darker side of society and was setting a straight course into crime.

Admittedly, I have absolutely no idea at what point I made the conscious decision to change my course and accept the reality that my father and mother were good examples of how *not* to live. I don't think it was an epiphany, I believe it was more of a gradual awakening.

Through most of my early years I was a bitter and negative person who lived as though the cup was absolutely half empty and didn't seem to have much of a shot at changing any time soon. Then fate began to change my life for me. I met a young woman who shortly thereafter became my wife. She had come from a loving family and soon demonstrated that there was a different, better lifestyle that could be lived.

It took a little while but I began to see there was a choice I needed to make if there was to be any opportunity to improve my situation. It was here that the emergence of my inner strength began.

Numerous self-help books and years of therapy helped me stay away from the prison bars that could easily have been my undoing, and to continue building the strength I'd found.

It has taken most of my adult life to actually see that the cup is really half full and it was within my power to fill it to the brim if I wanted.

A huge turning point for me was when I fully committed to go back to school. School had never been a good experience and I truly avoided the idea of getting into something that I was convinced would be painful and would likely be a profound failure. It had been an ongoing discussion for many years, but each time I found a reason not to move forward.

Interestingly, it was my daughter who informed me that there was a school in town for "old folks" like me. Although, that part was purely a generational perspective, I was, in fact, well into my fifties by that time. I will thank her always for that little push that was necessary for me to feel that it might be possible.

The story then took a remarkable and quite unforeseen turn.

I was barely in my master's program, which I was doing surprisingly well at considering my past learning experiences, when a couple of professors approached me and suggested that I continue on with my education. They told me that I definitely was appropriate material for a doctoral program. Without reservation, I will share with you that this was one of the most acknowledging moments of my life. I had come a long, long way in my own self-improvement and in finding a keen sense of inner strength.

I knew that I'd need a lot of help, but my professors were very willing to help me through the rigors of the doctoral program. These were by far the loftiest goals I'd ever set for myself. I am who I am today because of my rocky start and the courage I had to jump into the darkness and trust my higher power. For me, building a strong base of confidence where before there was none was an enormous step toward discovering and developing my inner strength.

WRIGHT

So have you arrived at the personal goals you set for yourself those many years ago?

LINDEN

A person can set goals like those, but in truth, it is a life journey with many goals that get accomplished. The path I've chosen has had many speed bumps along the way, but has been significantly smoother than it might have been had I made different choices.

What I have done is reach a place where I truly enjoy being able to give back and share my experiences with those who want to make positive life changes for themselves, which, as I found, very often include a career change. My own success is really vicarious through my clients. My quest was to design a program that had the potential to change how people felt about job searches.

The realization of my success culminated when clients completed my training program, went out to implement what I had shown them, and then reported back to me stating, "I've never had so much fun looking for a job in my life." Of course, not everyone with whom I've consulted came back with that response, but to hear those words from anyone was more than I expected. It has been spectacularly rewarding.

What I've discovered over the years is that uncovering one's inner strength springs from a deep examination of the self. Then, once a heightened awareness of who you are is identified, that can then be the foundation for doing that which is your true passion.

When these two elements are combined, people have likely arrived at a point in their own development that allows them to be self-actualized and feel a personal sense of inner strength.

WRIGHT

What do you think are the main differences between your advice and that of other people who are in your field?

LINDEN

As I mentioned before, many people are not aware of what they don't know with regard to career and job changes. As a result, they are using only the tools and techniques they know and what they believe is available to them. This is where my extensive research has paid off. I have been thoroughly engaged in discovering and developing this chunk of information that most people usually go out of their way to avoid, let alone develop as a skill.

A good example would be the vast number of career consultants and advisors who have stated and written articles on the concept that job searchers should "get used to a lot of rejections" as a fact of life for people looking for work. Some people are okay with this. But, by and large, the people with whom I've worked have expressed that they were already in a tough emotional state of mind resulting from being without a job or laid off in the first place.

I have known hundreds upon hundreds of individuals who, when faced with a campaign of rejections, find it just too much to deal with and simply give up.

Another popular approach is to look for a "silver bullet," or some other shortcut to help them avoid actually having to look for work. Eventually, they must conduct a search and not surprisingly, job search is, in fact, a job. It is a significant job of marketing the self, which most will feel is distasteful at best. What most people don't know is that it is not at all a time that has to be fraught with rejections, as many professionals in the career management field would suggest. With more effective approaches, better strategies, and more sophisticated tools, a person conducting a search can greatly minimize the expected high volume of rejections that typifies old style searching.

This alone has changed the perception of the normal drama that is affiliated with job search.

There is another key bit of knowledge. While most people know about résumés, interviews, and networking as the core things that are necessary when it comes to looking for work, very few people know that the approach is often more important than the tools. I found that structuring a job search as if it were a business project makes a tremendous difference in results. In this way, more strategic thinking and calculative—rather than speculative—planning comes into play and the results are much more effective.

Yet another crucial ingredient that nearly every searcher I've ever worked with was not aware of (and likely didn't know how to apply) was the element of quality assurance.

WRIGHT

How does quality assurance fit into finding a job?

LINDEN

Few people think there is much of a correlation. I would submit that there is a significant connection. I've always said that if people can't measure their efforts, then they will not easily be able to manage their job search. If people are not managing their search, it's probably managing them and thereby entrusting their future to the winds of fate. I find that to be a rather huge gamble. In most instances that's because people do not know how to measure a job search project.

The manufacturing experience earlier in my career was largely in the world of quality. I took the same ideology as exemplified by such quality greats as W. Edwards Deming and applied it to search techniques and tools. For instance, one of Deming's core teachings was about process improvement. A job search is a process and if the searcher does not routinely examine it to determine how and where it may be improved, it is most likely that the same errors will occur over and over again with the same results. This has the strong possibility of taking a toll on a person's psyche, self-esteem, and inner strength over time without their even knowing it. This can be particularly troubling if the searcher is not aware he or she is making the errors in the first place.

Another core teaching of Deming's was the necessity for building quality into the product, not just assuming that quality was inherent. An example of a product in job searching might be the résumé. If the quality isn't there from the get-go (for example, typos and other errors or inconsistencies), the end result will likely suffer. Again, many people may believe they have a résumé that is error-proof. They never discover the product was not up to the standard it needs to be effective. Meanwhile dozens of useless résumé documents may be out there under-performing.

I recall an excellent example of a person who wrote she had excellent attention to detail skills. However, she had misspelled a word and spell-check didn't pick it up. It's not difficult to imagine where most, if not all, of her résumés ended up.

Those people I've coached who have done a good job of measuring the effectiveness of their process (is it working the way they want) have been able to implement process improvement and change the outcome in a variety of ways. This usually manifests in far fewer rejections and timesaving, with the corresponding increase in self-esteem and inner strength.

WRIGHT

How can job searchers measure something they have little control over?

LINDEN

You bring up an interesting misperception. For the most part people think hiring is nearly all in the hands of the company doing the hiring and that they have little control over the market, company layoffs, and the people who do the hiring. That is not entirely true.

Searchers can be in control of much more than they are aware of. For instance, a person can *monitor* the market trend and future trends of the careers he or she is in with regard to expansion or shrinkage.

Good planning, in advance of trends, helps people avoid being caught off guard. This is especially true when companies are downsizing. As I found out, planning isn't always a part of the mix for some folks. A client had come to me saying he'd worked with other career counselors and was sure that I wouldn't be able to help him any more than the others had. That was certainly a different *approach* than most, but I went on and asked what he needed. He said that he needed some help with his interviewing. I asked him when his interview was scheduled and he responded, "In a couple of hours!" I did what I could with my one meeting and later found that he got the job. That part was great, but I wouldn't want to make a habit of it!

Searchers can actually *measure* the results of the affect of their résumé submissions and other search tools. Measurability is a key factor in results. All they need is a quality standard to work from. "Eventually," is not a measurable standard. However, the standard of attaining one solid interview for every ten targeted résumés sent is measurable and is one that works. If the résumé is not producing the desired results within the standard, it is likely that something is amiss with the document and it needs adjusting.

Another example of a job search quality standard is in the area of interviewing. One offer for every three interviews is a solid guideline. Again, if the effort is not producing these results, root cause analysis is critical in determining what is not working and then make the appropriate correction.

These are only a couple of examples of things that can be measured and when this thinking is applied across the board of the total search project, the results are very self-empowering.

With a little knowledge, the unemployed person can find his or her inner strength and get through a typically difficult time with a minimum of downtime and stress.

WRIGHT

This is an interesting subject. Is there anything else that you want to share about finding your inner strength?

LINDEN

As a strong proponent of life-long learning, I have come to believe that it is important to be open to alternative possibilities and to make the effort to close the gap between what is known and what isn't.

The knowledge is there to bring about transformational personal change if we are but willing to walk through the door.

My material is not so unique that it's never been thought of before. Most of it is surprisingly easy. Nearly every client with whom I've worked at one point or another has stated, "I can't believe I've never seen this. It all makes sense!" How I've put it all together is likely the thing that does the job.

The natural thing to do is to look at career or job change as though it were a linear activity, which is seemingly easier and feels more logical. Most would prefer that job and career change to be simple, not complex. But, in truth, the nature of job and career transition is more closely defined as a circular system of dynamically integrated parts and is complex.

With that in mind, it's important to be aware that treating the various elements as individualized pieces of the whole is not as helpful to the person doing the searching.

My research looked at the job search process elements at a deeper level, as a fully integrated system. Using Wheatley's concept of giving primary value to the relationships that exist among seemingly discrete parts, I found the search process to be much more effective if seen and practiced through a quantum theoretical lens with an underlying principal of dynamic connectedness. In other words, you have to look at the whole and realize that all the parts, which seem separate, are actually all deeply interconnected. That's made all the difference.

Now, the person who is just trying to get a job to make a buck need not delve into quantum mechanics to regain employment. But, he or she is more likely to find order out of chaos by following the "yellow brick road" laid out by the research results in order to help get where he or she wants to be. It is then when the job seeker is more likely to arrive at a sense of independence, self-empowerment, and discover an inner strength through learning.

WRIGHT

Well, Dr. Linden, this has been a very, very interesting conversation, especially given the fiasco of 2008 that has cost hundreds of thousands of people their jobs. I really appreciate your bringing all of this new information to me. It may not be new to others, but it certainly is new to me. I have enjoyed this conversation and I'll just bet that our readers will too.

LINDEN

Well, certainly this is the time for it, that's for sure.

WRIGHT

Today we've been talking to Larry J. Linden PhD. According to Benson and Klipper, job loss is among the top ten losses in life. To further complicate things, most people are very good at something, but job searching is usually not on that list. Dr. Linden has always believed in the adage that knowledge is power and if so, then learning how to conduct an effective and much less stressful job search, which takes about half the time as most, can be really empowering. More than ten years of research has gone into designing a personal development program with the emphasis on career management that has helped people to be much better at something that few people are very good at. Dr. Linden says, "I've been privileged to touch the lives of many people who came away with a sense of confidence, enhanced inner strength, and self empowerment. That for me has become personally gratifying. I can just imagine that after this conversation this is very true.

Dr. Linden, thank you so much for being with us today on *Discover Your Inner Strength.*

LINDEN

Thank you very much for inviting me.

AN INTERVIEW WITH...

Brian J. Marinelli

Brian Marinelli International LLC
P.O. Box 16335
Tampa, FL. 33687
813.975.8462
brian@brianmarinelli.com
www.brianmarinelli.com
www.keystocharisma.com

ABOUT THE AUTHOR

Brian J. Marinelli is an award-winning professional speaker, published author, charisma coach, and interpersonal communications expert.

He has authored the course, Keys to Charisma (www.keystocharisma.com), been a contributing author to the book Share and Grow Rich, and has written numerous booklets on communication and personal development skills.

Brian conducts public and private talks and seminars at a variety of corporations, associations, educational institutions, and special events. He has spoken for Baywinds Adult Learning Centers, Toastmasters International, The Knowledge Shop, The Great American Teach-In, Speaker Services, and many others.

A gifted presenter, Brian is the originator of the groundbreaking workshops *Unleash Your Winning Personality* and *Fabulous First Impressions* that have been attended by hundreds of people since 2002.

As a Toastmaster, Brian has won several speech competitions; and is a recipient of the Competent Toastmaster Award and the Advanced Toastmaster Award from Toastmasters International.

Brian is the Founder and President of Brian Marinelli International LLC; a company specializing in helping individuals and businesses develop more productive and fulfilling relationships allowing them to achieve their goals in an ever changing world.

THE INTERVIEW

DAVID WRIGHT (WRIGHT)

Today we're talking with Brian J. Marinelli. Brian is an award-winning professional speaker, published author, charisma coach, and interpersonal communications expert.

He has authored the course, *Keys to Charisma* (www.keystocharisma.com), he was a contributing author to the book, *Share and Grow Rich*, and has written numerous booklets on communication and personal development skills.

Brian conducts public and private talks and seminars at a variety of corporations, associations, educational institutions, and special events. He has spoken for Baywinds Adult Learning Centers, Toastmasters International, The Knowledge Shop, The Great American Teach-In, Speakers Services, and many others.

A gifted presenter, Brian is the originator of the groundbreaking workshops, *Unleash Your Winning Personality* and *Fabulous First Impressions*, which have been attended by hundreds of people since 2002.

As a Toastmaster, Brian has won several speech competitions; and is a recipient of the Competent Toastmaster Award and the Advanced Toastmaster Award from Toastmasters International.

Brian is the Founder and the President of Brian Marinelli International LLC, a company specializing in helping individuals and businesses develop more productive and fulfilling relationships, allowing them to achieve their personal and professional goals in an ever-changing world.

Brian, welcome to *Discover Your Inner Strength*.

BRIAN MARINELLI (MARINELLI)

Well, thank you David. It's a pleasure to be speaking with you today.

WRIGHT

So, how do you define charisma?

MARINELLI

There are many different ways to define charisma, but I define charisma in two distinct ways: *academically* and *elementally.* The academic version, as described in *Webster's New World Dictionary*, defines charisma as a special quality of leadership that captures the popular imagination and inspires allegiance and devotion, or as a special charm or allure that inspires fascination or devotion. But that's really the technical definition for charisma; I prefer to define charisma in its elemental form. I think the best way to define charisma is by asking the questions: What makes people so magnetic? What is the characteristic these people exhibit that draws us to them? What is that special magnetism they have and where does it come from? How do they develop this magnetic personality, and how can we do the same thing? This may sound like many different questions, but it really is the same question, just restated in different ways—what is it that these people do that makes them so charismatic, and how do they do it?

The simple answer is that charismatic people have high self- esteem—that is obvious. We also surely recognize that people with charisma and personal magnetism present an aura of strength, power, and certainty. Inherent within themselves is a profound sense of self-confidence, self-worth, and self-assuredness, which comes directly from *high self-esteem*. In fact, everything from self-image to self-worth to self-respect to self-importance, and ultimately self-confidence, stems unquestionably from maintaining a healthy amount of self-esteem. Therefore, I assert that excellent self-esteem is the seed to charisma.

WRIGHT

So, is charisma something one is born with or can it be learned?

MARINELLI

I get that question all the time, and have found that the majority of people tend to believe that charisma is something that one is born with—you have it or you don't. Yet, the reality is that the exact opposite is true. Anybody can learn the secrets to becoming a more charismatic person. Granted, there may be certain individuals who have a natural proclivity to charisma; just as there are child prodigies who are gifted in mathematics, science, or music at a very early age, but those are extremely rare cases. My experience and research has revealed that charisma and personal magnetism are abilities that a person can develop over time.

In my seminars, I use the analogy of Olympic high divers as an example to prove to my audience that they have the ability to create a magnetic and charismatic personality. Look at Olympic high divers—they climb up on platforms to what appears to be death-defying heights, and dive into the water below with such precision, grace, and poise, that it almost seems superhuman. What we don't see though is all the work that is required to accomplish an athletic feat of this magnitude.

High divers practice every single day for years and years, pushing their bodies and minds to the absolute limit, simply to get the chance to go to the Olympics and even then, they may not make the cut. The point is that person did not become an Olympic high-diver overnight.

Obviously, I am not suggesting that we need to train like Olympic high-divers here. What I am saying is we can learn to develop our skills to establish a winning, charismatic personality, just as an athlete learns how to develop his or her skills in a particular sport.

It is important to realize that charisma is not due to some innate ability, it is a skill set that can by taught to anybody.

WRIGHT

Do you believe that people with charisma possess something the rest of us don't, and if they do, what is it?

MARINELLI

Well, I wouldn't say charismatic people possess something the rest of us don't; they have just polished and honed those skill sets as I previously described. We all have these skill sets; we just haven't sharpened them and formed them in the same way they have. Besides developing a series of skill sets, the major difference between charismatic individuals and other people is *mindset*.

Charismatic people hold themselves in high regard and, at the same time, hold other people in high regard too. I am not saying people with charisma view themselves in an egotistical or arrogant way. I am saying that they view themselves as important members of society. They believe they have value, and believe other people have value too. Generally, they subscribe to a specific belief system that is rooted in mutual respect for one another. This specific mindset is what charismatic people believe at their core—a belief that people are significant, and this is what magnetically attracts us to these individuals. After all, we all want to feel like we are important, right? We want to feel like we have purpose, worth, and that we are appreciated for what we have to offer to the world. Charismatic people's convictions about themselves, life, and other people cause them to have a positive self-image, once again stemming from outstanding self-esteem.

You might be wondering how vital self-confidence is to this equation. Having tremendous self-confidence is definitely a chief component in self-esteem. Those who have superior self-esteem tend to have superior self-confidence as well. If you acquire reasonably good self-confidence, your self-esteem will rise exponentially. I suppose the best way to describe it is like this: charismatic people have fantastic self-esteem and the manner in which they express this wonderful self-esteem is through self-confidence. Therefore, if you develop magnificent self-confidence you will also develop magnificent self-esteem as well.

WRIGHT

Is there one main cornerstone principle or habit that a person must cultivate in order to become a charismatic individual?

MARINELLI

Yes, David, there is. The key is *value*. We talked previously about the emphasis of feeling that you have value; charismatic people clearly understand the importance of establishing this sense of significance in another person. You should make a conscious effort to show people that you recognize and respect them, that you value them and the contribution they make. Developing this habit benefits you too, for when you let other people know that you realize the value they have, you in turn raise your own individual worth in their eyes as well.

Let me give you an example of how this principle can positively affect your life, especially in relation to your charisma quotient. My grandfather, Jerry Norton, built a multi-million dollar billboard company in Cincinnati, Ohio, from the ground up. Starting with just a few pieces of lumber, a couple of plots of land, and a spirit of determination, he grew his business into a thriving enterprise, among some very stiff competition in Ohio at the time. He was not only financially successful and well respected in the industry but he also had tons of friends. People clamored to be around my grandfather, not because of his wealth but because of his good will, jovial demeanor, and compassionate nature.

My grandfather never talked much about business around relatives; as a result, it wasn't until I got older that I became aware of how successful he actually was. Finally, one day I asked him, "Grandpa, what is the secret to your success?" I thought it would involve having the right contacts, being written up in trade journals, or being a dynamic salesperson. My grandfather replied, "Son, if you truly want to be successful in business and in life, remember this: treat everybody you meet exactly the same, whether they're digging ditches, or they're the president of a multi-million-dollar corporation, because whatever they're doing it is important to them." My grandfather lived that philosophy to the day he died; this is why he continues to be admired and missed by those who knew him.

Abraham Lincoln had a great quote; he said, "If you would win a man to your cause, first convince him that you are his sincere friend." The cornerstone to charisma is all about making other people feel important and significant by confirming to them that you believe they have value.

WRIGHT

So, what makes your perspective unique from others in the self- improvement field?

MARINELLI

My perspective is unique in a variety of different ways; however, I will just touch on the main aspect that sets me apart from my colleagues.

I would say that most of the books and seminars on the market today are grounded in *theory*. Unfortunately, theory rarely works in the real world. Theory is a concept that sounds plausible and logical, but usually fails miserably when put into practice. And this is the major problem with theory—it is not proven. Most of the time a theory's foundation is centered on assumption and speculation, where a certain set of circumstances or situations need to be present in order for that model to work properly. However, the real world is unpredictable. My techniques and methods, on the other hand, deal with *results*—results that are gained through life experience and application. You will not find old, outdated, rehashed hypotheses or ivory tower philosophy in any of my material.

WRIGHT

Would you provide our readers with a breakdown of your philosophy on how to create a charismatic personality and personal magnetism?

MARINELLI

I break my philosophy down into six main parts, and each section builds on the one that precedes it. Let us look at each one of these parts individually, along with a brief description of what each one entails.

- *Defining Charisma*: This is where I describe the academic and elemental versions of charisma, as we discussed earlier. However, we have the opportunity to go into much more detail in my seminars and my *Keys to Charisma* course. In essence, I break it down into its bare components so people know where I am coming from before outlining specific strategies and techniques for developing a charismatic and magnetic personality that shines.

- *How to Get People to Like You*: In this section, I explain seven specific ways to get people to like you. Primarily, it revolves around the idea of instilling a sense of value in people, showing them that you value them, and that they should value you too. I provide students with techniques designed to be utilized in their dealings with people regardless of the situation or environment.

- *Creating Rapport*: Once you get people to like you, the next step requires strengthening your connection with them in order to cultivate a relationship. This is where rapport comes into play, whether the relationship you are trying to develop is business, social, or romantic. I furnish my students with a fixed set of behaviors that they can use in conjunction with the strategies on creating value discussed in the previous section to add validity to their words. The best tool I know for creating rapport is by showing people that you can walk your talk.

- *Powerful Communication Strategies*: Here I delve into communication strategies that allow people to present their ideas, thoughts, and beliefs in an effective and efficient manner. If you sincerely want to be charismatic, you must communicate not only through your words but also through your actions.

- *Unstoppable Self-Confidence*: I outline an amazingly simple and practical system to generating and producing instant self-confidence. Several people have told me that they think this one technique alone was worth the price of the entire course.

- *Characteristics of Charismatic People*: Finally, I clarify for my students why these methods work. I explain the *why* instead of just the *how*. I am unique in this respect because when you understand why my philosophy works, you can implement the techniques and strategies I teach with greater success.

WRIGHT

You mentioned the importance of good communication skills as a key ingredient to charisma. Would you elaborate on that point and maybe present us with a few insights on how a person can become a more effective communicator?

MARINELLI

I believe your success as a communicator has a direct effect on your success in life. Communication skills are an essential ingredient to charisma. If you want people to view you as an individual with a high degree of personal magnetism, then you must be able to communicate your ideas and thoughts effectively with power, confidence, and conviction.

Communication comes in three distinct forms. Most books, seminars, and courses simply deal with only two of the three forms of communication: *verbal* and *non-verbal*. Verbal deals with words, tone, pitch, and rate of speech. Non-verbal refers to body language, which includes things such as stance, facial expressions, and gestures. However, there is a third form of communication that most people forget about or do not know exists; and this third form of communication is *actions*.

I do not see many other speakers or authors talking about the importance of actions in respect to communication, but I believe they should. You know the old saying: "Actions speak louder than words." After all, your actions show your true character as an individual—what you think and what you believe. If your *actions* do not coincide with what you say, the credibility of your words may be called into question. So remember, there are three forms of communication, and to be an effective communicator you must focus on all three: *verbal, non-verbal,* and *actions.* Does that make sense?

WRIGHT

Absolutely, I never thought of it in quite that way before.

MARINELLI

The question that is then invariably asked is, "What is the secret to using these three forms of communication to become a brilliant conversationalist?" The secret to being an influential and powerful communicator is *listening.* Listening is the number one fundamental to successful communication.

In fact, if you want to be charismatic, it is required that you develop good listening skills, otherwise you will not be able to respond verbally, non-verbally, and with your actions in an appropriate manner. By listening to people, you can determine the most skillful way to handle crucial business and social situations competently.

I have discovered that there are three levels of listening.

- *Awareness:* The listeners who are practicing awareness listening are conscious that someone is speaking to them but they are not paying attention to the conversation. Their body language and responses show that they are ignoring the individual talking and could care less about what this person has to say. Usually, these people display their disinterest through their actions. For instance, shuffling papers, looking at their watch, staring out the window, or other menial tasks while you are trying to engage them in conversation are all good examples of someone practicing awareness listening.

- *Superficial:* Superficial listeners are paying attention but only minimally interested in what the other person is saying. In reality they are waiting for their "turn" to speak and are really only interested in what they have to say. The sad part about this is the majority of people listen in this manner. I do not think individuals do this intentionally—it's subconscious. Remember, when we are trying to formulate our own thoughts, we cannot attentively listen to the person who is speaking.

- *Active Listening*: Active listeners are paying total attention to the other person and interested in what he or she has to say. They listen carefully in order to fully absorb the information the person speaking is offering them. They give specific cues that they care about what this person is saying by nodding their head, using proper facial expressions, and keeping their eyes on the individual talking. Sometimes the listener will respond with short verbal comments like "I understand," "How interesting," "What happened next?" "Uh-huh," "Yes," and, "How did that make you feel?"

If you want to be viewed as a brilliant conversationalist, you must first work on and polish your active listening skills. Charismatic people fully grasp that listening is the source and means of their inevitable failure or success in interacting with people.

WRIGHT

You also discussed that charismatic people have exceptional self-confidence. We all know that self-confidence is a crucial element to success in life, however, establishing self-confidence is a tremendous challenge for a large number of people. Do you have any advice for our readers on how someone can begin to obtain outstanding self-confidence?

MARINELLI

That is an excellent question. When I first started studying success over fifteen years ago, that was something I wrestled with constantly. Probably, like many other people, I tried everything under the sun to become more self-confident with minimal success. I think you would agree with me, David, that the way you feel about yourself on the inside affects the way you appear on the outside. Therefore, I started to wonder if there was an approach that allows people to work from the *outside in* instead of the *inside out* in order to increase self-confidence. In other words, is there a process that would allow me to present a self-confident outer image while at the same time change the way I feel on the inside in relation to my self-image—kill two birds with one stone, if you will.

After much research, I found that such a system did indeed exist, and its foundation is rooted in *physiology*. What exactly is physiology? Physiology is the way you walk, talk, breathe, stand, and move. Moreover, there is a direct link between physiology and self-confidence. In fact, physiology not only affects your outward appearance but also affects how you feel on the inside as well. So, if your physiology contains elements that display a sense of confidence (spine erect, shoulders back, head up), you will feel confident. On the other hand, if your physiology is one of uncertainty (shoulders slumped over, head down, shuffling your feet), you will feel insecure. I know this may sound like a Pollyanna theory but I promise you it is not. I can actually take you and the readers through an exercise that will prove that everything I am saying is true:

- Assume a physiology that displays a sense of insecurity, uncertainty, and doubt (shoulders slumped over, head down, etc.). Think of all the worries, problems, and troubles in your life.
- Focus in on this disheartened and doubtful state of mind until you can really feel it within yourself. (Don't worry—I will bring you out of this state later in this exercise.)
- Without changing your physiology or demeanor in any way, switch to a state of certainty, assuredness, and self-reliance. Do not change your posture, breathing, or anything else about your physiology in any way. Just allow your mind to focus in on the aspects of being confident but do not let your body react to the feelings your brain generates.

Even though I am not standing right there next to you I'll bet you are having a hard time—if not finding it impossible—to get into a confident state of mind while standing in an insecure manner.

Now, try this:

- Assume a physiology that displays a sense of certainty, positivity, faith, and assuredness (shoulders back, head up, etc.). Think of your convictions, values, and the belief you have in yourself.
- Focus in on this feeling of power, confidence, and poise until you can really feel it within yourself.
- Without changing your physiology or demeanor in any way, switch to a state of uncertainty, insecurity, and doubt. Do not change your posture, breathing, or anything else about your physiology in any way. Just allow

your mind to focus in on the aspects of being unsure of yourself, but do not let your body react to the feelings your brain generates.

Once again, I'll bet anyone following along with this exercise are finding it difficult to switch back to the state of doubt and uncertainty while standing in a confident manner. Just as it is difficult, if not impossible, to remain in the confident state with a physiology that reeks of insecurity, the opposite is also true. Do you agree with me David?

WRIGHT

Absolutely, I tried as you were saying it. It's almost impossible.

MARINELLI

I would like to provide the readers with a technique I call the *"As If"* method, that puts people into a confident state in just a minute or two:

- Close your eyes and imagine how you would feel if you were completely self-confident. How would you walk, talk, stand, breathe, move, and act? Imagine what you would do if you were totally self-assured. Even if you don't know what you would do, pretend that you do know and envision this in your mind.
- Savor this image for a moment, allow this feeling of power to surge throughout your entire body and let your physiology react to it. Take the time needed to visualize and focus in on this scene until you have a sharp, clear image of it in your mind and can almost taste the experience.
- Open your eyes. Take notice of the way you are standing, the way you feel, and the confidence you now have about yourself and your abilities. Look at yourself in the mirror. Do you have a look of conviction and confidence that is now represented in your face and body? Have your thoughts changed since the beginning of this exercise and if so, how? Take note of your mindset and physiology and the changes that have occurred.

At this point you should be displaying a confident physiology and outward appearance that contain the elements of conviction, certainty, and faith. Be aware of the sense of power, purpose, and strength that now exists inside you too. If you faithfully practice the method I just described you will have better self-confidence in a short amount of time, I have used this technique myself, as have my clients, with tremendous success.

I recommend practicing the *"As If"* method every morning for the next couple of months to solidify it in your personality as a habit. By using this formula, you will increase your self-confidence and in turn, your self-esteem will increase as well.

WRIGHT

Seems like it could help people in developing self-confidence.

MARINELLI

Basically, you are retraining your mind to develop a more positive self-image; however, you are changing your self-image by changing the way you move your body.

WRIGHT

It is obvious that charisma is vital to success; however, is charisma the only thing a person needs to be successful?

MARINELLI

No; while charisma is an important aspect of being successful, it is not the only thing. Charisma will not make up for incompetence, lack of skill, talent, laziness, malicious intentions, or unethical practices.

For instance, recently I was watching a documentary on television about con artists and they reviewed stories of people who were bilked out of their life savings by unscrupulous investors. When they asked these seemingly intelligent men and women how the fraudulent financial advisors fooled them, time and time again the victims responded by saying, "He had so much charisma and personal magnetism you felt like you could trust him completely as if he was your best friend." I believe this example proves the power of charisma; however, keep in mind that eventually these thieves were apprehended and are now serving long prison sentences for their criminal misdeeds.

The point I'm trying to make here is that charisma can be extremely powerful and can even turn the tide in certain instances; but if used in an unethical manner, sooner or later it will come back to haunt you. Of course, charisma can also be used for ethical and responsible purposes too.

Let's say you were going in for a job interview, and it is between you and another candidate for this specific position. You both have the same credentials, the same experience, the same skills. Who will be chosen for the job? More than likely, the person with the most charisma will probably end up getting the position. So, to summarize, charisma is a major factor in being successful, but it is not everything.

WRIGHT

Why do you believe that such a high number of people have poor human relation skills?

MARINELLI

The reason why such a vast number of individuals have poor human relation skills is because we do not teach good human relation skills to people. Think about it. We teach everything else in school—reading, writing, math, science, and a host of other subjects—but we do not teach human relation skills, even though we should. In fact, that is my mission David—to instruct as many people as I can on how to create more productive and fulfilling relationships in all areas of their life. Whether I am speaking at an association, corporation, school, or college I enjoy having the opportunity to share this material with a variety of people. Therefore, I do not consider myself a *motivational speaker*; instead, I prefer to view myself as a *motivational teacher.*

WRIGHT

How and when did you discover that speaking was your passion and why did you choose charisma and interpersonal communication as your main topics?

MARINELLI

Well, it came about as a personal quest for me David. Ever since I was young, I have always been fascinated about what makes people tick. Growing up, I had very few friends, if any at all. I marched to the beat of a different drummer than most of my classmates. I spent the majority of my free time involved in mostly artistic endeavors such as drawing, theatre, and music. The high school I attended was very involved in athletics and if you weren't involved in a team sport, you were pretty much ostracized. I thought that going away to a university after graduating high school would be my saving grace. I had heard that in college, you could march to the beat of a different drummer and no one cares. Maybe that is true on some college campuses but that certainly wasn't my experience. When I went away to school, I chose a small college that turned out to be extremely cliquish and once again, I didn't really fit in. So, it was extremely difficult and hard for me to make friends; in turn, I became exceedingly depressed. I actually failed out of my first year of college and dropped out. Though, I want to point out, I did go back to college the following semester and ended up graduating from an excellent university a few years later.

However, that summer, after failing out of college, I retreated to my parent's house in Fort Myers and cocooned myself away from the rest of the world. It was during this solitary existence of mine when I discovered books by Og Mandino, Claude M. Bristol, Norman Vincent Peale, Dr. Robert Schuller, and Anthony Robbins. As I read these books I began to realize that I could change my life, I controlled my destiny; I decided that my past was not going to determine my future.

During that summer of 1992, I had the opportunity to see Tony Robbins speak in Chicago. For three days I sat riveted as Tony spoke about how he had gone from being a dismal failure to a phenomenal success and how we had the power to do the same thing. Looking around at the crowd and seeing the impact his words were making upon the other participants astonished me. At that moment, I knew what I wanted to do with my life. I wanted to be a professional speaker; I just felt it in my bones. I committed myself to learn everything I could about the secrets to success and to, share this knowledge with as many people as I could; giving them the tools needed to turn their lives into masterpieces.

WRIGHT

So, what inspires and drives you to be successful?

MARINELLI

I am inspired, driven, and passionate about people, and sharing what I have discovered with them. I consider it an obligation on my part.

Let me relate a story that took place early in my speaking career that might help clarify what I mean when I say people are my passion. I had been a professional speaker for about two years, and I had always gotten excellent responses from my audience. Well, one night I was giving a seminar where everything just seemed to go awry. I think every professional speaker out there, even the most successful, has at least one story about a talk that fell apart; this one is mine. The group I was speaking to were absolutely awful. In fact, people asked for their money back right in the middle of the speech. I have no doubt that if the audience had things to throw at me, I would have been driven off the stage by a hail of missiles. I died a death on the platform that evening that was a professional speaker's nightmare. I watched as my seminar imploded right before my very eyes. This had never happened to me before and it has never happened since. I made it through the rest of the evening but let me tell you, it was no easy task.

Afterward, I was on the platform licking my wounds when a man who had been sitting in the back of the room all night approached me and asked, "Mr. Marinelli, may I speak to you for a second?" I didn't really feel like talking to anyone;

certainly, the only reason this man had come up to me was to give me more grief about my speech. I sighed and replied, "Sure." Then this participant totally stunned me by saying, "Thank you."

I must admit I was rather perplexed by his response. He continued, "I've been attending therapy and seminars for several years now and you helped me more this evening with your words than anybody in the past ever has." I was speechless. Here I had just given the worst talk of my life and this person was thanking me for helping him. Maybe I did not make a connection with the rest of the audience that night; still, whatever I said had obviously connected with this individual. It was at that moment that I realized that you never know who you are going to touch with your message. That is the reason why I say that people—specifically sharing the secrets of success with people—are my *passion.*

WRIGHT

What do you believe is the secret to enjoying continuous achievement and success on a consistent basis in life?

MARINELLI

If people truly want to accomplish all their hopes, dreams, and desires in life consistently, I highly recommend they become a student of success. Students of success continue to educate themselves on the *science of achievement.*

If you visited my home, you would see that I have wall-to-wall bookshelves. In fact, every wall in my house has a bookshelf attached to it somewhere. I literally have hundreds of books on self-improvement and personal growth. People always ask me, "My goodness, do you really read all these books?" My answer is "Yes." It may seem like an obsession; however, it is not an obsession, it is a *quest.* Not to mention, since I now speak to people, it has also become a quest to provide my students with the best ideas, advice, strategies, and techniques I can uncover.

The late Dottie Walters, a first-rate speaker, bestselling author, and marketing genius, has a great quote that I love. She said, "Success is not a doorway, it's a staircase." You are always moving to or away from another level in your life. I meet people all the time who say they are stuck in a rut, however, once I start talking with them, I find out very quickly why they are stuck in a rut. They have stopped learning; consequently, they are not growing, expanding, or improving in any way. As human beings, we are designed with an underlying objective to unearth our full potential, improve our lives, and discover our inner strength; and you can only do that by becoming a never-ending student of success.

WRIGHT

What a great conversation, Brian. I really appreciate the time you've taken today to answer all these questions. You've given me and I'm sure the readers a lot to think about.

MARINELLI

Well, I appreciate you giving me the opportunity to share my philosophy in a format like this.

WRIGHT

Today we've been talking with Brian J. Marinelli. He's the Founder and President of Brian Marinelli International, a company specializing in helping individuals and businesses develop more productive and fulfilling relationships, allowing them to achieve their personal as well as their professional goals in an ever-changing world.

Brian, thank you so much for being with us today on *Discover Your Inner Strength.*

MARINELLI

Thank you, David.

CHAPTER Six

Leadership for Global Competitiveness

AN INTERVIEW WITH...

Mona Pearl

40 East Chicago Ave., #400
Chicago, IL 60611
312.642.4647
MonaPearl@BeyondAStrategy.com
www.BeyondAStrategy.com

ABOUT THE AUTHOR

Mona Pearl is a global business expansion and negotiation strategist. She has started and operated three businesses of her own. From operations to organization to bottom line results, Mona has led high performance teams and found new and creative ways to make money and increase market share. Using actionable market research, a network of high-level global contacts, and her cross-industry expertise, Mona Pearl develops competitive global strategies for leading multinational corporations, mid-market companies, as well as entrepreneurs to create significant and sustainable growth. Mona uses her expertise in strategic global competitiveness to extend market reach, enhance leadership, and engage the stakeholders along the value chain of growing their business.

As an international businesswoman, she knows that cultural differences can make or break a business deal. Mona's language abilities include: English, French, German, Hebrew, Rumanian and Spanish. Mona holds a master's degree from DePaul University in Chicago. Mona has also written and published numerous articles for industry publications.

DAVID WRIGHT (WRIGHT)

Today we're talking with Mona Pearl. Mona is a cross-cultural speaker, trainer, and strategist. She has done business in over twenty countries, lived on three continents, and is able to communicate in five languages. She provides her clients with the golden key to make the right decisions when expanding their business into other countries in a cost-effective way, while being competitive, so they can accelerate sales and make money. Mona says that what got American business people to be successful in the United States won't get them success internationally. They require a global mindset and a different set of skills. And she can help them develop these skills and acquire global leadership.

An applied program of education, training, and personal development enables one to learn and master the nuances of other cultures, be able to work in multi-cultural teams. The program leads to understanding and successfully dealing with the perspective of business partners in many lands.

We have an expert with us today to talk about that very subject, "developing a global mindset—what you need to know before going global."

Mona, welcome to *Discover Your Inner Strength*.

MONA PEARL (PEARL)

Thank you, it's great being here.

WRIGHT

Mona, you say that US mid-market companies need a wake up call to look into international markets. Why now?

PEARL

Now more than ever is the right time to enter global markets. Did you know that very soon 80 percent of the world's consumers will be outside the United States? Look at the new reality and think how you can turn it into an opportunity for your company. The rest of the world is catching up and is getting richer, so in order to maintain your leadership position you need to consider expanding internationally. It is time to stop focusing on insecurities and a U.S.-centric approach, and start competing for the growing global market.

Over the last three decades, the world has shifted from a collection of regional or national economies to a truly global economy as a result of technology, trade agreements, lower tariffs, better transportation, and easier communication. Many other nations have engaged in global business for decades now. The future lies in international commerce in both goods and services. Don't be left behind and let your competition build their reputation, strengthen relationships, and get all the business. Whoever enters the market first is the winner! Why not take advantage of the opportunities of the global economy and expand your business?

WRIGHT

Are U.S. businesses in danger of losing their competitive advantage? If so, how can you help?

PEARL

At the dawn of the twenty-first century, the United States is still the most competitive economy in the world. However, international competition is intensifying across the globe. To maintain our leadership position we need to continue to adapt and innovate. Increasing worldwide competition demands that we respond more rapidly, innovate faster and add more value. This is not only what is expected by *American* consumers, but also by the growing customer base overseas for goods and services provided by American companies and workers.

How we respond to these challenges and opportunities brought by an interconnected worldwide economy will shape the prosperity of Americans for generations to come. Meeting this challenge requires creativity, commitment, and experience.

Experience as well as a global network of relationships developed and nurtured throughout the years is essential. In order to be a successful player in the global arena, one has to develop relationships across borders. I have had the unique opportunity to work with multinational teams since the early nineties, while being exposed to a variety of industries, practices, corporate cultures, and other cross-cultural environments. The fact that I combine hands-on experience and the ability to solve problems and eliminate cultural barriers while helping my clients focus on their business and succeed in their goals is a definite advantage.

I believe in working hard and smart. As much as companies face similar challenges, they are different in the solutions they require. I treat each client as unique and never take a one-size-fits-all approach. There is no one formula that provides a "quick fix." I listen and provide creative and resourceful solutions that help my clients achieve bottom line results while minimizing embarrassment.

WRIGHT

How does your unique background give you insights that can help companies overcome cross-cultural barriers?

PEARL

Since a country's language expresses and represents its culture, being well versed in several languages gives one the insights into the deeper values and fundamentals of a country and the way its people expect to conduct business. It is not just a matter of subtle nuances and words that are used in business transactions, but also behavior and negotiation styles. My laser-focused listening ability and cultural lens allow me to identify and observe certain things that may be hidden to others.

This proved to be essential on an assignment in Spain. I traveled with a company's representatives to Spain to finalize a business transaction. (Yes, the perks of travel.) The Spaniards were wonderful hosts, and for about two and a half days they graciously showed us around. We were invited to the company president's home, met his family, and were invited to lavish meals. We had yet to touch on any business details and the U.S. team was getting impatient, confused, and anxious. Although they enjoyed being catered to, their reason for being there was bottom line results. They were discouraged and saw no point in staying any longer, but I talked them out of leaving and asked them to be patient. Just before dinner on the third night, we reached an agreement on the terms and conditions, and the deal was sealed.

There are different styles of negotiations and doing business. Cultural differences can make or break a deal. Other cultures may actually want to get to know you as a person before they do business with you.

I had the good fortune to be exposed to this multicultural world, and this is an asset that I bring to the table that is so useful to my clients. I become their trusted advisor who helps them avoid costly mistakes and make money.

WRIGHT

What are the main challenges globally that you see American companies facing in the next three years?

PEARL

I foresee five main challenges: the growing competition from other nations (and not only in technology), dependence on foreign manufacturing and resources, energy issues, credit and finance issues, and the lack of globally oriented talent.

Overcoming these challenges will be a direct result of how serious American companies are about competing globally and how well they are prepared to be successful. We have no choice but to be successful in everything we do to maintain our leadership position.

From Wall Street to Main Street, the affect of worldwide markets is enormous and U.S. companies need to create and sustain a competitive edge by accessing the growing worldwide marketplace. With the significant expansion of free trade agreements in recent years, the globalization of markets can no longer be ignored. American businesses have only just begun to market their products and services to new customers around the world. Competition in technology, manufacturing, and talent will widen the gap between the United States and other countries. These other countries are already on our doorstep, so it is not up to us to make the decision whether to compete globally or not. We have no choice and therefore, U.S. companies need to leverage competition and design and implement cost-effective strategies to enter the international marketplace.

Other countries have been increasing their global trade for years now. They get their education at the best universities in the United States and basically duplicate and adapt our methods to their country's needs in a very clever and sophisticated way. Although the United States is still the leader, we don't do enough long-term planning and we have a lack knowledge about what the other countries are doing in the same industry. With the emergence of the BRIC (Brazil, Russia, India, and China) countries, the United States is no longer the only market leader, although it is still the value leader. Doing business globally is an absolute necessity, and it would be very costly to not make the right decisions. American companies need to change their mindset and integrate a global strategy into their yearly planning to increase sales, generate economies of scale to manage risk, and raise profitability.

WRIGHT

How will leadership have to change?

PEARL

In the era of globalizing business, the concept of "headquarters" is changing and people no longer think in terms of "home" countries or "foreign" markets. A whole new mindset is emerging that embraces profit and competition as well as sustainability and collaboration. Therefore, leaders who will succeed have to be of a global mindset. This means they have to:

- Change thinking patterns and strategies from a domestic to a global focus.
- Manage uncertainty and fear while constantly adapting to change and accepting it as part of a process.
- Combine the various cultures and values of the corporate workforce into a unique global organizational culture.
- Become keenly interested in learning from a culturally diverse workforce to appreciate and embrace the differences.
- Develop the ability to work with people of other cultures as equals and accept the differences.
- Learn how to cooperate with partners worldwide by successfully managing global teams and alliances.

The challenge is to get middle-market C-level executives to address these issues, hire the right talent, and realize that success in the United States is not necessarily a prescription for global success. Traditional success strategies may not get you there in the international markets. If you want to transform your company to thrive and be a global player, you need to focus on different areas of competency and be open to change.

WRIGHT

Mona, what are five biggest mistakes companies make when going global?

PEARL

The five biggest mistakeş are:

1. *Not having the right people in the right positions when deciding to take operations globally.* Your VP of sales who did a great job in the U.S. market is usually not equipped with the tools and skills to open global markets. If the company is financially sound, you can probably hire an individual to be in charge of global business development. An alternative is cross-cultural training. A third choice would be to hire a local person in the market(s) you are pursuing. Which choice is best for your company? If you make the wrong decision it can be very costly as well as embarrassing. It may even profoundly affect your chances of ever getting back into that market.
2. *Not having clear objectives and a road map.* Don't skip this critical step! You can significantly increase your chances of success by starting with researching the market and the competition, and setting clear objectives,

timelines, milestones, and metrics. Make sure you define and target the right market(s) for your product or service. Don't just follow the crowds. Also, choose the appropriate mode for entering a particular foreign country or region. Not having a good road map can turn out to be very costly.

3. *Forgetting the fundamental importance of cultural differences.* There is no one way of doing business, and the American way is definitely not the only way. When venturing globally, one has to be sensitive to nuances in order to get the deal done. Many business transactions have been halted or terminated due to cultural misunderstandings or, to be a bit blunt, cultural ignorance. Managers in an international business environment should not only be sensitive to cultural and language differences, but should also adopt the appropriate policies and strategies for coping with them.

4. *Making decisions based only on widely known information.* One size does not fit all. Follow a strategy that fits the product or service, have a business objective, and make sure that your strategy is aligned with the target country or region. Practices may need to vary by country. Marketing a product in Venezuela may require a different approach from marketing it in Switzerland; managing U.S. workers may require different skills than managing Egyptian employees. Maintaining close relations with a particular level of government may be very important in Mexico and irrelevant in the U.K. If you disregard one component of this important triangle—a strategy that fits the product or service, a business objective, and cultural alignment—you are sure to dramatically increase your chances for failure.

5. *Being overconfident in one's global expansion skills.* Seek professional advice to navigate the unknown and use other people's experience to help you succeed and follow a smooth path. A little humility goes a long way in combating overconfidence. Remember that what got you to be successful in the United States in most cases won't get you there internationally. At the most fundamental level, the challenges arise from the simple fact that countries are different. Countries differ in their cultures, political systems, economic systems, legal systems, and levels of economic development. Many of these differences are very profound and enduring.

WRIGHT

How can you help make the road smoother for your clients?

PEARL

My years of gaining experience and working with companies that were involved in international business have given me insights and perceptions that help me simplify the road map for my clients. It's also easier if you're an outside observer to separate the trees from the forest and prepare a plan. Not everything is as complex as it appears and when you don't have the emotional attachment and the fear, insecurity and concern that things may not work out, it helps to steer companies in the right direction. The world out there has been global for many years—it's just that the United States hasn't seriously participated. There is an entire world out there that needs to be looked at as an opportunity to grow your sales and expand your business.

For example, when a global corporation acquired a local Chicago company it wanted to send a group of managers to the United States and came to me for help. By asking a series of questions, I made sure that the company was sending the most suitable people to the United States, and we provided them with the best education and training to conduct business here. In addition, a special program for their U.S. counterparts was implemented to help them deal with the new group that became part of the daily business environment.

To succeed in the global competitive marketplace, you must possess a wide array of skills, which may be different from the skills you need in order to succeed nationally. Fortunately, in many cases, the work done in the diverse workplaces of the United States prepares business people to succeed in the global arena.

WRIGHT

What are some of the tools, tactics, and tips for mastering business successfully across cultures?

PEARL

Factors such as political-economic environments and market structures affect international marketing decisions and make the process of locating international customers different from domestic marketing. One country's distribution system might be more conducive to deploying your own local distributor network, while another might best be penetrated with a local agent. There is no single way to find a customer who will buy your product or service. Some companies make their first sale after months of careful planning; others try it through an unexpected knock at the door.

When sizing up the markets and identifying the one(s) for you, you may need to take into consideration the fact that people's habits and needs are different than in the United States. The usage of the same product may be different, the price point may have to be changed, and modifications to the product itself may be necessary.

Decide how you will get into the market and what the most cost-effective strategy for your product or service is. Although there are many ways to identify and target your potential customers, there are three basic channels for export: 1) Direct sales, in which you make the sale directly to the foreign customers, 2) indirect sales, in which you sell through a U.S.-based intermediary, and 3) indirect sales, in which you sell through a foreign agent or distributor. In addition, you may want to consider owning a manufacturing facility in that country, a strategic alliance, a merger, or an acquisition. Which is right for you? Doing your homework may save you time, money, and embarrassment.

You may need to sharpen your diplomatic skills and learn cross-cultural negotiation through training and gathering of cultural intelligence. In making the connections, how do you meet the people you can trust? Many of the companies I have worked with used my services to locate trusted parties overseas. It may take years of building relationships but it can serve my clients very well, and save them time and in many cases, unnecessary expense. *Bottom line: your proven U.S. success strategies may not work in other countries.*

WRIGHT

Why is cross-cultural training so important?

PEARL

Global competition, air travel, and modes of communication have made international business both feasible and necessary. At the same time, it's important to recognize the direct costs of lost opportunities are higher than ever before. They include the loss of business and failed ventures in the targeted country, and loss of reputation. U.S. firms lose over $4 billion a year on failed foreign assignments and initiatives. These losses may be eliminated or reduced dramatically through proper cross-cultural training. Successful business interactions that result in profitable deals, manager productivity, cost-effective expatriation, and a smooth transition to the prospective country or region are the main benefits of investing in pre-departure cross-cultural training for the managers involved.

Successful adjustment to the many complex demands of an unfamiliar culture is a significant achievement and requires thorough preparation. Managers need effective training in the language and customs of their country of destination. They need a regimen that helps them develop the skills needed to communicate effectively and to function purposefully in an otherwise alien environment. Such a regimen, referred to as cross-cultural or intercultural training, is often carried out prior to the departure of managers, and before they are assigned to an overseas location. In addition to training managers, there is a need to train the senior executives who will be engaged in negotiations and planning, to make sure the first steps are done right, and to not jeopardize the future of business deals.

WRIGHT

What is the role of "culture shock"?

PEARL

Culture shock is one of the more expensive and least understood aspects of international business. In short, it refers to the sudden realization of being unprepared for exposure to an alien environment. The experience often consists of three distinct phases, though not everyone passes through these phases and not everyone is in the new culture long enough to pass through all three:

1. *The "Honeymoon Phase."* During this period, the differences between the old and new cultures are seen in a romantic light and wonderful. For example, an individual who moves to a new country might love the new foods, the pace of life, the people's habits, the buildings, and so on.

2. *The "Negotiation Phase."* After a few days, weeks, or months, minor differences between the old and new culture are resolved. One may long for food the way it is prepared in one's native country, may find the pace of life too fast or slow, may find the people's habits annoying, etc.

3. *The "Everything is Okay Phase."* Again, after a few days, weeks or months, one grows accustomed to the new culture's differences and develops routines. By this point, one no longer reacts to the new culture positively or negatively, because it no longer feels like a new culture. One becomes concerned with basic living again, as though one was in one's original culture.

Reverse culture shock happens upon returning to one's home culture after having grown accustomed to another culture. It can produce the same effects as described above.

Some people find it impossible to deal with culture shock. They give up trying to assimilate and return to their home country. Others become so magnetized to the foreign culture that they feel they must permanently move there to relieve the <u>stress</u>.

WRIGHT

What are the negative effects of culture shock and what should companies do to minimize them?

PEARL

Research indicates that expatriate failure rates among U.S. companies due to culture shock range from 10 to 20 percent. Unlike European and Japanese businesses, the United States is relatively new to global enterprise. Other countries, because of their smaller markets, have long had to look beyond the domestic arena.

Many expatriates will experience their first taste of culture shock on the job. To minimize the shock cultural induction courses, which typically last two to three days, are conducted by qualified cultural trainers. They emphasize the importance of an open-minded attitude in the foreign workplace. They also teach managers how to avoid putting up cultural barriers the first day on the job. Management styles are a constant source of stress and cultural discord among expatriates and their hosts. For instance, in American business settings goals and objectives must be reached by the quickest and most efficient route; the single-minded pursuit of profit is invariably the motivating force. By contrast, the French are suspicious of profit. They are driven much more by the notion of perfection and tend to think in terms of concepts.

To operate competitively in today's global market, employees need to be culturally sensitive and flexible in their business dealings. The time has come to move the U.S. international experience onto the fast track, but companies cannot afford not knowing how to navigate the international waters. With cross-border emigration continuing its upward trend around the world, companies need to ensure that their people adjust to the new work environment as quickly as possible. Foreign Service premiums and hardship allowances continue to be paid, but these perquisites should be increasingly supplemented with cross-cultural training courses.

WRIGHT

In addition to "culture shock," what other obstacles do U.S. managers face in the international arena?

PEARL

Business managers in the United States, though very successful in this country, often appear woefully inadequate when it comes to conducting business in other countries. In a foreign venue, they often lack the skills necessary to: 1) understand the culture in which they are assigned to live, work, and negotiate, 2) communicate effectively within the workplace, and 3) carry out their business objectives.

While differences in business methods can strain business relationships, differences in management styles can lead to lost productivity. For example, in Indonesia, China, Japan, and Latin America, subordinates expect to be given clear instructions and directed forcefully; otherwise they will sit back and do nothing. Managers in the United States, on the other hand, expect staff to take the initiative. Business methods such as brainstorming and teamwork, which may be carried out through a variety of management styles and are integral parts of the American management philosophy, are anathema to the Italian, Portuguese, and other cultures.

For a nation that has contributed so much to the world business culture, freedom, and free markets, we are culturally challenged, and we create needless obstacles due to a lack of knowledge of foreign social customs and languages. Not every American businessperson needs to learn multiple languages; however, the exposure to these languages—not just the sounds but also body language and ways of expressing appreciation—and learning not to ridicule people who don't act like we do, would be very helpful and profitable. Lack of knowledge leads to blunders and hence misunderstandings, which in turn waste time and money.

Finally, the recruitment and selection of expatriate managers requires an understanding of the unique demands of international jobs. The expatriate is faced with numerous cross-cultural challenges including language, customs, different work ethics, homesickness, family and spousal adjustment, and differences in the standard of living. Unfortunately, U.S. firms continue to use domestic criteria for recruitment and selection in spite of the multitude of obstacles expatriates face during international assignments.

WRIGHT

What distinguishes the U.S. global experience from that of other nations?

PEARL

Exposure to foreign cultures is a main component of globalization for the United States, as contrasted with countries across Europe or Latin America. Corporations that are highly involved in global business will find that actions taken in countries outside the United States can have unforeseen domestic affect. Whether American companies go global by design as part of their corporate strategy, or whether they suddenly awaken to the fact that they have a global workforce (e.g., through M&A) and customer base, they need a process for determining what training programs are needed and who should be trained. To be best prepared for globalization and its affects, then, American companies need to undertake a more extensive program of global training.

Normally, cycles of training occur throughout corporations on the latest business emphasis. American companies, eager to increase their competitiveness, usually concentrate training on areas they consider to be weaknesses. However, for American executives working globally, the fundamental reason for insufficient global training is that HQ does not always believe global training is necessary. The assumption is that American ways and business practices are the norm, both in the United States and abroad and that a manager who is successful in New York or Los Angeles will also be successful in Tokyo, Shanghai, or Moscow.

By contrast, companies in Japan and the U.K. see global experience as an integral part of the employees' management development and advancement. In other words, in these countries, if managers want to become top-level executives, they must have global experience. Therefore, companies in other countries are more discriminating in selecting their global managers.

WRIGHT

What needs to change in the way Americans approach international business?

PEARL

If American companies are to flourish, their perspective needs to be global—not only in driving toward higher profits, but in the sense of a set of operating principles that can guide to a greater understanding of their foreign counterparts, which, through mutual interdependence, can then lead to higher profits. To attain a global perspective, many American managers will need to adapt their current operating principles to a more encompassing, more cosmopolitan viewpoint of business. Much remains to be done in both corporate and entrepreneurial America for this global perspective to take hold. What is necessary is almost a complete transformation of the American way of doing business.

The international environment is characterized by dynamic issues. It is highly fluid, marked by the participative exchange of people, ideas, intellectual property, processes, money, and expertise. Responding to change in a global context is no longer a progressive or incremental process; rather, it is punctuated by a rapid and dramatic fluctuation in conditions.

Americans evoke strong stereotypes in the minds and hearts of people in foreign countries, and yet only few American businesspeople are aware of how they are viewed by their foreign counterparts. Knowing whether this view is positive or negative is crucial to the success of any business relationship—new or ongoing. Further, the typical American styles of negotiating and doing business can be huge obstacles overseas.

WRIGHT

What are some of the main differences between American business styles and those of other countries?

PEARL

The main differences are:

Direct and open communication. The Japanese, Germans, and many other cultures do not appreciate the approach of "tell it like it is," or "what's the bottom line?" These approaches may cause discomfort or embarrassment and give the impression of being too pushy or even hostile.

Impatience. The phrases "Get it done yesterday" and "Lead, follow, or get out of the way" represent acceptable ways of operating in the fast-paced American business environment. In a global context, these attitudes may lead to the perception that the American is rushing through the negotiation and has no interest whatsoever in getting to know the other side and building a relationship.

Negotiation styles. American businesspeople commonly negotiate alone and not in teams, perhaps due to the U.S. individualistic and competitive environment, or perhaps due to their entrepreneurial spirit. However, the perception on the other side may often be that the American negotiator does not take the situation seriously and is not properly prepared with the necessary expertise and support personnel to conduct meaningful business.

Emphasis on the short-term. U.S. corporations tend to look at the short-term, especially in comparison to the Eastern cultures. There is a tendency to think in terms of the immediate deal rather than developing a business relationship that will bear long-term benefits. The impression this leaves with other cultures is that the American is simply out to "make a fast buck" for the company.

U.S.-centric attitude. This attitude is best exemplified with a joke that has been around for many years: What do you call a person who speaks several languages? A polyglot. What do you call a person who speaks two languages? Bilingual. And what do you call a person who speaks one language? American. Americans have limited experience with other cultures due to the enormous market size and opportunities within the United States. The perception by other cultures is that Americans are culturally myopic and arrogant about their nationality, and that they refuse to learn a foreign language, understand local customs, or accept another country's approaches to business or personal life.

The tag-along-lawyer. In the United States, we are used to detailed and written contracts for almost everything. We are also used to lawsuits—suing over anything and everything. Other cultures perceive us as being distrustful. Rather than trying to develop personal relationships that lead to trust, lawyers are brought along and legal documents are presented. In some countries, this attitude is feared; in others, it is ridiculed.

WRIGHT

What does it take to communicate well in a multinational team environment?

PEARL

Communicating well in a multinational team environment requires a global mindset. Webster's dictionary defines the word "mindset" as a "fixed mental attitude formed by experience, education, or prejudice." In other words, a mindset is a predisposition to see the world in a particular way that sets boundaries and provides explanations for why things are the way they are, while at the same time establishing behavioral guidance. A mindset acts as a cultural filter through which we look at the world. It becomes a way of being rather than a set of skills. It is an orientation to the world that allows some people to see certain things that others do not see.

A global mindset means that we scan the world from a broad perspective, always looking for unexpected trends and opportunities that may constitute a threat or an opportunity to achieve our personal, professional, or organizational objectives.

A world teeming with businesspeople of many cultures requires a particular sensitivity on the part of managers and leaders seeking to be successful overseas. Those who work in or closely follow international affairs need to develop competence in anticipating the way that persistent structures of the mind (i.e., mindsets) affect their international interactions. As many international managers will not have prepared for such involvement before starting their careers, they may find that they now have to add something new to their arsenal of intellectual skills if they are to pursue their specialties and interests effectively across international boundaries.

WRIGHT

What are some of the components of a global mindset?

PEARL

Managers with global mindsets are those who:

- Have a much broader perception of the world.
- Mirror the globe microcosmically while concentrating on the broader picture.
- Accept and embrace global changes and see them as opportunities rather than obstacles.
- Trust process rather than structure to deal with the unexpected in life and make the best out of it.
- Thrive on diversity and teamwork as tools to accomplish objectives and goals.
- Always rethink and evaluate steps and barriers by finding new meanings and changing their direction and behavior accordingly. Rules are not carved in stone and may be adapted to the challenges of the changing global environment.
- Are doers, yet are willing to occasionally step back and go with the flow.
- Accept paradox and work to understand complexity in a way that has purpose and direction.
- Live life on many levels and consider the world their playground and their school.
- Don't resist life, but embrace the changes and challenges life may offer.

Global mindsets are not exclusive, but inclusive. People with exclusive global mindsets risk alienating many people in the world on whom they are dependent. When they think too small, they exclude purposes and goals that are important to others and undermine their ability to be effective global leaders.

WRIGHT

What does the training entail that fosters such a mindset?

PEARL

An applied program of education, training, and personal development enables one to learn and master the nuances of other cultures, leading to understanding and the ability to deal successfully with prospective business partners in many lands. It's important for any training to be centered on the individuals in terms of what they need to know and how to best present the knowledge and skills to be learned. What sets global training apart from other programs of corporate training is an increased focus on the background and culture of the individuals.

Global training can be divided into three steps:

1. Developing and refining an awareness of existing cultural differences.
2. Increasing specific knowledge and understanding of the individual's culture and how their values may influence the training process.
3. Assessing, re-designing, and customizing training content based on the previous two steps.

The content has to incorporate a body of cultural knowledge, openness to other cultures, and cultural empathy. It also has to focus on adaptive problem-solving skills for both managers and employees. These skills encompass a flexibility that will enable them to redefine strategies and reinvent structures within the global organization. The prerequisite for training is a commitment to invest time and money in development and in the company's global training effort.

It's important to note that global awareness is not the exclusive domain of managers on expatriate assignments. A common company language at home is necessary for the discussion of global business opportunities. Therefore, training should not be limited to top-level or international marketing personnel, but should extend to those who design and manufacture products sold abroad.

WRIGHT

What is the basic goal of global training?

PEARL

The basic goal of global training is to develop skills and increase the ability to lead and execute global strategies. Gathered from personal experience and field research, the training should:

- Change thinking patterns and strategies from a domestic focus to a global mindset.
- Help people manage uncertainty and fear while learning to adapt to change and accepting it as part of a process.
- Combine the various cultures and values of the corporate workforce into a unique global organization culture.
- Develop the interest to learn from a culturally diverse workforce to appreciate and embrace the differences.

- Develop the ability to work with people of other cultures as equals and accept the differences.
- Teach how to cooperate with partners worldwide by successfully managing global teams and alliances.

Properly trained, people can reach commonly defined goals with people from cultures other than their own while treating the other's culture with deep integrity. Global training also facilitates the transfer of knowledge or skills so they can be used appropriately in the receiving environment. Finally, global training creates a climate in which changes in attitude, behavior, and perceptions are achieved through the sharing of knowledge and technology in a culturally appropriate way.

WRIGHT

What sets global training apart from other training programs?

PEARL

What sets global training apart from other programs of corporate training is an increased focus on the background and culture of the trainees. Trainees need to understand that they will most likely work in multinational teams and face various cultures throughout their career. In addition to training, an ongoing coaching relationship is needed to help with specific incidents, issues, and transformation. One size does not fit all.

I am not trying to modify behavior; rather, I am suggesting a new paradigm in which HR management is linked to strategic business objectives. This will not only drive management development on an individual basis, but the organization's collective capability and commitment to using all strategies to build a competitive edge.

WRIGHT

What are some of the desired training outcomes?

PEARL

Important training outcomes are cultural sensitivity and empathy, integrity, and sharing of knowledge and technology in the receiving environment. The greatest challenge for trainees is truly understanding other cultures and the frameworks with which people from other countries develop and share ideas. Companies that currently provide some cross-cultural training need a more systematic approach. They should start by assessing all employees to determine who needs global training and what training should be provided so they can design an effective multicultural training program.

Taking American ideas into other countries without taking cultural differences into consideration is generally detrimental in global management. American corporations need to train their employees to expand their horizons beyond the domestic and to think and work from a global perspective.

The fact that many Americans believe that they have nothing to learn from other cultures is a major barrier. American managers involved in international business activities are often sent abroad with little, if any, training. Too often, management appears confident that an individual's understanding and business knowledge will easily compensate for the lack of cultural understanding.

To circumvent this and other barriers to the successful conduct of business internationally, there is a growing need to learn how to manage decentralized, multi-centered, flat-layered organizations, sometimes with multicultural teams.

Training in contextual thinking skills is also of great importance. Managers need to learn to see the organization against the political, social, technological, or global background in which it operates. It is not enough to have the right goals and strategies to get to the right place. More importantly, executives need the ability to get there in the face of a lot of uncertainty. Training executives to enhance their personal effectiveness and international skills (e.g., how to work across cultures, how to adjust to change, and how to tolerate ambiguity) will require familiar methods and available technology, but used in a new global context.

A degree of psychic flexibility that is rare among today's corporate troops is also called for to meet global challenges. For example, global executives will have many more opportunities to cope with the unforeseen, to admit failure, and to live with ambiguity.

Along with being able to discern how a company fits in a global economy, tomorrow's executives will need sharper personal insights in order to succeed. They will need to look inward as well as outward in order to become more self-aware and understand clearly their own personal values. Further, self-awareness will need to extend to what an executive does not know. Past strengths can be future weaknesses, and the key for the future executive in a global company is learning which is which. Global executives will have to know more about more things, but they may be much less certain of what they know. This translates into a need for humility and a need to learn.

The successful manager will be an adaptable, multidimensional thinker and have the ability to impel people toward a vision. Unfortunately, there are no hard rules for developing such a person, and it really depends on the person's background, openness, and other things that were mentioned before.

Imagine coming to work and finding in the lobby a team of bright, well-educated professionals with impressive credentials who are eagerly awaiting their opportunity to talk to you. Imagine as you greet them and begin to talk with them that these highly motivated individuals articulate great and lofty goals for your success. You are persuaded by their eloquence. Then, imagine that the members of this dynamic team have just informed you that they have brought with them several tons of their own equipment, now waiting at the loading dock, with which to help you achieve your success. At this you suddenly frown.

Of course you have been polite to greet them. Of course you have listened to them for a short while. That is certainly the civilized way to handle this sort of situation. But of course you are also skeptical since you do not know them. So you check with your colleagues. You call the head office, and no one among senior management knows them.

You become more skeptical, even cautious, and decide not to let them into the building beyond the lobby. In your search for someone who may know these people, you call the building's security office. The building supervisor dispatches an urgent message to all of your fellow staff, putting the entire building on a high-priority alert. A security detail seals off the loading dock, fearing the loaded truck that the team has brought with them. The police are quickly called to investigate.

With the police on the way, you rejoin your surprise visitors in the lobby accompanied by security guards. You press further for more details from the team members whose accents betray an obvious foreign origin. Image that.

A ludicrous detective plot? A far-fetched opening to a spy thriller? A bit of international intrigue? No, this is the beginning of an actual story about an American company and its bizarre and unfortunate attempt to do business overseas. This story is also an excellent illustration of the kind of problems a company and its managers can encounter when attempting business with prospective partners from another country.

The actual story involved a prominent American entertainment company, which shall remain unnamed, and a German industrial firm, noted for its precision manufacturing of highly technical equipment. As the story unravels, the team of bright, well-educated engineers was sent from the parent firm in Germany to the American company in California. Accompanying the team of three German engineers were three tons of highly specialized gear that they had expected to deploy and operate for the benefit of the American CEO and his employees.

Unfortunately, only top management of both companies ever talked to one another about the prospective deal to set up the equipment demonstration. As both had talked, in person and by telephone, both had understood that each side was interested in seeing what the other had to offer. The conversations were in English. What happened? What went wrong?

In my estimation, there was no language barrier, but there was a cultural barrier. The details of this story reveal not only the necessity for clear communication between individuals of different countries (which may easily be addressed with language classes), but the clear need for an effective means with which to convey important concepts and meaning across two similar, though fundamentally different, cultures. The latter is the focus of my practice and contribution to companies going global.

My work will:

- Set out in detail the problems that beset American companies in their attempt to conduct business in overseas locales and with people of foreign origin.
- Discuss business problems in terms of their possible and probable solution.
- Undertake a thorough examination of culture and its interdependence with prospective world markets and an emerging global economy.
- Distill a set of helpful steps from the most likely solution that can help the business.
- Organize these steps into a useful training program—a guide to help business managers successfully communicate across cultures.

WRIGHT

So what are the key steps you find yourself doing with every team to prepare them for success in foreign markets?

PEARL

I use three steps. The first one is to define the corporate strategy and make sure it is a good fit with the current corporate culture, the people involved, and the target country or region. The second step is increase specific knowledge and understanding of the individual's culture and how their values may influence the strategy and the tactics. The third one is basically assessing, redesigning, customizing, and executing a strategy for success.

WRIGHT

Earlier you said that nonverbal communication can make or break a deal when negotiating internationally. Will you give our readers a few examples?

PEARL

I definitely have quite a few examples, and successful communication and international business requires not only language capabilities and also nonverbal communication that includes body language, intonation, facial expressions, and far more. It helps interpret and emphasize the message being delivered and the other side may get the message as serious, threatening, comic, and so many other facets that are rooted in the receiver's culture.

For example, in most Latin cultures the proximity in which people stand is very close. In the United States, we need our space, or at least this is what we are told. I witnessed a lively negotiation between the U.S. businessperson and a Brazilian representative. From the observation deck it seemed that the Brazilian was chasing the American, trying to get close. What really happened was that as soon as the Brazilian crossed the perceived value the American had in mind, the American took a step or two back. It was pretty funny to observe and, as I joined the conversation, I made sure to create a balance in which all sides were comfortable.

Certain cultures use their hands and facial expressions to elaborate on their verbal message. In many cases it creates a drama-like environment where you see a whole group of people using high-pitched voices; their hands are in constant movement and their heads as well. The Eastern cultures do not appreciate that and it seems pretty foreign and unnecessary. So sometimes it can be funny and sometimes it's pretty sad. People who know the nonverbal cues of another culture would be better liked by people of that culture and will have greater chances of succeeding in a transaction.

WRIGHT

This is quite an interesting topic. It's one that the United States is going to have to learn. Who in the world is going to teach them?

PEARL

Apparently, yes, and as much as the United States is a leader in everything else I think we are a little bit behind in this case and it's time to catch up.

WRIGHT

Well, Mona, I really do appreciate all the time you've taken to answer these questions. The information is fascinating, at least I find it fascinating, and I'm sure that our readers will as well. I want to thank you for taking so much time with me to answer these questions today. It's really been a pleasure.

PEARL

Thank you, David. I hope this can be of help to many, many U.S. corporations.

WRIGHT

Today we've been talking with Mona Pearl. Her programs of cross-cultural leadership education, training, and personal development enable her clients to learn and master the nuances of other cultures, to be able to work in multi-cultural teams and succeed in global markets. Her programs lead them to understanding and successfully dealing with prospective business partners all over the world, while successfully managing the complexities, contradictions and conflicts associated with going global.

Mona, thank you so much for being with us today on *Discover Your Inner Strength*.

PEARL

Thank you, David.

CHAPTER Seven

A Values-Based Approach

AN INTERVIEW WITH...

Dr. Stephen Covey

www.stephencovey.com

ABOUT THE AUTHOR

Stephen R. Covey was recognized in 1996 as one of *Time* magazine's twenty-five most influential Americans and one of *Sales and Marketing Management's* top twenty-five power brokers. Dr. Covey is the author of several acclaimed books, including the international bestseller, *The 7 Habits of Highly Effective People,* named the number one Most Influential Business Book of the Twentieth Century, and other best sellers that include *First Things First, Principle-Centered Leadership,* (with sales exceeding one million) and *The 7 Habits of Highly Effective Families.*

Dr. Covey earned his undergraduate degree from the University of Utah, his MBA from Harvard, and completed his doctorate at Brigham Young University. While at Brigham Young University, he served as assistant to the President and was also a professor of Business Management and Organizational Behavior. He received the National Fatherhood Award in 2003, which, as the father of nine and grandfather of forty-four, he says is the most meaningful award he has ever received.

Dr. Covey currently serves on the board of directors for the Points of Light Foundation. Based in Washington, D.C., the Foundation, through its partnership with the Volunteer Center National Network, engages and mobilizes millions of volunteers from all walks of life—businesses, nonprofits, faith-based organizations, low-income communities, families, youth, and older adults—to help solve serious social problems in thousands of communities.

DAVID WRIGHT (WRIGHT)

We're talking today with Dr. Stephen R. Covey, cofounder and vice-chairman of Franklin Covey Company, the largest management company and leadership development organization in the world. Dr. Covey is perhaps best known as author of *The 7 Habits of Highly Effective People,* which is ranked as a number one best-seller by the *New York Times*, having sold more than fourteen million copies in thirty-eight languages throughout the world. Dr. Covey is an internationally respected leadership authority, family expert, teacher, and organizational consultant. He has made teaching principle-centered living and principle-centered leadership his life's work. Dr. Covey is the recipient of the Thomas More College Medallion for Continuing Service to Humanity and has been awarded four honorary doctorate degrees. Other awards given Dr. Covey include the Sikh's 1989 International Man of Peace award, the 1994 International Entrepreneur of the Year award, *Inc.* magazine's Services Entrepreneur of the Year award, and in 1996 the National Entrepreneur of the Year Lifetime Achievement award for Entrepreneurial leadership. He has also been recognized as one of *Time* magazine's twenty-five most influential Americans and one of *Sales and Marketing Management's* top twenty-five power brokers. As the father of nine and grandfather of forty-four, Dr. Covey received the 2003 National Fatherhood Award, which he says is the most meaningful award he has ever received. Dr. Covey earned his undergraduate degree from the University of Utah, his MBA from Harvard, and completed his doctorate at Brigham Young University. While at Brigham Young he served as assistant to the President and was also a professor of Business Management and Organizational Behavior.

Dr. Covey, welcome to *Discover Your Inner Strength*.

DR. STEPHEN COVEY (COVEY)

Thank you.

WRIGHT

Dr. Covey, most companies make decisions and filter them down through their organization. You, however, state that no company can succeed until individuals within it succeed. Are the goals of the company the result of the combined goals of the individuals?

COVEY

Absolutely—if people aren't on the same page, they're going to be pulling in different directions. To teach this concept, I frequently ask large audiences to close their eyes and point north, and then to keep pointing and open their eyes. They find themselves pointing all over the place. I say to them, "Tomorrow morning if you want a similar experience, ask the first ten people you meet in your organization what the purpose of your organization is and you'll find it's a very similar experience. They'll point all over the place." When people have a different sense of purpose and values, every decision that is made from then on is governed by those. There's no question that this is one of the fundamental causes of misalignment, low trust, interpersonal conflict, interdepartmental rivalry, people operating on personal agendas, and so forth.

WRIGHT

Is that primarily a result of an inability to communicate from the top?

COVEY

That's one aspect, but I think it's more fundamental. There's an inability to involve people—an unwillingness. Leaders may communicate what their mission and their strategy is, but that doesn't mean there's any emotional connection to it. Mission statements that are rushed and then announced are soon forgotten. They become nothing more than just a bunch of platitudes on the wall that mean essentially nothing and even create a source of cynicism and a sense of hypocrisy inside the culture of an organization.

WRIGHT

How do companies ensure survival and prosperity in these tumultuous times of technological advances, mergers, downsizing, and change?

COVEY

I think that it takes a lot of high trust in a culture that has something that doesn't change—principles—at its core. There are principles that people agree upon that are valued. It gives a sense of stability. Then you have the power to adapt and be flexible when you experience these kinds of disruptive new economic models or technologies that come in and sideswipe you. You don't know how to handle them unless you have something you can depend upon.

If people have not agreed to a common set of principles that guide them and a common purpose, then they get their security from the outside and they tend to freeze the structure, systems, and processes inside and they cease becoming adaptable. They don't change with the changing realities of the new marketplace out there and gradually they become obsolete.

WRIGHT

I was interested in one portion of your book, *The 7 Habits of Highly Effective People,* where you talk about behaviors. How does an individual go about the process of replacing ineffective behaviors with effective ones?

COVEY

I think that for most people it usually requires a crisis that humbles them to become aware of their ineffective behaviors. If there's not a crisis the tendency is to perpetuate those behaviors and not change.

You don't have to wait until the marketplace creates the crisis for you. Have everyone accountable on a 360-degree basis to everyone else they interact with—with feedback either formal or informal—where they are getting data as to what's happening. They will then start to realize that the consequences of their ineffective behavior require them to be humble enough to look at that behavior and to adopt new, more effective ways of doing things.

Sometimes people can be stirred up to this if you just appeal to their conscience—to their inward sense of what is right and wrong. A lot of people sometimes know inwardly they're doing wrong, but the culture doesn't necessarily discourage them from continuing that. They either need feedback from people or they need feedback from the marketplace or they need feedback from their conscience. Then they can begin to develop a step-by-step process of replacing old habits with new, better habits.

WRIGHT

It's almost like saying, "Let's make all the mistakes in the laboratory before we put this thing in the air."

COVEY

Right; and I also think what is necessary is a paradigm shift, which is analogous to having a correct map, say of a city or of a country. If people have an inaccurate paradigm of life, of other people, and of themselves it really doesn't make much difference what their behavior or habits or attitudes are. What they need is a correct paradigm—a correct map—that describes what's going on.

For instance, in the Middle Ages they used to heal people through bloodletting. It wasn't until Samuel Weiss and Pasteur and other empirical scientists discovered the germ theory that they realized for the first time they weren't dealing with the real issue. They realized why women preferred to use midwives who washed rather than doctors who didn't wash. They gradually got a new paradigm. Once you've got a new paradigm then your behavior and your attitude flow directly from it. If you have a bad paradigm or a bad map, let's say of a city, there's no way, no matter what your behavior or your habits or your attitudes are—how positive they are—you'll never be able to find the location you're looking for. This is why I believe that to change paradigms is far more fundamental than to work on attitude and behavior.

WRIGHT

One of your seven habits of highly effective people is to "begin with the end in mind." If circumstances change and hardships or miscalculations occur, how does one view the end with clarity?

COVEY

Many people think to begin with the end in mind means that you have some fixed definition of a goal that's accomplished and if changes come about you're not going to adapt to them. Instead, the "end in mind" you begin with is that you are going to create a flexible culture of high trust so that no matter what comes along you are going to do whatever it takes to accommodate that new change or that new reality and maintain a culture of high performance and high trust. You're talking more in terms of values and overall purposes that don't change, rather than specific strategies or programs that will have to change to accommodate the changing realities in the marketplace.

WRIGHT

In this time of mistrust among people, corporations, and nations, for that matter, how do we create high levels of trust?

COVEY

That's a great question and it's complicated because there are so many elements that go into the creating of a culture of trust. Obviously the most fundamental one is just to have trustworthy people. But that is not sufficient because what if the organization itself is misaligned?

For instance, what if you say you value cooperation but you really reward people for internal competition? Then you have a systemic or a structure problem that creates low trust inside the culture even though the people themselves are trustworthy. This is one of the insights of Edward Demming and the work he did. That's why he said that most problems are not personal—they're systemic. They're common caused. That's why you have to work on structure, systems, and processes to make sure that they institutionalize principle-centered values. Otherwise you could have good people with bad systems and you'll get bad results.

When it comes to developing interpersonal trust between people, it is made up of many, many elements such as taking the time to listen to other people, to understand them, and to see what is important to them. What we think is important to another may only be important to us, not to another. It takes empathy. You have to make and keep promises to them. You have to treat people with kindness and courtesy. You have to be completely honest and open. You have to live up to your commitments. You can't betray people behind their back. You can't badmouth them behind their back and sweet-talk them to their face. That will send out vibes of hypocrisy and it will be detected.

You have to learn to apologize when you make mistakes, to admit mistakes, and to also get feedback going in every direction as much as possible. It doesn't necessarily require formal forums—it requires trust between people who will be open with each other and give each other feedback.

WRIGHT

My mother told me to do a lot of what you're saying now, but it seems that when I got in business I simply forgot.

COVEY

Sometimes we forget, but sometimes culture doesn't nurture it. That's why I say unless you work with the institutionalizing—that means formalizing into structure, systems, and processing the values—you will not have a nurturing culture. You have to constantly work on that.

This is one of the big mistakes organizations make. They think trust is simply a function of being honest. That's only one small aspect. It's an important aspect, obviously, but there are so many other elements that go into the creation of a high-trust culture.

WRIGHT

"Seek first to understand then to be understood" is another of your seven habits. Do you find that people try to communicate without really understanding what other people want?

COVEY

Absolutely. The tendency is to project out of our own autobiography—our own life, our own value system—onto other people, thinking we know what they want. So we don't really listen to them. We pretend to listen, but we really don't listen from within their frame of reference. We listen from within our own frame of reference and we're really preparing our reply rather than seeking to understand. This is a very common thing. In fact, very few people have had any training in seriously listening. They're trained in how to read, write, and speak, but not to listen.

Reading, writing, speaking, and listening are the four modes of communication and they represent about two-thirds to three-fourths of our waking hours. About half of that time is spent listening, but it's the one skill people have not been trained in. People have had all this training in the other forms of communication. In a large audience of 1,000 people you wouldn't have more than twenty people who have had more than two weeks of training in listening. Listening is more than a skill or technique; you must listen within another's frame of reference. It takes tremendous courage to listen because you're at risk when you listen. You don't know what's going to happen; you're vulnerable.

WRIGHT

Sales gurus always tell me that the number one skill in selling is listening.

COVEY

Yes—listening from within the customer's frame of reference. That is so true. You can see that it takes some security to do that because you don't know what's going to happen.

WRIGHT

With this book we're trying to encourage people to be better, to live better, and be more fulfilled by listening to the examples of our guest authors. Is there anything or anyone in your life that has made a difference for you and helped you to become a better person?

COVEY

I think the most influential people in my life have been my parents. I think that what they modeled was not to make comparisons and harbor jealousy or to seek recognition. They were humble people.

I remember one time when my mother and I were going up in an elevator and the most prominent person in the state was also in the elevator. She knew him, but she spent her time talking to the elevator operator. I was just a little kid and I was so awed by the famous person. I said to her, "Why didn't you talk to the important person?" She said, "I was. I had never met him."

My parents were really humble, modest people who were focused on service and other people rather than on themselves. I think they were very inspiring models to me.

WRIGHT

In almost every research paper I've ever read, those who write about people who have influenced their lives include three teachers in their top-five picks. My seventh-grade English teacher was the greatest teacher I ever had and she influenced me to no end.

COVEY

Would it be correct to say that she saw in you probably some qualities of greatness you didn't even see in yourself?

WRIGHT

Absolutely.

COVEY

That's been my general experience—the key aspect of a mentor or a teacher is someone who sees in you potential that you don't even see in yourself. Those teachers/mentors treat you accordingly and eventually you come to see it in yourself. That's my definition of leadership or influence—communicating people's worth and potential so clearly that they are inspired to see it in themselves.

WRIGHT

Most of my teachers treated me as a student, but she treated me with much more respect than that. As a matter of fact, she called me Mr. Wright, and I was in the seventh grade at the time. I'd never been addressed by anything but a nickname. I stood a little taller; she just made a tremendous difference.

Do you think there are other characteristics that mentors seem to have in common?

COVEY

I think they are first of all good examples in their own personal lives. Their personal lives and their family lives are not all messed up—they come from a base of good character. They also are usually very confident and they take the time to do what your teacher did to you—to treat you with uncommon respect and courtesy.

They also, I think, explicitly teach principles rather than practices so that rules don't take the place of human judgment. You gradually come to have faith in your own judgment in making decisions because of the affirmation of such a mentor. Good mentors care about you—you can feel the sincerity of their caring. It's like the expression, "I don't care how much you know until I know how much you care."

WRIGHT

Most people are fascinated with the new television shows about being a survivor. What has been the greatest comeback that you've made from adversity in your career or your life?

COVEY

When I was in grade school I experienced a disease in my legs. It caused me to use crutches for a while. I tried to get off them fast and get back. The disease wasn't corrected yet so I went back on crutches for another year. The disease went to the other leg and I went on for another year. It essentially took me out of my favorite thing—athletics—and it took me more into being a student. So that was a life-defining experience, which at the time seemed very negative, but has proven to be the basis on which I've focused my life—being more of a learner.

WRIGHT

Principle-centered learning is basically what you do that's different from anybody I've read or listened to.

COVEY

The concept is embodied in the Far Eastern expression, "Give a man a fish, you feed him for the day; teach him how to fish, you feed him for a lifetime." When you teach principles that are universal and timeless, they don't belong to just any one person's religion or to a particular culture or geography. They seem to be timeless and universal like the ones we've been talking about here: trustworthiness, honesty, caring, service, growth, and development. These are universal principles. If you focus on these things, then little by little people become independent of you and then they start to believe in themselves and their own judgment becomes better. You don't need as many rules. You don't need as much bureaucracy and as many controls and you can empower people.

The problem in most business operations today—and not just business but non-business—is that they're using the industrial model in an information age. Arnold

Toynbee, the great historian, said, "You can pretty well summarize all of history in four words: nothing fails like success." The industrial model was based on the asset of the machine. The information model is based on the asset of the person—the knowledge worker. It's an altogether different model. But the machine model was the main asset of the twentieth century. It enabled productivity to increase fifty times. The new asset is intellectual and social capital—the qualities of people and the quality of the relationship they have with each other. Like Toynbee said, "Nothing fails like success." The industrial model does not work in an information age. It requires a focus on the new wealth, not capital and material things.

A good illustration that demonstrates how much we were into the industrial model, and still are, is to notice where people are on the balance sheet. They're not found there. Machines are found there. Machines become investments. People are on the profit-and-loss statement and people are expenses. Think of that—if that isn't bloodletting.

WRIGHT

It sure is.

When you consider the choices you've made down through the years, has faith played an important role in your life?

COVEY

It has played an extremely important role. I believe deeply that we should put principles at the center of our lives, but I believe that God is the source of those principles. I did not invent them. I get credit sometimes for some of the Seven Habits material and some of the other things I've done, but it's really all based on principles that have been given by God to all of His children from the beginning of time. You'll find that you can teach these same principles from the sacred texts and the wisdom literature of almost any tradition. I think the ultimate source of that is God and that is one thing you can absolutely depend upon—"in God we trust."

WRIGHT

If you could have a platform and tell our audience something you feel would help them or encourage them, what would you say?

COVEY

I think I would say to put God at the center of your life and then prioritize your family. No one on their deathbed ever wished they had spent more time at the office.

WRIGHT

That's right. We have come down to the end of our program and I know you're a busy person. I could talk with you all day, Dr. Covey.

COVEY

It's good to talk with you as well and to be a part of this program. It looks like an excellent one that you've got going on here.

WRIGHT

Thank you.

We have been talking today with Dr. Stephen R. Covey, cofounder and vice-chairman of Franklin Covey Company. He's also the author of *The 7 Habits of Highly Effective People,* which has been ranked as a number one bestseller by the *New York Times*, selling more than fourteen million copies in thirty-eight languages.

Dr. Covey, thank you so much for being with us today.

COVEY

Thank you for the honor of participating.

Trust Yourself to Think Bigger & Live Bolder

AN INTERVIEW WITH...

Margie Warrell

Margie Warrell International LLC
PO Box 8102
McLean VA 22106
214.686.4155
margie@margiewarrell.com
www.margiewarrell.com
findyourcourage.com

ABOUT THE AUTHOR

Margie Warrell is a coach, speaker, and author who is passionate about empowering people to think bigger, live bolder, and achieve outstanding results in their careers, relationships, and lives. The author of *Find Your Courage* (McGraw-Hill), Margie empowers individuals and organizations internationally to live and lead with greater clarity, confidence, and courage.

THE INTERVIEW

DAVID WRIGHT (WRIGHT)

With me today is Margie Warrell, an ICF Certified Coach, best-selling author, and speaker who is recognized internationally as an expert on living and leading with courage.

Margie has come a long way from her childhood in rural Australia to being a best-selling author and recognized by Cambridge *Who's Who* as a leader in her field internationally. Combining a background in Fortune 500 business with graduate qualifications in psychology, in 2006 Margie co-authored *101 Ways to Improve Your Life* with Jack Canfield, John Gray, and other leading success experts. In 2007, her second book, *Find Your Courage* (McGraw-Hill), became a bestseller and a USA Best Book Awards finalist.

Margie is known for her ability to get to the heart of what holds people back and limits their success. She has presented her programs to audiences internationally with clients that include NASA, British Telecom, ExxonMobil, and Accenture. Margie has also been interviewed on over two hundred television and radio programs including NBC's *Today Show,* and *The Daily Café.*

When it comes to living boldly, Margie walks her talk. Not only has she travelled the globe extensively—from the Middle East to Papua New Guinea—but she is also "mum" to four equally adventuresome young children. Needless to say, Margie is passionate about empowering people to think bigger, live bolder, and achieve outstanding results in their careers, organizations, relationships, and lives.

Margie, you have written and spoken extensively on the topic of living and leading courage. Why is courage something you are so passionate about?

MARGIE WARRELL (WARRELL)

Courage is vital because fear can hold people back in very profound ways. Only by having the courage to rise above fear in our conversations, aspirations, and actions can we do all and be all we are capable of.

My passion for living with courage and empowering others to do so has come through my professional experiences and personal challenges. I have spent a lot of time in many countries and experienced incredibly diverse cultures, and along the way I've met people with very different values and perspectives on life. But everywhere I have gone, the one universal factor I have found that holds individuals, communities, organizations, and even countries back is fear. Whether it is fear of change, fear of challenging the long-held status quo or cultural tradition, fear of being ostracized by one's family, losing face or looking foolish in front of one's peers, or simply fear of making a mistake, all human beings struggle with fear in some way, shape, or form. Only by rising above our deepest fears and the self-doubts they fuel can we as individuals, and humanity as a collective, hope to enjoy a deeper sense of fulfillment in our lives and make a meaningful contribution that leaves the world better off for our having been part of it.

WRIGHT

What has been your own experience with fear and, more importantly, learning how to overcome it?

WARRELL

I had a pretty wholesome childhood growing up as one of seven children on a dairy farm in rural Australia. Although my family was very loving and supportive, I often felt a nagging sense of self-doubt. I wrestled with fear—fear of not being good enough or pretty enough, fear of criticism, fear of being left out or unpopular, fear of looking foolish in front of those I wanted to impress, fear of not having what it takes to succeed in life, and failing in my endeavors.

Of course, like most kids, I had dreams about what I wanted to do when I "grew up," yet at the same time I had a whole bevy of limiting beliefs about what was possible for me. To rephrase a few words from Marianne Williamson, "Who was I to be brilliant, gorgeous, talented, and fabulous and amazingly successful?"

But I worked hard at school, got great grades, and at eighteen left home to attend university in Melbourne, four hours' drive away. I think that was my first big act of courage because it was scary moving to a large city where I knew no one, having to fully support myself and taking the super fast track to independence. But tough though they were, those first couple of years away from home taught me an invaluable life lesson—unless you risk failing at something, you will never succeed at anything.

Three years later, after graduating and working multiple jobs, I again stepped outside my comfort zone—this time donning a backpack and heading overseas on a shoestring budget to explore the world. During my travels through Southeast Asia, Europe, North America, and India, I learned another important lesson on courage: when we step beyond our comfort zone, we discover strengths we may otherwise not have known we had.

In the years that followed, I embarked on numerous other adventures through the Middle East, Africa, Asia, and South America. I also began my career in business, was married, and soon after, headed to Papua New Guinea for three years where I worked in marketing. Later I returned to study psychology and then began one of life's greatest adventures—parenthood!

Along the way, I had to deal with my share of change, heartache, disappointment, uncertainty, and risk. But through it all, I continually discovered in myself resilience and capability beyond what I thought I had. This served to both deepen and reinforce my belief that our experience of life shrinks or expands in proportion to our courage. I also learned another universal life lesson—while you can't always choose your circumstances in life, you can always choose your response to them.

WRIGHT

So are you saying that you believe courage is the antidote to fear?

WARRELL

I sure am. You see, courage is not the absence of fear or self-doubt—courage is action in its presence. That's why without courage, people end up settling for far less than what they truly want, selling out on their dreams, and living mediocre lives instead of extraordinary ones. They languish for years (decades even!) in jobs they don't enjoy, in relationships that leave them yearning for deeper intimacy, and "getting by" in lives absent of purpose and devoid of passion. Without courage, our lives become ruled by fear and weighed down in resignation, excuses, and regret. So only by living with courage can one ever hope to savor the rich sense of joy and satisfaction that only a life well lived can bring.

WRIGHT

Do you think that people these days are more fearful than they used to be?

WARRELL

Terrorism, recession, fundamentalism, identity theft, corporate downsizing, melting ice caps, child predators, online predators, super bug predators . . . every day the headlines scream at us to batten down the hatches, sanitize our hands, our minds, our voices, and avoid any possibility of rocking our boat or the boats of others. So yes, absolutely, I believe that we live in a culture of fear that urges us to avoid risk, trust sparingly, and stick with the status quo wherever possible. It's for this very reason, though, that we need to be increasingly vigilant of fear-mongering, discerning about which fears we pay heed to, and mindful of the oppressive impact that living in fearfulness can have.

Regularly I meet people living under a dark cloud of anxiety whose lives are fuelled by fear rather than possibility. It permeates every corner of their life, from how they raise their children to how they engage with their neighbors, their boss, their family, organization, and the world in general. Little by little, fear creeps its way in, metastasizes, and leaves people selling out to the path of least resistance— political correctness and convenient mediocrity. They tiptoe through life keeping their sights set low to minimize the risk of failure and social embarrassment.

WRIGHT

Margie, what do you say to readers who often find themselves wrestling with their self-doubts and feeling anything but fearless in the face of the challenges they are facing?

WARRELL

Courage is not about fearlessness at all. Unfortunately though, people often make the mistake of thinking that because they sometimes feel anxious and afraid, overwhelmed with self-doubts, or lacking the confidence they perceive in others, that they don't have what it takes to be courageous themselves. But that is simply untrue.

Courage doesn't always come in hero form and some of the greatest acts of courage are from those who have been most afraid. Nelson Mandela said it beautifully when he wrote, "I learned that courage was not the absence of fear, but the triumph over it. The brave man is not he who does not feel afraid, but he who conquers that fear." Do you think the young man who stood in front of that huge army tank in the middle of Tiananmen Square wasn't feeling fearful? Not a chance. I'm sure he had fear coursing through every vein in his body. But he also had the power of his convictions steeling him to hold his ground, vulnerable in the face of that huge armored tank and the might of the Chinese military behind it, and to make a stand for justice, for basic human rights, and freedom of speech.

So I don't just believe that courage is a "nice to have" ingredient for creating a successful life—it's the core ingredient. As the Greek philosopher Aristotle observed way back in the fourth century, "Courage is the first of human qualities because it is the one quality which guarantees all others." And so if we are going to enjoy our lives fully and achieve the kind of success we want—whether in our relationships, our careers, our businesses, or any single area of life—we must be willing to step forward in the presence of the many fears that would otherwise have us sitting passively on the sidelines and playing safe.

WRIGHT

So are you also saying that feeling fear is a good and normal emotion?

WARRELL

Absolutely I am. If we didn't feel fear we'd be like Spock, the one-dimensional *Star Trek* Vulcan—either that or dead. Which is precisely my point—it's not about whether you feel fear or not, it's about what you do with it. The fact is that fear is a naturally occurring human emotion, and while some people may naturally be bolder and others more cautious, no human being is immune to it. We wouldn't want to be immune to it because fear is an emotion that is wired into us in order to protect us from harm and enable us to thrive in the world. Heck, if we didn't feel fear, the human race would have been devoured by hungry, saber-toothed tigers back in our caveman days.

So the question is not about whether fear is a good thing or a bad thing, but rather whether the fears you feel every day are serving you by keeping you safe from real danger and allowing you to thrive in life and love or whether they are hindering you—keeping you from taking the actions needed to enjoy deeper fulfillment and greater success (however you choose to define it).

If you look around at people who are regarded as having lived very successful lives—whether in this current generation or throughout history—you will note that every single one of them had to rise above their own fears, take risks, and be daring in their own way. Margaret Thatcher, Galileo, Oprah, Abraham Lincoln, Helen Keller, Gandhi, Lance Armstrong, Mikhail Gorbachev, Edison, Mother Teresa, Columbus—all of them had to overcome their own doubts in order to take on challenges that many people would have said were too large to even consider. They didn't focus on probabilities; they focused on possibilities.

But it's not about being famous or powerful or better than anyone else—it's about being the best possible version of yourself and fulfilling your own unique potential in the world. Opportunities to do that arise every single day, such as: every time you challenge the way something has "always been done," when you pick up the phone and extend an invitation to someone you'd like to know better, when you express an opinion that may ruffle feathers, end a relationship that isn't working to create space for one that will, pursue a dream that requires trading the safety of the known for the possibility that life might hold something bigger and better in store for you.

At the end of the day, it's not lack of opportunity or connections or lucky breaks or education or prosperity that keep people from leading truly successful lives, it's a lack of courage to go after it. The only difference between the people who lead an *extra*-ordinary life and those who live an ordinary one is the *extra* courage they bring to it.

WRIGHT

It's not always easy to admit feeling afraid. For some it's even a sign of weakness. So how important is it for people to acknowledge that they feel fearful?

WARRELL

It's very important. In his groundbreaking book, *Emotional Intelligence,* Daniel Goleman wrote that only by developing a strong awareness of the emotions we are feeling at any given time can we manage them and be effective in our dealings with others in our success overall. In short, if you don't own your fears, they will own you and sabotage your efforts to succeed!

So it's important to identify the fears—however subtle—that are niggling in the backwaters of your mind and then to decide whether they are valid and worthy of attention or not! As Mark Twain once wrote, "I have known a great many troubles in my life. But most of them never happened." The gutsiest people I know are people who absolutely feel fear, but who then make very conscious choices not to let their fears keep them from confronting their challenges powerfully and taking on new ones that stretch them and call on them to grow as a human being.

WRIGHT

Earlier you referred to courage in relation to three areas: our conversations, aspirations, and actions. Will you elaborate on each of these areas beginning with why courage is so important in our conversations?

WARRELL

The quality of our relationships is determined by the quality of the conversations we have in them. Think for a moment about your most valued personal relationships and you will notice the correlation to the quality of the conversations you have in them. They are conversations that don't just stay at the superficial "keeping up appearances" level but go deeper, beyond the trite and mundane down to concerns that are real and feelings that are authentic. Issues are put on the table rather than being left to fester indefinitely. Likewise, in your professional relationships, while they may not always be as intimate, there will also be a high degree of openness, respect, authenticity, and trust. On the other hand, if you flip the coin and think about the relationships you have that are either the most strained or conflict-ridden, it's because there has been a lack of quality, caring, and mutually respectful conversations taking place.

But here's the hitch and the reason why courage has everything to do with the quality of our relationships. Speaking up about issues that inevitably arise in any ongoing relationship—whether in the boardroom or the bedroom—takes real courage. It can be very unnerving to share how you genuinely feel or ask for what you really want from someone (versus what you think you might be able to get). Likewise, it can be downright terrifying to address a long-standing issue that's been sitting there like a big white elephant in the corner of the room for so long that you've almost come to think of it as normal. These conversations can be very intimidating and so we need to be very courageous to have them!

Finding the courage to engage in conversations that put you at risk—whether of confrontation, causing offence, rejection, or criticism—requires being honest with yourself about the price you will pay by not having them. Acknowledging the cost of sticking with the status quo will help you to rise above your fear of speaking up. Sometimes these fears can manifest in your body—from a mild case of butterflies to an outbreak of shingles (believe me, I know people who've had just that!). So only by acknowledging those fears and then making the commitment to yourself to speak your truth, be real, and risk the possibility of confrontation can you have the conversations needed to strengthen your relationships and resolve the issues that threaten to undermine them.

WRIGHT

What do you see as the keys to having "courageous conversations"?

WARRELL

There are four important keys to having an "effective," courageous conversation. I deliberately throw the word "effective" in there because sometimes when people speak up to let someone else know what they "really" think it only results in damaged trust, resentment, and relationship breakdown. Needless to say, that's obviously not the result you are looking for. The four keys are:

1. Identify your highest intention
2. Manage emotions
3. Rework your story
4. Speak to the listening

The first core component that's incredibly important is to identify your highest intention for the conversation. That is, get clear about what positive purpose you are hoping to achieve. Needless to say, unless the intention you have going into the conversation is a positive one and you are clear that what you need to say is ultimately going to be of service to you *and* to the other person, then your conversation is unlikely to produce a positive outcome in the longer term.

Of course, when it comes to human beings, emotions can quickly hijack a conversation and derail it from reaching a positive outcome. So managing your own emotions and responding effectively to the emotions of others is a second important key for an effective, courageous conversation. You see, different emotions predispose us to different actions. If you are angry or resentful, then your instinctive response is to inflict hurt onto the other person in some way, whether by a snide remark, the "silent treatment," or outward aggression. If you are fearful, then you will either respond by moving to silence (playing it safe and saying nothing at all) or to violence, donning your verbal boxing gloves, intent on fighting your way to victory. The problem is that if you end up the "winner," then, by default, someone else has to be the "loser." Sure, you've won the battle but at what cost? On the other hand, if you let your fear of confrontation keep you from expressing your opinion, then that's also going to do you a disservice. Ultimately, issues that aren't talked out are acted out and tend to resurface in harmful and hurtful ways.

So if there is something you genuinely want to say, chances are there is someone who genuinely needs to hear it. Often, when I'm working with managers and even senior leaders, one of their biggest challenges is "discussing the indiscussible" because they want to avoid the repercussions of causing offence and upsetting people. So they choose the more convenient and hassle-free path (at least in the short-term) of just ignoring the issues. They decide instead to wait for the next opportunity to have the person transferred (or to be transferred themselves!). Where's the integrity in that? So while managing emotions that have the potential to hijack a conversation is important for everyone, it is essential for anyone who wants to be a successful manager or leader.

The third key is to take a step back and challenge the beliefs you have about your predicament—to rework your "story." Our stories are the melting pot of assumptions, prejudices, and attitudes that we all have about everything in the world around us, about others, about ourselves and about the challenges we face throughout life. Often though, we fall into the trap of thinking that how we see a situation is the way it actually is; but not so. We don't see the world as it is; we see it as we are. We don't own the truth, just our story of it!

Just as it's vital to challenge your "story" about your predicament and the assumptions you have that underpin it, it's equally essential to try to understand how other people might view it and to uncover their story. This takes courage and humility because it requires acknowledging to yourself first of all, and then to others, that maybe you don't own the "whole truth" and there may very well be more to this situation than you have seen or been acknowledging.

For instance, how have you contributed to the status quo? What have you done or failed to do? It's very easy to point the finger and lay the blame squarely at the feet of others, but until we own up to the fact that we have, through our words and actions and lack thereof, contributed to our circumstances, we won't be effective in fixing what isn't working. Coupling this with active listening that's driven by a genuine desire to not only understand *what* the other party thinks, but *why* the person came to think it creates a powerful combination that serves to build trust, lower defenses, and shift the negative emotions that may be hanging over the issue. As my colleague and co-author, Stephen R. Covey, states in his book, *The 7 Habits of Highly Effective People,* "Seek first to understand before being understood."

The fourth and final key is to speak to the listening. In other words, to say what you want to say in such a way that minimizes the gap between what you want others to hear and know and what they actually understand.

Have you ever made a comment or a joke that someone else either didn't understand or took the wrong way? What occurred was a lack of understanding on your part—whether reasonable or not—about how that person would perceive, interpret, or understand what you said. You see, too often we think that what we are saying is what the other person is hearing. In reality, the real meaning of communication is defined not by what is being said but by what is being heard. Understanding someone else's story and the frame of reference from which they are listening allows us to communicate what we need to say in a way that the other person will understand without getting defensive.

Masterful communicators know that they are responsible for how others listen to them and are very intentional about speaking to that listening.

WRIGHT

Will you share a few key strategies readers can use to help them get their point across without upsetting the people they are talking to?

WARRELL

Sure. There are many different models on how to have what I call a "courageous conversation," but one that I think is simple to remember and follow is based on three core types of conversations. These are:

a. *Descriptive Conversations:* These basically describe "where am I?" or "where are we?"
b. *Speculative Conversations:* These speculate about what the ideal outcome could be. They answer the question, "What do I/we *really* want?"
c. *Action Conversations:* These identify which actions need to occur to get from current Point A to ideal Point B. That is, "How do I/we get there?"

Begin with what I call "Descriptive Conversations" that convey your viewpoint on the situation or problem in a way that leaves open other possible interpretations and doesn't apportion blame. Start by stating the facts first and then proceed to sharing your opinion about them. You see, if you treat your opinion as though it were a fact (e.g., "You clearly aren't committed to the success of this project or business or relationship") then you are guaranteed to irritate the other person. So begin by pointing out the undisputable facts like, "During the last week you have failed to attend three meetings" or "Last week you said that you didn't to invest time in xyz," and then move on to share your opinion in such a way that leaves open the possibility that there is another explanation or interpretation of the facts. For instance, "I may be misinterpreting things but I'm beginning to wonder about your level of commitment to this project" or "I know there's more than one way to see every situation but I can't help but feeling like you aren't fully onboard." Get the drift?

Second, move on to "Speculative Conversations" that focus on the future rather than on the past. It's easy to get stuck in a blame game where the goal is to see how much blame you can pile at each other's feet. But since when has stone-throwing been a productive pursuit? Rather than focusing on the past and what "shoulda-coulda-woulda" happened, focus on the future and on what you would like to have happen going forward. Collaborate and speculate on what the ideal outcome could be.

Finally, move from speculating about the ideal outcome or solution to identifying what has to happen (or stop happening!) to move from you are now to where you to be. With "Action Conversations," it's important to set clear expectations and be specific in both what you commit to and what you ask for.

Make sure there are concrete timelines. Then put in place accountability systems to ensure that all parties are honoring their commitments. If you can't figure out exactly what needs to be done to resolve things, at least commit to staying in regular dialogue.

WRIGHT

So we've covered the role of courage in conversation; what's courage got to do with our goals and aspirations?

WARRELL

Michelangelo once said, "The greater danger is not that our goals are too lofty and we fail to achieve them; but that they are too small and we do." Our aspirations are what we dream about—what excites and inspires us. Unfortunately, for many people, somewhere along the path from childhood to adulthood they downgrade their dreams and goals to ones they judge to be safer bets. After all, dreaming is risky and not all our dreams come true. But the problem is that unless we have the courage to ask ourselves, "What do I *really* want out of life?" and then let our imaginations take flight, we are never going to create "the life of our dreams."

The same applies to any area of life in which we aren't fully satisfied, since in any area of life in which we lack vision, we also lack power. It all begins with clarifying whatever it is that truly inspires us—however unique or different that may be from what inspires those around us. Truth be told, it matters not what you dream of but rather that your dream provides you with a deeper sense of purpose and passion and delight in being alive. After all, the word "inspire" comes from the Latin for "to breathe life into." What would breathe new life into you?

Of course, about two seconds after we connect with what inspires us, our fears rear their risk-aversive heads reminding us of the dangers that lurk ahead should we be bold enough to pursue those dreams. But to that, I have to quote English poet Robert Browning who wrote, "The aim, if reached or not, makes great the life." The truth is that whether or not you achieve all your goals and dreams is not as important as the fact that you have had the courage to try. When you look back on life one day, at least you won't have to think, "I wonder what might have happened if I'd tried?" Fear regret more than failure. Life's far too short to be lived meekly.

WRIGHT

This brings us full circle to the third key area of courage. Why does it take courage to take action?

WARRELL

When we take action, we are really putting our money where our mouth is and putting ourselves—our ego, reputation, and yes, even our money—on the line. That is why a rewarding life takes courage. It requires us to feel our fears and then to step forward despite them. Yes, it's risky, but then what worthwhile endeavor isn't? The way I see it is that the biggest risk any of us take is to take no risks at all. It takes just a quick look through the history books to see that we human beings fail far more from timidity than we do from over daring.

WRIGHT

So Margie, is there a simple step-by-step process that people can follow to step into courageous action?

WARRELL

Yes. And you can create it yourself by answering the following five questions:

1. *What do I really want?* And when I say "really," I mean *really* want. If you could have the ultimate relationship or job or career or business or lifestyle, what would it be? Don't let "what's realistic" keep you from thinking big. There are things that you, and only you, can do. Sure, you may not always succeed in accomplishing your dreams, but you have absolutely zero chance of accomplishing anything worthwhile if you are too afraid to dream big in the first place. As the saying goes, if you don't know where you want to go, any road will take you. So instead of succumbing to the committee of disparaging little voices in your head that ask, "Who are you to do that?" respond with "Who am I *not* to!"

2. *Where have I been letting my fears and doubts keep me settling, procrastinating, and being stuck in inaction?* Often we don't like to admit where our fears are holding us back. But only when we start owning our fears do they stop owning us. So really delve deep into this question. Ponder what you would do if you had no fear of failing. Reflect on what you would change if you didn't doubt your ability to manage the challenges that change would bring. Ask yourself what possibilities would open up if you could trust yourself that no matter what happened, you could handle it. Then make a firm commitment to reclaim the power you have been giving your fears and to stop allowing your fears to run your life.

3. *What's the price I will pay for not making changes?* Write down how you will feel about yourself six months from now and then five years

from now if you stick with the status quo. The cost you pay can come in many forms but your own sense of self-worth is up there at the top. This is followed closely by the quality of your relationships, to being the role model your kids need you to be, your enjoyment of life, regret, stress, lost opportunity, financial hardship, an absence of fulfillment, and a limit to the difference you can make for others. Too often we convince ourselves that we really are content with the status quo when in truth we know, in our heart of hearts, it actually sucks and we are settling big time. So being honest with ourselves about the profound cost of inaction is a crucial step toward courageous action.

4. *What are the initial steps I need to take?* Often when people think about achieving a big goal they quickly find themselves overwhelmed with just how much must be done to accomplish it. So it's really important when you are starting out to break down your goal into smaller bite-sized steps. As Martin Luther King once wisely said, "You don't have to see the whole staircase. Just take the first step." So write down what those first few steps will be and assign each a deadline. In other words, don't just think it, ink it! The most important thing here is to take some action—any action—however seemingly small and insignificant! All that matters is that it's in the direction you want your life to travel. After all, if you keep doing what you've always done, you'll keep getting what you've always gotten.

5. *How can I create an environment that keeps me on track?* When you have an environment around you that supports you and brings out your best, it makes it easier to persevere when the going gets tough and ultimately to prevail. So be very intentional in setting up systems and support networks that help keep you on track and accountable. Share your goals with those around you, ask your friends and family to help hold you accountable, join a support group, or hire a coach. Schedule time with yourself to regularly review your progress and reflect again on these questions.

Also, be vigilant of those people and the forces in your environment that could jeopardize your success. People who are unsupportive, cynical, resigned, and discouraging can be like a lead chain around your ankle when it comes to moving forward. Einstein once said, "Free spirits have always encountered violent opposition from cynical mediocre minds." So do what you need to do is minimize the impact of the mediocre minds in your life. If that means spending less time in the company of certain energy-draining people, then so be it. It's your life on the line here! Likewise, if there are other forces in your environment that could pull you off track—a lack of proper planning, organization or dysfunctional systems—attend to them. Don't underestimate the impact your physical, social, and emotional environment can have on your wellbeing, productivity, and motivation to stay on track toward your goals.

WRIGHT

Margie, you've shared so many empowering strategies and perspectives for living more boldly. But it's got me wondering, do you ever find it hard to be courageous yourself?

WARRELL

Daily—sometimes even hourly! Why do you think I wrote a book called *Find Your Courage*? The reality is that if it were easy to walk the path of courage, everyone would be doing it. All around us people would be powerfully addressing the issues that weigh them down. There'd be a sudden drop in anti-depressants, as people took ownership for what wasn't working in their lives and began to make a stand for what they wanted and cared about. Our corporations and governments would have leaders doing the right thing versus what was politically expedient. Instead of righteously marching into battle, we'd first be trying to better understand why the other party loathed us so much to begin with. Ahhh . . . if only the path of courage were an easy one to follow.

It's not easy to be courageous and I don't find it any easier than the next person. But because I know how incredibly stifling it can be to allow fear to rule our lives I work hard at stepping over my fears as they arise—whether fear of saying no, being criticized, having an awkward conversation, or failing outright—and take action anyway. Of course, like all human beings, sometimes I slip up. But making mistakes is all part of the human experience. They always offer us an opportunity to learn about what doesn't work, to evolve as a human being, to practice humility, and to do better next time. Life is one long series of lessons in how to be brave in the face of all it brings our way.

Helen Keller once said, "Life is a daring adventure or nothing." And so that's the spirit I try to bring to the challenges and opportunities that life presents me with. Life flies by so fast and our years on earth are so few. I've often heard it said that in the twilight of life people regret far more the things they didn't do than those they did, which is why, whatever your age or circumstances, it's so important to connect with what inspires you, acknowledge your doubts and fears, and then to step boldly forward despite them—in the small things as much as the big—trusting that whatever challenges come your way through life, you have all the strength, courage, and wisdom within you to meet them.

CHAPTER Nine

Your Strength Will Set You Free

AN INTERVIEW WITH...

Sara Canuso

A Suitable Solution
200 South Broad St., Ste. 440
Philadelphia, PA 19102
215.356.2854
sara@asuitablesolution.com
www.asuitablesolution.com

ABOUT THE AUTHOR

Sara Canuso, President of A Suitable Solution, educates men and women—from business executives to solopreneurs to college students—on how to make the most of the Impact of Image. Her insightful keynote presentations, business seminars, and one-on-one coaching deliver new ideas and practical tools in the areas of creating powerful first impressions, developing a positive self-image, dressing for success, and inspiring confidence.

As an Image and Body Language Specialist, Sara empowers individuals to use non-verbal communication effectively with others and to understand not only what others say, but to discover the unspoken messages and feeling behind their words and actions.

Sara's informative and popular business columns on the Impact of Image in corporate America have appeared in the *Philadelphia Maven, Legal Intelligencer, Philadelphia Business Journal,* and the Burlington County Bar Association's newsletter, *The Straight Word.*

DAVID WRIGHT (WRIGHT)

Today we're talking with Sara Canuso. She is President of A Suitable Solution and advises some of the Philadelphia region's most successful men and women. As a speaker, writer, teacher, and motivator she provides clients with the skills, principles, and habits needed to project confidence and to thrive professionally. Her program, "A Polished Professional Image for Workplace Success," is sought after by the region's top businesses in helping to give new associates a more confident professional persona. Sara is the creator of "Campus to Corporate," a program held in area colleges to help students prepare to enter the workplace. She is a certified seminar leader and is known throughout the region for her informative and popular column in *Maven Magazine* Philadelphia, and her "Winning Look" articles have appeared in the *Legal Intelligencer* and the Burlington County Bar Association's newsletter, *The Straight Word*.

Sara, welcome to *Discover Your Inner Strength*.

SARA CANUSO (CANUSO)

Hello David. Thank you so much for having me.

WRIGHT

So why do you think it takes most people so long to find their strengths, their purpose, and passion?

CANUSO

Well, David, I think we first have to take into consideration that according to proven statistics, by the time we are eighteen we have heard the word "no" more than two hundred thousand times! When we are young, our insecurities are so often hard to overcome that it is difficult to have the confidence in ourselves to move forward and envision a successful future. Very often, our strengths are just so beaten down that they are just too hard to find.

WRIGHT

What do you feel are the problems people face in trying to be successful?

CANUSO

A majority of people do not stay focused long enough to finish projects, so they do not get a sense of fulfillment; then doubt sets in for any future accomplishments. I always use the following analogy: There was a famous tightrope walker who never fell off the wire. When he was asked how he managed to stay on the wire and never fall, he said, "The key is, I never look back, to the side, or down. I keep my eye focused on the destination." When I first heard that, it was a wow moment for me because, I thought, this is really how life is. We tend to look back at our past, we tend to look to the side at people who are distracting us or at people who are telling us no, we can't do it. This really throws us off balance. We truly just have to get into the habit of saying, "I'm looking forward and trusting my God-given talents."

WRIGHT

It's known on the corporate streets that your programs are always a sellout and your audiences leave with a newfound empowering feeling about themselves. Why is that?

CANUSO

When people attend my programs, they leave with having received something that has made an immediate impact in their lives. I teach them to realize that they alone are responsible for and in control of their happiness and their success. We all tend to do it, David—at times, we tend to think we're not happy because of various circumstances such as "my sibling is causing me heartaches" or "my spouse is not treating me right" or "I am not being treated fairly at work." We also tend to listen to too much of what others say and what they think we should be doing to create a life of happiness and fulfillment.

WRIGHT

You help clients with creating lasting first impressions, but I can see how it goes beyond clothing and outward appearance. How do you begin with someone who has little or even no confidence?

CANUSO

It's funny—I go into companies and work with new associates on creating polished professional images, and employers ask me if I can tell their new associates how to dress and what to wear. In reply, I always ask, "Well, what are we placing into the suits?" For me the clothing is the icing on the cake. I have attendees go to the core of their being to find out once and for all their talents, their likes, their strengths, and, just as important, their dislikes. We then begin to work on people skills, body language, principles, and skills that start to build a foundation for a life of success.

WRIGHT

I've been listening to self-image conferences for years and years. Is it really true that people make up their minds about others in the first seven to fourteen seconds?

CANUSO

Yes, that is a fact. Is it fair? Perhaps not, but it is a reality.

WRIGHT

That's scary isn't it?

CANUSO

It is very scary. I share with people—especially my students in my Campus to Corporate program—that after all the years spent studying, all the nights you were awake with brain freeze and worrying about exams (and we won't even discuss the expense), yet within seven seconds you walk into an interview or into a meeting and someone decides whether or not to do business with you. The person makes that decision whether or not you are smart, whether or not you are intelligent, trustworthy, and honest. So many people in corporate life will spend hours planning for a meeting and preparing their presentation, yet they give very little thought to what they're wearing, how they're walking into a room, their posture, their handshake. I try to have people come to the realization that all of that work is just going by the wayside. Over 55 percent of communication is non-verbal, so why are they paying so little attention to their non-verbal skills? This is why I have people start to focus on their non-verbal skills as well as their verbal skills.

WRIGHT

So, about this thing of strengths—even football coaches and basketball coaches now tell that they don't even bother with weaknesses, they only work on the kid's strengths. The question is how does one go about finding their strengths?

CANUSO

We all have strengths and talents. Some people are just born salespeople and most of us have to be taught techniques to bring out those strengths. Just as a baby taking those early steps, we sometimes fall on our face. Remember the song, "Pick Yourself Up," from the 1936 Ginger Rogers, Fred Astaire movie *Swing Time?* The lyrics that were repeated during the song were, "Pick yourself up, dust yourself off, and start all over again." That is a true concept for living. Repetition builds confidence and confidence brings success.

I've always been fascinated with people's success stories and how many enterprises they were in that failed before they were successful. The thread that runs through every success story is that they never gave up. Once you find your strengths and start to focus, you begin to build a strong foundation and a life of passion, purpose, and success. When you do what you love, you get up each morning and cannot wait to start the day.

I switched careers and I'm doing what I love. I have to honestly say that since I decided to follow my passion and work with my strengths, I have not gotten up one day without excitement and enthusiasm, because I am getting up and I am doing what I love. My day just never seems like work.

WRIGHT

So why do you think people give up on their hopes and dreams, only to go back to doing the same thing that they hate?

CANUSO

What happens is that we become so comfortable with what we're familiar with and what we're in a habit of doing—it's the same routine and it's easier to fall back into a routine. It's easier to fall back into familiarity and convenience and it's just easier to go back to what we're accustomed to. With so many years of learned behavior we just automatically fall back into some of our habits, whether they're good or bad.

When you feel yourself continually returning to what you hate, you have to just stop yourself. Believe it or not, it only takes a few seconds to say, "Hold it! Take a couple deep breaths. I'm not going back there. I am not going backward. I am staying the course to my dreams and goals."

WRIGHT

A wise man once told me one time that if I should ever be walking down a country road and see a turtle sitting on the fencepost, I can bet my bottom dollar that he didn't get up there by himself. So what or who pushed you over the edge of making the decision to follow your dream?

CANUSO

I have been blessed with so many people who have touched my life and left their mark and who always seemed to have my interest at heart that it would take another two chapters to explain their impact.

The one who stands out is an eleven-year-old boy. I hired Giulian to water our garden at our summer home because we were not there during the week. He was focused and had the confidence to turn a simple watering job into a business. He stayed the course and actually had to hire two additional friends to help him with his growing business. Each week I watched him come by and in amazement I just thought, "Now, how does an eleven-year-old find that kind of motivation and here I sit after all these years still questioning my thoughts and my dreams?" That is when I made the choice to claim the life I was meant to live. Once I made that decision, I began to soar.

David, it is a decision—you've got to make a decision that this is your life. This kind of decision is one you must make once and for all.

Once I made that decision, I went beyond my dreams and still each day I look for other possibilities I haven't even tapped into. From that point on, I reached out to successful people who knew the challenges of starting a business and asked for their thoughts and suggestions. I am fortunate to have an entrepreneur for a brother who was amazing at keeping me on track during the days I seemed to be totally derailed. Ironically, my former employer of thirty-two years, who was always there coaching me, now claims the student has become the teacher and wants to work with me on future projects.

Best of all, I have a husband who has never made me doubt myself and has always shared great support, love, and belief. I'm sure there were days when he thought my decisions were crazy, but he never questioned my actions. That's really something great to have because we go through life and people question, "Well, what are you doing this for—are you crazy?" I'm sure you've gone through periods of your life where people have doubted you or questioned your decisions; you just have to decide that it is your life and you are free to make your own decisions.

Family and friends are a necessity in helping to build your strength, since they are the ones who act as your support and reinforcement as you are building your strength for a better life. I could never have done it without them.

WRIGHT

Absolutely.

So how can people begin to find their strengths, their passion, and purpose?

CANUSO

Well, it's critical that people begin by listing and eliminating all negative thoughts that they've accumulated in their mind—they take up too much valuable space. It is the same principal as a computer. When your computer catches a virus, it's on overload, it's not going to run, and it's either going to crash or run slower. Our minds are no different. So, we need to take the time to scan our minds, grab a piece of paper and a pen, and write down any negative thoughts we've had, regardless of how silly we may think they are.

Some examples are: I hate the way people talk to me. I hate the way I speak. I hate my hair. I hate my siblings. I hate the way I do presentations.

After you write all of your negative thoughts down, you take the paper, tear it up in a million pieces, and you physically throw it in the trash because, David, that's exactly where these negative thoughts belong—in the trash.

I just cannot begin to tell you how my clients, and how attendees in my program, take a deep breath after doing this exercise. Then a big sigh of relief is heard. A weight has now rolled off their shoulders and they are ready to soar. Now, with all the negativity eliminated, they have room to start filling themselves with positive thoughts and positive energy.

How far do you think you would go in a car without fuel? When I ask people that they laugh. I always ask, "Do you put fuel in your car?" The answer is always yes of course, after giving me a look of confusion. So why wouldn't you fuel your mind? What I have people do is to start each day by writing at least fifteen positive affirmations about themselves, their dreams, their goals, and things they haven't accomplished yet.

Some examples are: I am confident. I am receiving a promotion. I am a writer. I am inspiring. I am gifted. I am talented. What happens is that you can write the same things day in and day out, but here's what happens: you get up in the morning and you say, "I know what I am. I know what I want to be." You then are able to start your day by fueling your mind, body, and spirit and this is what gives you the energy to go through the day.

WRIGHT

So how important are first impressions when trying to succeed in business?

CANUSO

Critical. You walk into a room and, as I said, within seven seconds someone is deciding if he or she wants to do business with you. This is where inner strength comes into play. You have the strength and the confidence to project a great first impression. I always ask the question, "What is the first impression you have of yourself?" This is where it all begins, this is where the confidence comes in—you have a great first impression of yourself, you have a look of confidence, a look that exudes trust and respect. You walk into a room and immediately there are people who want to do business with you or associate with you before you've even spoken a word.

Would you give your time, money, or business to someone who walked in looking as though he or she was in a confused state of mind or who projected little interest or confidence? Times have changed and people are more in tune and nervous about the economy. They are really watching over their business and their future. Think of yourself David; would you want to do business with someone who is already a success or who looks confident—someone you know and you can go to sleep at night knowing that you have your business or your money with a person who knows what he or she is doing?

So, first impressions are critical. Even more so than that, let's go back to asking what is the first impression you have of yourself? Do you see how it all follows? You're eliminating the negative thoughts you have of yourself, and you're fueling yourself every day with a positive image and positive thoughts you have of yourself.

WRIGHT

Yes, I never understood why people have to put on judicial robes when they think of themselves, when they don't do it when they think of others.

So what would your final thought be to share with our readers to help build their strength?

CANUSO

I would say to spend more time with yourself and get to know what you're here to do and how you should be living the life you've always dreamed of. We just don't spend enough time with ourselves. And, just as we need to exercise and feed our body every day, we need to feed our minds, our souls, and our spirits on a daily basis.

The other thing I always suggest is to surround yourself with positive people and positive thoughts. One of the probably most difficult things for me was to realize that I had to eliminate some people from my life—they were draining my energy. Once I eliminated them from my life, I could feel more energized. I had just never realized how draining they were.

Spend more time reading and listening to other people—listening to other people's stories, and listening to inspiring people who have had to beat all the odds and yet made it to where they are today as successful people. A book that continues to inspire me when I have doubts is *The Ten Things I Learned from Bill Porter.* It is a *must* for inspiration on strength. Not only have so many people beaten the odds, but they also found their dreams and made a difference.

WRIGHT

They are great motivators.

CANUSO

You know what, David? They *are* really great motivators. There are so many stories around. These stories give you the inspiration to realize, "Wow, look at how this person did it, and here I sit feeling sorry for myself, or not thinking that I have the courage or the strength." So that's what I would suggest—spend more time with yourself, do more reading, and listening to people who are just truly inspiring.

WRIGHT

So considering all of your experiences in the business world, and these years—especially the last two years, doing what you're doing now—what do you now know for sure?

CANUSO

This is always my favorite question. I now know for sure that what is meant to be is up to me, I have the right to live a life with passion, purpose, and excitement, and every day is an opportunity for me to make a difference and enjoy so many people and opportunities that pass my way every hour, every second of the day.

David, the key is to be aware and to be open to what the universe is offering to you. So many times, we're just not paying attention. I have found that once I took responsibility for my life, and once I really started to pay attention to my surroundings, I realized that there were so many doors open to me, that I now step into opportunities I never thought of stepping into before. Now I pay attention to everything the universe has to offer me.

WRIGHT

Well, what a great conversation. I really do appreciate all this time you've taken with me today to answer these questions.

CANUSO

Thank you. And my best to all who are taking the time to find the life they were meant to live.

WRIGHT

You've given me a lot to think about and I know you will give the readers the same.

CANUSO

I hope so. It's my belief that not one person should spend another day without claiming the gifts, strengths, and talents he or she was given and should be enjoying and sharing.

WRIGHT

Today we've been talking with Sara Canuso, President of A Suitable Solution. She advises some of the most successful men and women in business. She's a speaker, writer, teacher, and motivator. Sara provides her clients with the skills, principles, and habits needed to project confidence and to thrive professionally. I don't know about you, but after listening to her, I think she knows what she's talking about.

Sara, thank you so much for being with us today on *Discover Your Inner Strength*.

CANUSO

Thank you, David.

CHAPTER Ten

Activating Your Best Self

AN INTERVIEW WITH...

Mike Jay

1132 13th Ave
Mitchell, NE 69357
877.901.Coach (2622)
www.mikejay.com

ABOUT THE AUTHOR

Mike Jay is a professional business coach, consultant, and "happeneur." An award-winning United States Marine and collegiate athlete, he initially parlayed his leadership experience into agribusiness innovation and management success in medicine, hospitality, and business services. In 1999, he founded a world-class business and executive coach-training system. Through more than ten thousand hours of coaching sessions, Mike has served business leaders in some twenty-seven countries. He is consistently on the leading edge of leadership innovation, culture change, and "emergenics"—a field he created to explore the nature of creating fewer problems than you solve. Mike coined the term *generati* and has dedicated his life to generative leadership.

DAVID WRIGHT (WRIGHT)

Today we're talking with Mike Jay. In his work as a professional coach, he uses a "strengths-reformed" approach to support clients in developing their inborn talents into effective, conscious strengths. These attuned strengths then allow clients to achieve flow states and release free energy that clients can use to improve resilience and adaptability. Mike's unique, real-world background gives him the opportunity to support clients as they design away their weaknesses and choose instead to invest their time, energy, efforts, and actions to create effortless contributions in life, work, and in the society at large.

Mike Jay, welcome to *Discover Your Inner Strength*.

MIKE JAY (JAY)

Thanks for inviting me, David. I'm glad to be here.

WRIGHT

So, why is discovering your inner strength important?

JAY

Well, one of the things that is really important, which you noted in the brief introduction, is the question of how we design away our weaknesses. To do that, we have to first discover what we're really good at. We have to discover what our innate or inborn gifts are that most people tend to take for granted. Our society at large is very good at pointing out the areas in which we're not good. These are areas most people would call a gap. It's also easy to be critical in today's turbulent and uncertain world.

In taking a positive approach, we can say that each person has a particular set of talents that are most likely innate and inborn. These talents, when coupled with the development of knowledge and skills over time, comprise strengths in our lives through the use of those talents—a key leverage point I'll talk about a bit later.

There is an unconscious misunderstanding of what our strengths are. There is also the application of what society says is a *standard of behavior* that everybody is supposed to meet. If you don't meet this set standard, you should go out and try to remedy that. Well, what does this do? For the most part, it pits us against our limitations because very few of us match up to the wonderful ideal standard of perfect behavior that society has created over time. This is especially the case in contemporary times in which complexity is increasing exponentially every day.

By contrast, the starting place in our *reforming* approach is to urge you to do whatever you can—engage a coach, a mentor, a developmental team, your best friends, people around you, even ex-bosses—to find out what others think you are really good at. What does that look like behaviorally? In other words, what is their perception of your strengths? We couple that with your own exploration of these same questions and hone in on what it is that you're really, really good at.

Abraham Maslow was a famous psychologist who said something I particularly like. I paraphrase his quote like this: a person who is good with a hammer goes looking for nails. We normally do that unconsciously, however, and what I ask is, what if we were to make that process conscious? What if we knew what to say yes to because it is in complete alignment with what we are really good at, and conversely, what to say no to?

I do realize that people are not always in a situation where they can use their strengths because situations today often call for a very complex approach. Most of the time we have a limited capability to meet all of the needs of our situation, and we have to find others to help us or to collaborate with. But if we know our strengths, then we know what to say yes and no to. And because we're not informed through our limitations but reformed through our strengths, we also know *what help to ask for from whom* by saying, "I'm really good at this. It looks like you're pretty good at that. Why don't we get together and see if we can attack this monster challenge together?"

Until we discover our inner strengths—until we are crystal clear about what our gifts are and what we're good at—there's a tendency in society today for us to operate under the illusion that we can do anything if we just try hard enough. I think that's a real error.

WRIGHT

From your perspective, why is it easier to make our limitations or weaknesses disappear instead of working on them?

JAY

I need to give a little context for this. I have always thought that it was easier and less resource intensive to *not* have to solve problems. If we could find a way to do that, then we would not have to resource the problem solving. So that's my bias coming from a business context.

My work with executives around the world has convinced me that because society projects this ideal image of an executive, a leader, a good boss, or whatever other role we're in, in one way or another we compare ourselves to that benchmark.

Then we create a gap survey and start trying to close the gaps. That's how people spend a significant amount of education or training dollars. I would imagine professional development, in all its forms, is close to a half-trillion-dollar industry these days. So consultants, coaches, trainers, educators, and academics have a vested interest in keeping us in the gaps, there is no question about that.

Marcus Buckingham, with his most recent book, *Go Put Your Strengths to Work,* finds that only 14 percent of the people he surveyed in the workplace are using their strengths. And that is actually a decrease from five years earlier when it was 17 percent. How can we account for that already low percentage and for its decrease still further? It's the societal message that if you've got a weakness, you need to take care of it—*you need to get fixed!*

Well, I take my clients in a different direction. I have a saying that urges the following: *inform through your limitations, reform through your strengths.* I find that we can make the consequences of your having a limitation disappear by helping you say yes and no to the *right* things, by helping you reach out to other people for assistance, by teaching you about resilience, and by teaching you how (when needed) to *up the downside* in a turbulent, changing environment. We can spare you the consequences of where your limitations automatically would put you—in places where you cannot do anything but force your limitations to play. What I suggest is that you look at this scenario differently.

In other words, say you have a limitation, and let's just pick one that I run into all the time: you're a strong leader, and you sometimes have a tendency to talk over people and not listen as well as you should. This probably describes half of the leadership in the country because there's a real benefit to being a strong leader. Yet at the same time, this style can be accompanied by limitations such as a lack of emotional intelligence or impulse control or other behaviors that have been *psychometrically detailed* as a *gap.* The analogy I use is of a person mopping the floor because there is a sink overflowing in the next room. I could go over and work with the person by getting a better mop or changing their mop stroke or teaching him or her how to do it faster or making other kinds of behavioral changes. Or, I could say, "Why don't we shut off that faucet in the next room?"

If we can make the problem disappear, or if we can lessen the problem so that we don't have to solve it—at least not solve it all the way—then whatever resources and energy we were going to put into problem-solving would be available to reform our weakness or limitation through a different approach. That's what I mean by eliminating or making our weaknesses disappear, instead of pursuing one behavioral approach after another to try to solve problems that we ourselves are actually creating *naturally.*

These inborn limitations are a root consequence of who we are, not because we are bad people, but because our strengths lie elsewhere. In my view, people do not look far enough *upstream* to realize that if you put yourself in a situation where you are constantly compressed as a strong leader, you will not behave very well. And there's no amount of behavioral change in the world that's going to help you much unless it is non-compression behavior, which is not natural for this type of leader in our example. In fact, it's going to deter you as a strong leader.

The thing to do is to look upstream, assess how you are getting into those difficult relational situations, see what you have been saying yes and no to that continually puts you in a compressed position, and then *relieve the problem through design, not through your real-time behavior.*

I believe we can get rid of most of the work that we do in trying to close the gap when, in fact, we're the ones who created it. As I used to tell managers whom I trained a number of years ago, "You guys have to be great firefighters if you're the ones going around lighting the fires. So let's stop lighting the fires."

WRIGHT

Will you give us a personal example of the mechanics of using strengths to, as you say, inform through limitations and reform through strengths?

JAY

I had a particular executive who "fell into" coaching as a result of my coaching a subordinate and getting the boss involved. We kept hearing stories about how this CEO seemed to be indecisive, stonewalling decisions, and not be able to do real-time work—the kind of work that people wanted in their organization. So subordinates felt bottled up as things, according to their perspective, were being stalemated. This is typical of the kind of situation I run into with coaching. After spending some time with this CEO, we discovered that he was masquerading as an extrovert when he was actually an introvert.

The second reason that the company didn't make many of the decisions they needed to make was that they were using what I call a Japanese style of management. The story goes that the Japanese would get a load of lettuce on the dock, and the people who were selling the lettuce wanted them to hurry up, inspect it, and take the lettuce for a certain price. The Japanese didn't want that price, so they just let the lettuce sit. The problem solved itself over a period of time.

That was what this person was doing. As a CEO in today's environment, you are bombarded from every part of your organization with a gazillion requests. How in the world do you filter and deal with those demands? The way this particular executive was dealing with them was to wait and see whether if he didn't deal with them, they would just go away. But he was doing this unconsciously, so he didn't understand the effect it had on others.

With design we worked to inform him about his limitations and the consequences of his decision model of not communicating with people. We then worked to reform him through his strengths. And what were his specific strengths that were operating unconsciously? He would think about things for a good while, analyze problems, gather more information, and not go off half-cocked with the fire-ready-aim sequence that in today's economy can get you into big trouble.

Because he was not consciously aware of his particular strengths, he was not able to inform those around them about the inherent limitations and consequences of the decision-making style of his personality type. So he was perceived as having these gaps as a leader. The others naturally jumped to their own conclusions about his capacities and even perhaps his motives.

We informed the CEO about his limitations and then reformed them through his strengths. He started talking to people and teaching them how to work with him. He asked them to be very clear about the decision they needed, to present the relevant data, and then come back in a couple of days and ask him for a decision. He said that unless they made more noise to this effect on the front end, there was not enough noise to cause him to pay attention. He was surrounded by so much noise as it was, and his pressure-prompted strengths could easily become limitations if the design or scaffolding of support around him was natural, rather than being *cynthesized* (a word I created to represent a creatively synthesized design).

We also taught people how to create a signal within the noise so that the CEO would not just hear the noise, but also see the signal. We simply reframed the entire thing. Did the CEO change? Not really. He's still the same person, doing the same things. But now, the way his behavior appears and is received is much different because he was able to say, "Hey guys, I'm not a stonewaller. I'm not a person who over-deliberates or is afraid of making decisions. It's just that this is the way I make decisions, and if you want to work with me in this decision format, here's how to do it." We turned the situation around and got rid of most his limitations by reforming this CEO through his strengths. We did this by using cynthetic design and not allowing him to be a victim of his natural design.

There are many things that each one of us can do creatively to recognize that even though strengths and weaknesses are on different sides of the same coin, this doesn't mean we always have to come up heads—or tails. We can pay attention to the other side and see what it is telling us in terms of feedback, and we can reform the tails side through the heads side. That's what I try to get people to think about instead going in and working, in this example, on changing the CEO's behavior to make him a quick decision-maker. That would go against who the CEO is and undermine the strengths that have brought the organization all the good things it has achieved under his leadership so far.

WRIGHT

So how deeply do you go to get to strengths? Is understanding your talents enough?

JAY

That's a good question because if we unpack strengths, they're made up of talent, which is innate, and knowledge and skill, which are both learned. But then there is also another piece that neuroscientists and people who study the brain have helped us to understand—we have to *use* the talent to develop it as a strength. I'm hoping that readers who have read this far will find this next point a takeaway that gives them an "ah-ha." It is possible, when we've unpacked the formula for using a talent, that if the context or environment we're in causes us to use a set of skills and knowledge repeatedly, there's a tendency for us to actually develop a *negative strength*. It's like criminals who are amazingly talented and especially good at what they do. Why are they not productive to society? Because they use their talent, developed by skills and knowledge into a strength, to con people or to produce a negative effect. Because of what we are exposed to or the circumstances we face over time, many of us have a tendency, unconsciously, to develop negative strengths. So while it is so important to unpack the components of our strengths, it is especially important to understand when our strengths start to have negative effects. I think that is the hardest thing for people to do.

Probably many of us, on reflection, would realize that we have strengths that, because of certain knowledge and skills we have used, have become negative. So how do we remake those?

First of all, you probably need to go back to the knowledge and skills components. Find out how much those are embedded in that talent, and then begin to reform the strength into a positive effect. To me, you're not working on a weakness in this case—you're working on a strength. To invest time here is therefore a real smart thing to do, because that talent can be seen as a positive contributor if you put the right knowledge and skills with it and *use* it effectively. So this is where I think people should be spending a significant amount of their time. Besides, when you work with your talents, rather than against them, you learn *very* fast!

Important to understand next is what creates a talent and how deep we need to go into the strengths formula. In my view, there is a deeper upstream way to get to where you can unpack talent. I see talent as a composite of our personality and our underlying motivation. This comes not only from significant research by Dr. Steven Reiss of Ohio State University, whose books include *Who Am I* and *Normal Personality,* but also the work of Joseph LeDoux. In his book, *Synaptic Self: How Our Brains Become Who We Are,* he explains that our brain neurons and neural network form through *selection and activity.* In other words, what gets used when we're smaller we keep and, over time, what is used grows. So, what caused the need to have this particular talent manifest in density over time? What was the selective piece that was used?

I believe the selective piece is what Reiss's research has shown, which is that our motivational architecture, which is largely unconscious, is pre-wired into our system, and those talents are formed through a composite, combinatorial set of effects, as the Gallup Organization and Marcus Buckingham and other researchers have discovered. These talents, then, are made up of a composite of underlying motivation and valuing activity. This explains not only why we do what we do, but also why we don't do what we know we should do.

Take my case, for instance. I know what food I should eat. I know how to use the glycemic index. I know I should eat more vegetables than meat, but I don't do it. Why? It's not because I don't know what to do. It's because I'm motivated in a different direction to continue to practice a certain way of eating that to me gives me the most return, the most bang for the buck, even though long-term I may be setting myself up for failure.

How many of us know that there's something we're doing every day that we should be doing differently? We know we should get up early and exercise. We know we shouldn't drive so fast. We know we should save money. The list goes on and on. The point is not in the knowing, it's in what it is that is unconsciously driving us. What Reiss found that unconsciously drives us are our motives.

The way we can go deeper into understanding a strength is to first unpack the strengths formula, second unpack talent, and then we can unpack and go to work on understanding the underlying motivation, which is the engine of strength and the engine of talent. Let's face it, if we're wired up in a certain way, it's going to take a different design process to bring change in our lives than if we continue to think that simply by knowing and having evidence of something it will cause us to act.

It's not in the knowing, but rather, it's what we're motivated to do and what our unconscious will have us do. What Reiss says is that we can unpack that and make the unconscious more conscious. Does that mean that with a snap of the fingers and some knowledge we can change? Not necessarily. But at least we become less victimized by what we don't know that is causing us to move in a different direction. That's what I mean by digging into and deepening our strengths by unpacking the strengths formula, unpacking talent, and beginning to look at unconscious motivation.

WRIGHT

So once you understand your strengths, how do you design a system that works for you in real time to match your capability with the requirements you have?

JAY

If we go back to your first question about why strengths are important, the number one reason is that we need to know them. That doesn't necessarily mean we can do anything about them, but we need to know them.

What I have done is create a cynthetic, in other words, a creatively synthesized design formula. It's not a formula based on natural design, which so many people talk about, because natural design has gotten us where we are now. If we're not happy where we are or successful where we are, then natural design is not aligned with the existential realities in our life. It's that simple. So we have to go to a simple type of cynthetic design. This is where coaching, mentoring, consulting, counseling, and even psychotherapy, if need be, all have pieces to contribute in designing the system. It also depends on what the existential realities are, what a person's capability is, and where the person is in his or her life journey.

The important thing, however, is to *not* fall victim to the typical coach, consultant, mentor, or psychotherapist who is going to use a blank-slate approach. The blank-slate approach says that if we just teach you enough and convince you to learn it, you will change. This is typical in society today—it's in all our education systems and it's the biggest part of that half-trillion dollar "self-development" industry!

The little formula I have devised begins with capability. You have to know your capability, and this starts with understanding and unpacking your strengths and talents and not deluding yourself about what it is that you can do. You cannot begin with what you say you can do—your *espoused theory,* as motivational researcher Chris Argyris calls it. Start with your *theory in the use*—what you actually do and what other people observe you doing. Much of the time what we think we do is not always entirely what other people in our life perceive us as doing. Our ego needs often delude us into continuing to move in the direction that it wants us to go, and so other people can give us real support in terms of understanding our capability. That's number one.

Number two is that we have to be really clear about our requirements—the existential realities in our life. Often they will shift as our context shifts. Realities at work are different from realities at home, with the children, with our mate, by ourselves, with our peers, and so on. So we have to understand what the requirements are contextually. What we're mainly talking about in the context of this book are our requirements in the workplace or in an organization.

You can find out what the requirements are from your boss, your customers, your peers, your children, your strategy and tactics—from all the different things that you have going on to create a picture of requirements. You now have a map of capability and a map of requirements. When you overlay those two, you're going to see that you've got some requirements left at the end of your capability map in almost every case. In many cases, you'll also have some capability that extends beyond your requirements in some areas. If you don't, then you're probably playing a pretty small game, and most of us today are not able to play that small a game, even if we want to. It's more likely that we're playing a much bigger game than we would like to.

What happens then is that the capability map does not cover all the requirements or it is way out of alignment. What does that mean? Well, that's what other people call gaps and what I call opportunity. At that point, if you have not BS'd yourself about the capability gap (and this is probably the number one reason to have a coach—as a BS detector!), then the first thing you need to do once you understand clearly your capability gap is to reach out to other people, other resources, other systems. There are many things that you can do.

In my case, for example, I'm low on social contact. When I unpack my talent, one of the things that shows up is that I don't like a lot of contact with people. On the one hand, because I'm an extrovert, I'm quick and I've got the gift of gab, people like me, and I'm charming (well, let's say at least until people get to know me). But when all is said and done, I'm ready to go work on some ideas. So when I unpack that, I realize that to be a successful person I have to reach out to people, just like I'm reaching out through this interview today to help me get my message across. Otherwise, my low social contact might prevent me from reaching out—yet the requirements say if people don't know about me they can't hire me. So how do I know what I need to do to reach out? I know what my capability is, I know what the requirements are, and I know what's missing. That enables me to design for what's missing instead of trying to change myself and working in that gap, which has very low efficacy since most of what I have to change there are my limitations.

I have an analogy that works for people who are familiar with Internet speeds. Back when we were starting on the Web, these things called limitations were like a 300-baud modem (if you can go back that far). But the one I thought was really fast back in the early days of the Worldwide Web was 14.4. A page would almost load in thirty seconds (there weren't any graphics at all in those days) and I thought that was really fast. Well, when you compare a 14.4 with a T-1 line today, that's what strengths and limitations look like. Using our strengths is like using an ultrafast T-1 connection. Using our limitations compares to the speed at 14.4, which is crawling speed.

When we use that fast path with strengths, what's freed up with that gain in efficiency is what I call free energy. If you try to run everything down that 14.4 pipe, it's going to take time and a *lot* of energy to stuff it through that small area. If you run it down the T-1, though, it's going to slide down there as you've never seen it slide. It's going to be effortless and easy. T-1 is the metaphor for our strengths, while our limitations are the 14.4. The 14.4 is an awfully small pipe that you have to stuff a lot through, and it takes a lot of energy in the process.

If you're trying to do that with limitations, you're going to eat up all your energy, whereas when you're using your strengths, most of the time you'll be spinning off free energy. Looking at Ilya Prigogine's work on dissipative structures (for which he won the Nobel Prize in chemistry), he said that a dissipative structure is any complex, adaptive system, such as a human being, which is organizationally closed and energetically open. What happens when you start stuffing a lot of energy into that organizationally closed system is it tries to dissipate the energy. Whatever it dissipates or uses is entropy. When the system gets stuck and too full of energy, it can no longer stay organizationally closed; it has to burst open. That's what's happening to most of us today. We're being forced into chaos as we try to scramble and use the amount of energy that's been stuffed into our system. Most of us are working in limitation, and that's why we have no free energy, or we can't dissipate the energy coming into our systems.

The only way to build a system is to use the effortless ideas of strengths. If we can stay in strengths, we're going to continually spin off free energy because it's easy to dissipate the energy that is coming in. This means that we can then (technically, with the second law of thermodynamics) uphill that free energy into new system design, and we can actually change, adapt, and be more resilient because we have the free energy to do so. If, on the other hand, people are compressed and loaded up with energy they can't dissipate and they spend time doing things they shouldn't be doing, they cannot change, they cannot adapt. They don't have the energy to do so because it's being sucked out of them every day in working through or with their limitations.

Our job is to design the system so our clients can access free energy. We may have to go back and redesign how they use and unpack their talents in light of the things they're motivated to do and what's easy for them. There's a concept that Elliott Jaques presented in his book, *Requisite Organization,* called flow, whereby people are carefully matched to the complexity and capability that they can handle. They're able to push a *right*-sized rock instead of being exhausted by trying to push one that's too big or bored with one that's too small.

Over time we change, we grow, we mature, we're able to push bigger rocks, and that's a key piece in our design. What we do is look at how big a rock you should be pushing. How big a rock would you like to push? How big a rock *can* you push? Then let's get as close as we can to that size. We may have you push the current rock for now but spin off enough free energy that you can begin to look at pushing a different kind of rock. Not only that, but in working in your strengths, we'll get you back into the happiness curve. Instead of working on your limitations so you can be successful, all the while dumping happiness because it's not fun to work in your limitations, our idea is to converge happiness and success. Working in strengths, we get those two paths pulling together *and* enable you to spin off some free energy so you can take on the world. You can also take on the unpredictable complexity that's coming at you.

WRIGHT

So how can people who have never before understood their true strengths function in a world where everyone focuses on weaknesses?

JAY

David, if you and I can answer that question we can get rich! Let me try to answer it. Our society basically functions from an idea that was probably misinterpreted from the early days of the Declaration of Independence, which is that all people are created equal. We have this idea that we come into the world as equals and anybody can learn anything. If we don't learn certain things we're just not trying hard enough or don't have good enough teachers or haven't read the right books or haven't gone to the right programs or don't have the right guru or haven't done yoga in the right way. There are a million reasons why we're not measuring up that society uses to reinforce this assumption that people can be anything they want to be.

My fear in the present political situation is that there are people in power who really believe that—they believe that if we spread money around we'll make racehorses out of plow horses. The worst thing we can do is put a racehorse in a plow harness or a plow horse on a racetrack, and that's what we'll be doing. We want to feed our racehorses and take care of them so they can run; and we want to feed our plow horses and take care of them so they can plow. This is a hard thing for people to swallow because everything that we do in the world makes us want to treat everyone equally. That's certainly a social, moral, and civilized thing to do. At the same time, we need to understand that people are different and that these differences begin at birth. There is plenty of research that refutes the humanist, blank-slate idea that all people are created equal and therefore they can do anything if enough time and money is spent on them, they are trained correctly, and if they are led and managed right. But there's a huge system with a lot of people in education, training, even politics and religion who have a vested interest in keeping it going.

A few of us, including some well-known and respected people, are beginning to understand that not everybody can do everything, and you give up your happiness in trying to be somebody you're not. We need a new idea of ego in the world so that you can accept yourself as you naturally are.

The late Albert Ellis spent fifty years doing a free clinic on Friday nights in Manhattan, and at the end of that time, he concluded there were two things you had to do to be okay—just two. The first is to accept yourself. The second is to accept others unconditionally.

I created an engagement model built around this system of discovery that looks like the Olympic logo of interlocking rings.

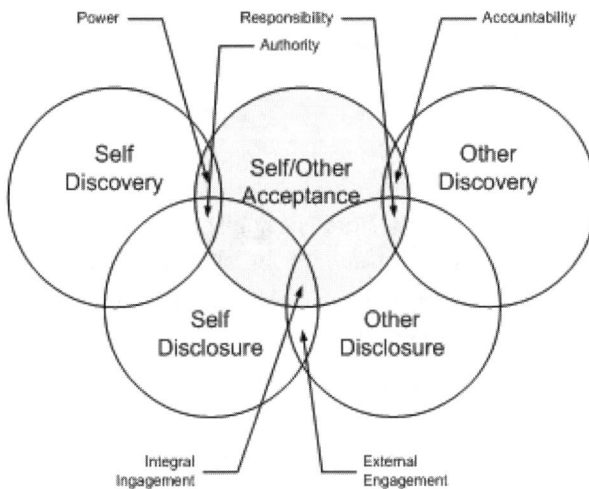

The two rings on the left are self-discovery and self-disclosure. The two rings on the right are other-discovery and other-disclosure. The ring in the center, linking them all, is self-acceptance and other-acceptance.

The hardest thing for us to do is get to the point of realizing it's okay that we're not like someone else. It's okay that we don't meet the societal ideal of the "organization man" or the great leader that we have pictured in our minds or whatever other standard we've ascribed to. If we can get to the point of accepting who we are—that we're different and unique, that we have a special set of gifts that when employed create the optimal contribution we can make to our fellow man and society and to ourselves—we have a chance at being successful *and* happy. That is the true grail.

There's a BBC documentary called *The Century of Self* that shows the one-hundred-year foundation we have in the psychology of the developed world about being something we're not. If I could urge our readers to do one thing, it would be to watch that program. It shows how Madison Avenue marketing and advertising are designed to keep you in the illusion that if you just do whatever it is they want you to do, you can have it all. What we need to discover is that being happy and successful *is* "having it all." This could include what we own or buy or not. It's being able to look at yourself in the mirror and know that you're living a *right* life—a life designed around who you are and what you are required to do without working on weaknesses all the time. That's when everything tips. We're not there yet, but I think people are starting to wake up to the fact that if they keep going in the direction they're headed, things aren't going to turn out the way they thought.

WRIGHT

So why don't more people get this idea—this set of ideas—which you're discussing?

JAY

It's counterintuitive, I think, because it has been so ingrained in our society and in much of our world that our egos are constantly pushing us to compare ourselves to other people—to be better looking, to be slimmer, to wear a certain style of clothes, to change our haircut, to walk a different way, to own a different kind of car. These are assumptions that we have been led to accept into our mental models of what is attractive and desirable—being like Mike (as in the old Michael Jordan commercials).

What I'm suggesting is not easy because it is essentially a battle against the ego. Many spiritual teachers talk about the ego, but they do so in a different way than I'm talking about it. What I'm trying to do is give people another way out. Is this direction spiritual? Absolutely, but indirectly so. Are we going after the ego? Yes, but not directly so. We're trying to convince people about things that they actually deep down already know, but haven't had pointed out to them because the din of noise in a society says you should be this or that. It's louder and is covering up the signal inside each one of us that says, "Wait a minute, I have certain gifts; there are some things I do better than anybody else. Why don't I spend my time doing those? Why do I have to be like John, Sally, Suzy, Vladimir, or Amit?" You know, we've got this ingrained in us. The ego investment in this mental model says it is a good thing because as an ego I get to go through life completely untested, running you every which way.

So is this going to be a hard set of ideas to get? Yes, because it's counterintuitive to your ego, and I think that's the most difficult thing that people have to realize. The unfortunate thing we've found through research and adult development is that not everybody has the ability to become self-aware enough to look at these ideas and say this makes some sense. The costs of our current way of living can be so high and the transition that people have to make to exit the ego world can be so long and protracted that most people will not do it. They've got too much invested in life as it is. That's what drives organizations and civilizations into the ground—they can't stop and they can't pull back. If you can get hold of these ideas, you can save yourself and your kids and your grandchildren. I can show you the way out, and you can live a lot happier life, but it does take some work.

WRIGHT

You've mentioned the "blank slate" concept. Why did blank slate assume such a large part of our present psychology?

JAY

Steven Pinker's 2002 bestseller, *The Blank Slate,* makes the case that human behavior is largely shaped by evolutionary psychological adaptations. In other words, there is a significant amount of scientific and academic support to blank slate. An example is what happened during World War II with the application of eugenics. Eugenics posited that a certain type of people was supposedly better than any other type. The idea was to wipe out everybody who wasn't of that type. Consequently, our society, both in academia and in moral terms, pivoted as far as possible away from eugenics and therefore from an understanding that people are born into differences. We began to figure out all kinds of ways and justifications for why everybody is equal.

Though the motivation for blank slate was not necessarily bad, you have to look at the long-term consequences of such an ideology, not just the short-term swing away from what was a horrible moral problem stemming from World War II. The consequences of our long-term adherence to blank slate are what we have today—the continued efforts, spending, and resource allocation to try to make people into whatever society is trying to make people into.

Dr. Clare Graves, noted scholar of the evolution of human psychology and culture, is often quoted as having said that at some point we need to realize that "people have a right to be who they are." There's not a whole lot we can do to change that, but what we can do is to build a scaffold of support in our organizations, our leadership, and our families that will allow people to become optimal in their contribution as who they are.

Reiss's research shows that even people of very little ability, even people with mental retardation, still show clear signs of how they are motivated. We literally can access every part of society, even folks born into disability, to help people have better lives. The way to do that is not to treat everyone the same, but to scaffold support in our social programs, organizations, and our personal lives. This takes a different mental perspective. It takes swinging back toward the center, away from the blank-slate polarity.

Actually, once someone comes out of the womb and is determined to be X or Y or Z, he or she has extreme adaptability. The human experience is extremely flexible in the way that a person's particular talents, motives, and gifts can be adapted into particular strengths. If we can find ways for people to work in those, regardless of their ability, they're going to have happier lives, and we're going to be more successful as a society. I think, for example, of a twenty-two-year-old woman who is cognitively disabled and has the mentality of a two-year-old. She's erratic in her behavior and is difficult to connect with. But she loves to shred paper. And so she has a "job" at a state agency where she spends her mornings as an ace paper shredder!

I really believe that we have to shift the goals of society. Instead of a goal of putting a computer on every desk or everybody owning a home, maybe society's goal should be to help people make optimal contributions and be happy. That's going to take a shift out of our present psychology, although we're already seeing signs of that when people talk now about positive psychology and resilience and optimism. I think we've begun the swing, but it's a matter of getting the word out more, which is what I'm trying to do here.

WRIGHT

So what do you think is the biggest mistake that people make around the use of strengths?

JAY

We have to be careful, because strengths have layers. A strength may look one way on the surface, and it's easy to be confused by what we call noise—the noise of strength. We may make assumptions about what people are capable of and how they can best use their strengths and not be sufficiently filtering out the noise. We need to understand what that signal is beneath the noise, and we do that by unpacking the strengths, by taking a look at talent, and by understanding what the upstream motivation is. Sometimes people do strengths work at the superficial level and don't get any traction with it. Until you put design with an understanding of capability and requirements—with capability being largely our strengths—you don't get far enough into the equation to get real traction. Then what happens is, people see a weakness as nothing more than the other side of a strength. They start overplaying a strength, which creates more weakness. Now what do you do? The person is shutting down a strength—to alleviate the weakness—and now you've got a double-jeopardy situation where you're not only supposedly working on a weakness, but you're actually having the person change an area of strength to a negative.

There's such a thing as a negative capability. The poet John Keats wrote about it this way: "I mean Negative Capability, that is, when a man is capable of being in uncertainties, mysteries, doubts, without any irritable reaching after fact and reason" (*http://www.mrbauld.com/negcap.html*).

In our society, especially Western society, we are so enamored with action, with jumping to the first conclusion that we see—what I call playing in the noise—that we do not use the negative aspects of capability, which includes sitting back and allowing space to be created for deliberation, for contemplation, for reflection, to delay, and to actually adopt a non-action approach. This is not negative in the sense of arithmetic or in the pejorative sense, but rather in the nonuse of a positive capability. In short, it's a movement away from being pulled too quickly into complexity.

An easy definition of complexity is an increase in the number of variables and in the delay between cause and effect. In complexity, we have more things to deal with and more delays. Well, humans are not good waiters, literally and figuratively. It's like taking a shower in Europe where the warm and cold water mix at the faucet. You turn on the hot, but it's not hot because the water heater is maybe half a building away. So you keep turning it hotter and hotter, and then all of a sudden the hot comes and burns you. You turn it down and it still burns you, and you keep turning it down. Then all a sudden the cold comes and makes you freak out again.

We've probably all had that experience before; that's what complexity does to us. If you jump to a quick conclusion—if you play in the noise and don't filter it—you're going to start making decisions. The more decisions you make, the more variables you introduce into the system, and the more complex things get. You can see the cycle here.

The idea that we can immediately discern people's strengths by their behavior, and that we can immediately understand clearly what may perhaps be a convoluted means by which they are trying to reach their ends, can add up to a process that is very disappointing to them.

We need to have an understanding of design, otherwise we can end up throwing resources at a gap—the gap between a person's capability and requirements—and these days we're running out of resources. So how do we apply the few resources we have to get the leverage we need and the right kinds of outcomes for people, systems, and society? Well, we have to take some time. We have to filter the noise, find the signal, and figure out the right levers to pull. The way we do that is to unpack the strengths equation, unpack talent, and begin to understand what those levers are and how to get traction with this "strengths way of being."

I think the reason that people are working in their strengths less and less (as reported by the research I mentioned above) is that some people are falling victim to this tendency to immediately jump at strengths, and they don't really know how to unpack them. They don't really understand what strengths mean, and you can't use strengths very much when you say yes and no to *wrong* things. Then people are forced to use their weaknesses or they don't know how to reform them through strengths. This is the danger that comes with a superficial view of strengths, and then we conclude that a strengths-based approach doesn't work and we move on to the next fad.

The *right* idea, then, is to deeply discover and accept our strengths, be able to see strengths in other people and differentiate ours from theirs, and find the leverage point in deploying our own strengths. Then we can apply the few resources that we do have available to us to linchpin the whole process.

WRIGHT

Well, Mike, this has been a great conversation. I have taken copious notes here today, and I've learned a lot about strengths and weaknesses. I really do appreciate all the time you've spent with me on these questions. I think our readers are going to have a lot to think about. I know I do.

JAY

Thanks, David. I appreciate your inviting me. I love telling this story. I'm passionate about it, as you can tell, and I hope something I've said today will lead our readers to an idea that can help them be more happy and successful. I really appreciate the opportunity to be a part of such a process.

WRIGHT

Today we've been talking with Mike Jay. As a professional coach, he uses a strengths-reformed approach to support his clients in developing their inborn talents and conscious, effective strengths. He helps them design away their weaknesses and choose instead to invest their time, energy, efforts, and actions to better use their strengths.

Mike, thank you so much for being with us today on *Discover Your Inner Strength.*

JAY

Thank you, David. I've enjoyed it.

CHAPTER Eleven

Using Strategy to Discover Your Inner Strength

AN INTERVIEW WITH...

Brian Tracy

www.BrianTracy.com

ABOUT THE AUTHOR

One of the world's top success motivational speakers, Brian Tracy is the author of many books and audio tape seminars, including *The Psychology of Achievement, The Luck Factor, Breaking the Success Barrier, Thinking Big* and *Success Is a Journey.*

THE INTERVIEW

DAVID WRIGHT (WRIGHT)

Many years ago, Brian Tracy started off on a lifelong search for the secrets of success in life and business. He studied, researched, traveled, worked, and taught for more than thirty years. In 1981, he began to share his discoveries in talks and seminars, and eventually in books, audios and video-based courses.

The greatest secret of success he learned is this: "There are no secrets of success." There are instead timeless truths and principles that have to be rediscovered, relearned, and practiced by each person. Brian's gift is synthesis—the ability to take large numbers of ideas from many sources and combine them into highly practical, enjoyable, and immediately usable forms that people can take and apply quickly to improve their life and work. Brian has brought together the best ideas, methods, and techniques from thousands of books, hundreds of courses, and experience working with individuals and organizations of every kind in the U.S., Canada, and worldwide.

Today, I have asked Brian to discuss his book, *Victory!: Applying the Military Principals of Strategy for Success in Business and Personal Life.*

Brian Tracy, welcome to *Discover Your Inner Strength.*

TRACY

Thank you, David. It's a pleasure to be here.

WRIGHT

Let's talk about your book the *Victory!: Applying* the *Military Principals* of *Strategy* for *Success* in *Business* and *Personal Life.* (By the way it is refreshing to hear someone say something good about the successes of the military.) Why do you think the military is so successful?

TRACY

Well, the military is based on very serious thought. The American military is the most respected institution in America. Unless you're a left liberal limp-wristed pinko most people in America really respect the military because it keeps America free. People who join the military give up most of their lives—twenty to thirty years—in sacrifice to be prepared to guard our freedoms. And if you ask around the world what it is that America stands for, it stands for individual freedom, liberty, democracy, freedom, and opportunity that is only secured in a challenging world—a dangerous world—by your military.

Now the other thing is that the people in our military are not perfect because there is no human institution made up of human beings that is perfect—there are no perfect people. The cost of mistakes in military terms is death; therefore, people in the military are extraordinarily serious about what they do. They are constantly looking for ways to do what they do better and better and better to reduce the likelihood of losing a single person.

We in America place extraordinary value on individual human life. That is why you will see millions of dollars spent to save a life, whether for an accident victim or Siamese twins from South America, because that's part of our culture. The military has that same culture.

I was just reading today about the RQ-1 "Predator" drone planes (Unmanned Aerial Vehicles—UAVs) that have been used in reconnaissance over the no-fly zones in Iraq. These planes fly back and forth constantly gathering information from the ground. They can also carry remote-controlled weapons. According to www.globalsecurity.org, the planes cost $4.5 million each and get shot down on a regular basis. However, the military is willing to invest hundreds of millions of dollars to develop these planes, and lose them to save the life of a pilot, because pilots are so precious—human life is precious. In the military everything is calculated right down to the tinniest detail because it's the smallest details that can cost lives. That is why the military is so successful—they are so meticulous about planning.

A salesperson can go out and make a call; if it doesn't work that's fine—he or she can make another sales call. Professional soldiers can go out on an operation and if it's not successful they're dead and maybe everybody in the squad is dead as well. There is no margin for error in the military; that's why they do it so well. This is also why the military principals of strategy that I talk about in *Victory!* are so incredibly important because a person who really understands those principals and strategies sees how to do things vastly better with far lower probability of failure than the average person.

WRIGHT

In the promotion on *Victory!* you affirm that it is very important to set clear attainable goals and objectives. Does that theme carry out through all of your presentations and all of your books?

TRACY

Yes. Over and over again the theme reiterates that you can't hit a target you can't see—you shouldn't get into your car unless you know where you are going.

More people spend more time planning a picnic than they spend planning their careers.

I'll give you an example. A very successful woman who is in her fifties now wrote down a plan when she was attending university. Her plan was for the first ten years she would work for a Fortune 500 corporation, really learn the business, and learn how to function at high levels. For the second ten years of her career she talked about getting married and having children at the same time. For that second ten years she would also work for a medium sized company helping it grow and succeed. For the third ten years (between the ages of forty and fifty), she would start her own company based on her knowledge of both businesses. She would then build that into a successful company. Her last ten years she would be chief executive officer of a major corporation and retire financially independent at the age of sixty. At age fifty-eight she would have hit every single target. People would say, "Boy, you sure are lucky." No, it wouldn't be luck. From the time she was seventeen she was absolutely crystal clear about what she was going to do with her career and what she was going to do with her life, and she hit all of her targets.

WRIGHT

In a time where companies, both large and small, take a look at their competition and basically try to copy everything they do, it was really interesting to read in *Victory!* that you suggest taking vigorous offensive action to get the best results. What do you mean by "vigorous offensive action"?

TRACY

Well, see, that's another thing. When you come back to talking about probabilities—and this is really important—you see successful people try more things. And if you wanted to just end the interview right now and ask, "What piece of advice would you give to our listeners?" I would say, "Try more things." The reason I would say that is because if you try more things, the probability is that you will hit your target

For example, here's an analogy I use. Imagine that you go into a room and there is a dartboard against the far wall. Now imagine that you are drunk and you have never played darts before. The room is not very bright and you can barely see the bull's eye. You are standing along way from the board, but you have an endless supply of darts. You pick up the darts and you just keep throwing them at the target over there on the other of the room even though you are not a good dart thrower and you're not even well coordinated. If you kept throwing darts over and over again what would you eventually hit?

WRIGHT

Pretty soon you would get a bull's eye.

TRACY

Yes, eventually you would hit a bull's eye. The odds are that as you keep throwing the darts even though you are not that well educated, even if you don't come from a wealthy family or you don't have a Harvard education, if you just keep throwing darts you will get a little better each time you throw. It's known as a "decybernetic self-correction mechanism" in the brain—each time you try something, you get a little bit smarter at it. So over time, if you kept throwing, you must eventually hit a bull's eye. In other words, you must eventually find the right way to do the things you need to do to become a millionaire. That's the secret of success. That's why people come here from a 190 countries with one idea in mind—"If I come here I can try anything I want; I can go anywhere, because there are no limitations. I have so much freedom; and if I keep doing this, then by God, I will eventually hit a bull's eye." And they do and everybody says, "Boy, you sure where lucky."

Now imagine another scenario: You are thoroughly trained at throwing darts—you have practiced, you have developed skills and expertise in your field, you are constantly upgrading your knowledge, and you practice all the time. Second you are completely prepared, you're thoroughly cold sober, fresh, fit, alert, with high energy. Third, all of the room is very bright around the dartboard. This time how long would it take you to hit the bull's eye? The obvious answer is you will hit a bull's eye far faster than if you had all those negative conditions.

What I am I saying is, you can dramatically increase the speed at which you hit your bull's eye. The first person I described—drunk, unprepared, in a darkened room, and so on—may take twenty or twenty-five years. But if you are thoroughly prepared, constantly upgrading your skills; if you are very clear about your targets; if you have everything you need at hand and your target is clear, your chances of hitting a bull's eye you could hit a bull's eye is five years rather than twenty. That's the difference in success in life.

WRIGHT

In reading your books and watching your presentations on video, one of the common threads seen through your presentations is creativity. I was glad that in the promotional material of *Victory!* you state that you need to apply innovative solutions to overcome obstacles. The word "innovative" grabbed me. I guess you are really concerned with *how* people solve problems rather than just solving problems.

TRACY

Vigorous action means you will cover more ground. What I say to people, especially in business, is the more things you do the more experience you get. The more experience you get the smarter you get. The smarter you get the better results you get the better results you get. The better results you get the less time it takes you to get the same results. And it's such a simple thing. In my books *Create Your Own Future* and *Victory!* you will find there is one characteristic of all successful people—they are action oriented. They move fast, they move quickly, and they don't waste time. They're moving ahead, trying more things, but they are always in motion. The faster you move the more energy you have. The faster you move the more in control you feel and the faster you are the more positive and the more motivated you are. We are talking about a direct relationship between vigorous action and success.

WRIGHT

Well, the military certainly is a team "sport" and you talk about building peak performance teams for maximum results. My question is how do individuals in corporations build peak performance teams in this culture?

TRACY

One of the things we teach is the importance of selecting people carefully. Really successful companies spend an enormous amount of time at the front end on selection they look for people who are really, really good in terms of what they are looking for. They interview very carefully; they interview several people and they interview them several times. They do careful background checks. They are as careful in selecting people as a person might be in getting married. Again, in the military, before a person is promoted they go through a rigorous process. In large corporations, before a person is promoted his or her performance is very, very carefully evaluated to be sure they are the right people to be promoted at that time.

WRIGHT

My favorite point in *Victory!* is when you say, "Amaze your competitors with surprise and speed." I have done that several times in business and it does work like a charm.

TRACY

Yes, it does. Again one of the things we teach over and over again that there is a direct relationship between speed and perceived value. When you do things fast for people they consider you to be better. They consider your products to be better and they consider your service to be better—they actually consider them to be of higher value. Therefore, if you do things really, really fast then you overcome an enormous amount of resistance. People wonder, "Is this a good decision? Is it worth the money? Am I going the right direction?" When you do things fast, you blast that out of their minds.

WRIGHT

You talk about moving quickly to seize opportunities. I have found that to be difficult. When I ask people about opportunities, it's difficult to find out what they think an opportunity is. Many think opportunities are high-risk, although I've never found it that way myself. What do you mean by moving quickly to cease opportunity?

TRACY

There are many cases were a person has an idea and they think that's a good idea. They think they should do something about it. They think, "I am going to do something about that but I really can't do it this week, so I will wait until after the month ends," and so on. By the time they do move on the opportunity it's to late—somebody's already seized it.

One of the military examples I use is the battle of Gettysburg. Now the battle of Gettysburg was considered the high-water mark of the Confederacy after the battle of Gettysburg the Confederacy won additional battles at Chattanooga and other places but they eventually lost the war. The high-water mark of Gettysburg was a little hill at one end of the battlefield called Little Round Top. As the battle began Little Round Top was empty. Colonel Joshua Chamberlain of the Union Army saw that this could be the pivotal point of the battlefield. He went up there and looked at it and he immediately rushed troops to fortify the hill. Meanwhile, the Confederates also saw that Little Round Top could be key to the battle as well, so they too immediately rushed the hill. An enormous battle took place. It was really the essence of the battle of Gettysburg. The victor who took that height controlled the battlefield. Eventually the union troops, who were almost lost, controlled Little Round Top and won the battle. The Civil War was over in about a year and a half, but that was the turning point.

So what would have happened if Chamberlain had said, "Wait until after lunch and then I'll move some men up to Little Round Top"? The Confederate troops would have seized Little Round Top, controlled the battlefield, and would have won the battle of Gettysburg. It was just a matter of moving very, very fast. Forty years later it was determined that there were three days at the battle of Gettysburg that cost the battle for the Confederates. The general in charge of the troops on the Confederate right flank was General James Longstreet. Lee told him to move his army forward as quickly as possible the next day, but to use his own judgment. Longstreet didn't agree with Lee's plan so he kept his troop sitting there most of the next day. It is said that it was Longstreet's failure to move forward on the second day and seize Little Round Top that cost the Confederacy the battle and eventually the war. It was just this failure to move forward and forty years later, when Longstreet appeared at a reunion of Confederate veterans in 1901 or 1904, he was booed. The veterans felt his failure to move forward that fateful day cost them the war. If you read every single account of the battle of Gettysburg, Longstreet's failure to move forward and quickly seize the opportunity is always included.

WRIGHT

In your book you tell your readers to get the ideas and information needed to succeed. Where can individuals get these ideas?

TRACY

Well we are living in an ocean of ideas. It's so easy. The very first thing you do is you pick a subject you want to major in and you go to someone who is good at it. You ask what you should read in this field and you go down to the bookstore and you look at the books. Any book that is published in paperback obviously sold well in hardcover. Read the table of contents. Make sure the writer has experience in the area you in which you want to learn about. Buy the book and read it. People ask, "How can I be sure it is the right book?" You can't be sure; stop trying to be sure.

When I go to the bookstore I buy three or four books and bring them home and read them. I may only find one chapter of a book that's helpful, but that chapter may save me a year of hard work.

The fact is that your life is precious. A book costs twenty of thirty dollars. How much is your life worth? How much do you earn per hour? A person who earns fifty thousand dollars a year earns twenty-five dollars an hour. A person who wants to earn a hundred thousand dollars a year earns fifty dollars an hour. Now, if a book cost you ten or twenty dollars but it can save you a year of hard work, then that's the cheapest thing you have bought in your whole life. And what if you bought fifty books and you paid twenty dollars apiece for them—a thousand dollars worth of books—and out of that you only got one idea that saved you a year of hard work? You've got a fifty times payoff. So the rule is you cannot prepare too thoroughly.

WRIGHT

In the last several months I have recommended your book, *Get Paid More and Promoted Faster* to more people. I have had a lot of friends in their fifties and sixties who have lost their jobs to layoffs all kinds of transfers of ownership. When I talked with you last, the current economy had a 65 percent jump in layoffs. In the last few months before I talked with you, every one of them reported that the book really did help them. They saw some things a little bit clearer; it was a great book.

How do you turn setbacks and difficulties to your advantage? I know what it means, but what's the process?

TRACY

You look into it you look into every setback and problem and find the seed of an equal or greater advantage or benefit. It's a basic rule. You find that all successful people look into their problems for lessons they can learn and for things they can turn to their advantage. In fact, one of the best attitudes you can possibly have is to say that you know every problem that is sent to you is sent to help you. So your job is just simply look into to it and ask, "What can help me in this situation?" And surprise, surprise! You will find something that can help you. You will find lessons you can learn; you will find something you can do more of, or less of; you can find something that will give you an insight that will set you in a different direction, and so on.

WRIGHT

I am curious. I know you have written a lot in the past and you are a terrific writer. Your cassette programs are wonderful. What do you have planned for the next few years?

TRACY

Aside from speaking and consulting with non-profits, my goal is to produce four books a year on four different subjects, all of which have practical application to help people become more successful.

WRIGHT

Well, I really want to thank you for your time here today on *Mission Possible!* It's always fascinating to hear what you have to say. I know I have been a Brian Tracy fan for many, many years. I really appreciate your being with us today.

TRACY

Thank you. You have a wonderful day and I hope our listeners and readers will go out and get *Focal Point* and/or *Victory!* They are available at any bookstore or at Amazon.com. They are fabulous books, filled with good ideas that will save you years of hard work.

WRIGHT

I have already figured out that those last two books are a better buy with Amazon.com, so you should go to your computer and buy these books as soon as possible.

We have been talking today with Brian Tracy, whose life and career truly makes one of the best rags-to-riches stories. Brian didn't graduate from high school and his first job was washing dishes. He lost job after job—washing cars, pumping gas, stacking lumber, you name it. He was homeless and living in his car. Finally, he got into sales, then sales management. Later, he sold investments, developed real estate, imported and distributed Japanese automobiles, and got a master's degree in business administration. Ultimately, he became the COO of a $265 million dollar development company.

Brian, you are quite a person. Thank you so much for being with us today.

TRACY

You are very welcome, David. You have a great day!

CHAPTER Twelve

The Pattern of Success

AN INTERVIEW WITH...

Scott V. Black

P.O Box 430
Kennedale, Texas 76060
Phone: 817-478-1858
MrBlack@empoweru.net
www.empoweruinternational.com

ABOUT THE AUTHOR

Scott V. Black is the CEO and founder of Empower U International. Scott founded Empower U Inc in October of 1994. He is certified as a Human Behavioral Specialist and as a Master Practitioner of Neuro Linguistic Programming (NLP) who has worked with tens of thousands of clients across North America. Scott has conducted Leadership training and inspired leaders internationally. Whether his is working with world class athletes, coaches, executives, or individuals He is committed to helping people get what they want in their professional and personal lives.

Scott's strong belief in the potential of the individual has moved his passion to train and coach business leaders and their teams to be all they can be. He is an inspirational leader who is committed to making this world better, one individual at a time. His mission is to get people emotionally involved with their cause – helping individuals and organizations take themselves to the next level. Where do those leaders who want to go to the next level go? Mr. Black and his world renowned Leadership Awakening training is the answer for those who are committed to "Raise the Bar"! Mr. Black brings Passion and commitment; he brings FIRE to every individual and organization he has the opportunity to inspire.

THE INTERVIEW

DAVID WRIGHT (WRIGHT)

Today we're talking with Scott V. Black. Scott is a "Passion Generator" and a "Hope Peddler." His mission is getting people emotionally involved with their cause—their life—and helping individuals and organizations reach their potential. He is an inspirational leader committed to passionately challenging leaders to be Under Construction, applying the principles of Constant and Never-Ending Improvement to their personal and professional lives. He is also the author of *Becoming your Dreams: Want it. Create it. Live it.* His company, Empower U International, offers the most powerful leadership training available today. Empower U's leadership training experience catapults individuals and corporations to "Raise their Bar" and become the "Best of the Best." Clients include MillerCoors, American Athletics Inc., Kraft, and hundreds of other national and international companies. He has conducted life-altering leadership training in three countries and all across North America.

Scott, welcome to *Discover Your Inner Strength*.

SCOTT V. BLACK (BLACK)

Thank you, David. I am honored to be a part of this book and to be included with some of the great authors and speakers who have been assembled for this outstanding cause.

WRIGHT

You say there is a pattern of success. What makes you believe that there is actually a pattern for this thing called success?

BLACK

Well, you know, David, I've been working with individuals, executives, and other leaders for almost twenty years now, and through all this work, I have learned many things about people. One of the main things I have identified is that there are patterns all around us. There are patterns for how we get to work, how we get to angry, happy, passionate, or to survival. There is a series of patterns that get us what we have.

One of the problems is that most people don't see the pattern. This is a problem if one wants to make some changes, to get out of our comfort zone—our normal way of doing things. If we don't realize there is a pattern at work, then how can we make changes to get us to a higher level? I see patterns in life that most people don't see and then I help people identify those patterns that are getting them what they are receiving. If you remember the movie, *The Sixth Sense,* the little boy could see dead people nobody else could see. Like the little boy in the movie, I too see things that other people can't see—these patterns.

There are all these patterns around us and in order for us to accomplish our dreams and to be successful we must identify those patterns of activity. I think it was Einstein who said that the definition of insanity is doing the same thing over and over and expecting different results. So if you don't like the results, change the approach; when you change the approach, you change the results.

Since most people are reacting to what is happening in their lives, instead of mapping or planning their activity to get desired results, they have a hard time believing that these patterns exist. In the training I do, I ask people in the audience if they have ever driven home before without realizing how they drove home. With some light laughter in the room, usually most raise their hand. Most of us have had that experience where we jumped into our vehicle and we stopped at all the stops, we turned at all the turns, and wound up at our house. Yet if we stop to think about it, we were not consciously aware of all the activity. We were mentally somewhere else while our body automatically did all the things that we needed to do to drive home.

There are four levels of learning and the highest level is "Unconscious Competence." In other words, you don't know what you know. We call this level, Mastery. We can actually function on autopilot as we drive home, in our marriages, at work, and in all areas of our lives.

So, there are patterns all around us. There's a pattern for the way we make ourselves passionate, there's a pattern for how we make ourselves depressed, there's a pattern for making ourselves amorous—there's a pattern for most of the things we do. Once we understand that these patterns exist, then we can activate the four-step strategy for working in patterns:

Step 1—Identify the pattern.

Step 2—Ask, "Is this getting me what I want?"

Step 3—If the answer is yes, then duplicate the pattern and document. We call this SOP—Standard Operating Procedure. By doing this you can almost guarantee duplication of results. If the answer is no, go to step four.

Step 4—Change the existing pattern and then go back to step one. Sometimes a slight change can bring about a great result. By making the process conscious, we are then in a position to do something about it.

One of the keys to living a successful life is to understand that these patterns exist and then apply the four steps for working with patterns.

In the years I've been working with individuals and organizations, I have come to understand that there is a simple pattern out there for becoming successful. We have a tendency to be procrastinators. We can make things so complicated that we don't have time to do what needs to be done. So the easy answer is, "I don't know." This is the number one way we procrastinate. If you "don't know," then you don't have to do anything about it. If you don't believe me, ask a small child where his or her shoes are as you are rushing out the door late to an appointment.

I like to subscribe to the KISS philosophy—Keep It Simple Scott. Life doesn't have to be as complicated as we make it out to be. In my years of working with people and organizations, I have uncovered the simple pattern of success: Want it. Create it. Live it.

First of all, you have to know what you want—you have to *want* it. Then secondly, once you know what you want, you have to begin with the end in mind and *create* it. Once you know what it looks like, sounds like, and feels like, the third, and probably the most difficult step, is to *live* it!

WRIGHT

So what is success?

BLACK

For me that is an easy question. My children know what the Black family motto is, "When you live your life like it matters, it does!" That is my focus on living a successful life.

As simple as that question is, it is an interesting question because so many people out there want to be successful but have not identified what that means to them. If you were to line up one hundred people twenty-five years old and ask them if they were going to be successful, I don't think you would get many "no's." Many people are active and very busy, but what if they are going in the wrong direction? Understand this simple truth: if you don't know where you're going, then any road will take you there. Once you do know where you are going and what you want, then the road narrows. It becomes easier to stay the course because you know you are heading in the right direction.

One of my favorite definitions of success is the one by Ralph Waldo Emerson:

"To laugh often and love much;
to win the respect of intelligent persons

and the affection of children;

to earn the approbation of honest critics

and endure the betrayal of false friends;

to appreciate beauty; to find the best in others;

to give of one's self;

to leave the world a bit better, whether by a healthy child, a garden patch or a

redeemed social condition;

to have played and laughed with enthusiasm

and sung with exultation;

to know even one life has breathed easier because you have lived . . . this is to have

succeeded!"

That is my favorite definition of success, but I'm going to tell you right now, David, it really doesn't matter what my definition of success is—what truly matters is those people who are reading this book. What is their definition of success? This is a really important piece; it's not to be glossed over, because if you don't have a definition of success, then how will you know if you're on the right path, or more importantly, how will you know if you're on the wrong path so you can get back on the right path?

For some people success could be a profitable business, a good family, maybe a relationship with God. There is no right or wrong here, but there needs be some defined data as to what success is. We will all be held accountable for what we did on this planet. So it doesn't really matter what people's definition is, what matters is that they have one. How do you get to a place where you have never been before or a place where you don't know what it looks like, sounds like, or feels like? In our two-and-a-half-day intensive Leadership Awakening training, people get to the core and they clearly define this for their life and their work. Once they define their success, they tap into a natural, internal power source that ignites their journey to achieve their dreams.

WRIGHT

I've heard people say that your training is unique but your message is simple. Would you tell me what they're talking about?

BLACK

I have been doing this intensive Leadership Training for almost twenty years. I have had speakers and trainers and people who have been through every type of training out there. When they are finished with our training, they are blown away by the growth that can take place in two and a half days.

I never get tired of hearing training junkies tell me, "This is the most powerful and most challenging training I have ever taken." Our training is very unorthodox and very unique. It's out of the box, and at times, it's confusing. Because people are so good at being who they are and doing what they do, I work hard to get them out of their normal pattern. I get people to buy into being uncomfortable for the entire process because that is where growth takes place—outside the comfort zone. How do we get people who are already doing a lot right—who are doing better than most—stirred up to the point that they are willing to raise the bar and give more? That question was a driving force for the process that we call Leadership Awakening.

Life can be confusing at times. Marriage, having children, being a light in a sometimes dark world, and not accepting the status quo can sometimes be confusing, unfair, and tough. How do people learn to move beyond, to stay committed, to give 100 percent, even when it doesn't make sense? That is easy—practice, practice, practice.

I remember the story of a man who went to New York to do some sightseeing. He jumped into a taxicab and he asked the driver what was the best way to get to Carnegie Hall. The driver responded, "That's easy—practice, practice, practice!"

In our training, we create an environment that is just like life. People experience more of the ups and downs of life in two and a half days than most experience in years outside this process. I have discovered that people learn best what they see, hear, and do. Our training is experiential, and it gets people applying "Emotional Intelligence" in all aspects of their life. People get to practice, practice, practice how to take their personal and professional lives to a completely new level, whatever circumstances life has thrown at them. Life gets so busy at times. We get things so convoluted, so complicated, and at times we can sometimes get a bit off course, even though compared to most we are doing great.

We take a very unique approach to get people on fire for their lives, to identify what's important, what stirs them, and what drives them. If today was your last day on this planet, ask yourself this question: did you live your life in such a way that you truly accomplished something—anything—that really meant something to you and to those who matter? We get people to this unique place in a very unorthodox way, but when the journey is completed and they look backward, they see that it is common sense!

WRIGHT

You discuss the importance of knowing what one wants. Why is it so important to ask oneself the basic question, what do I want?

BLACK

Knowing what people want is the key to their personal motivation. It goes back to my original statement on success. A lot of people get up each day, do what they do, go home at night, get up the next day and do it again, and again, and again. I always like to start my training by asking this simple question: What do you want? It is so easy to be busy and get caught up in the rat race that some call life. Too many people are like the hamster on the wheel, just going through the motions—working hard and expending a lot of energy, not having enough time to do everything that we think we need to be doing.

One of my favorite speakers, Zig Ziglar, said it best, "You can have anything in life you want, if you just help enough people get what they want." One of the first things I do is get down to the core of what people want. The best way to do that is to get people to identify what they want. That is the secret to motivation. David, most people don't know what they want, but they do know what they *don't* want. Most people can give you a list of what they don't want—I don't want to be at a dead-end job, I don't want to do this, I don't want to do that—but so many people are running through life unhappy because they don't know the answer to that one simple question: what do you want? Once they figure out that key question, then they ignite their internal engine. Nietzsche said, "He who has a *why* to live can bear almost any *how.*" When people know what they want, they get their "why." When we know our "why"—what we want—then we can move through any "how."

The core of any great transformational training is to get people emotionally involved with their life, their purpose, and what they want. It comes down to how we are made—how we work. We have a stem in our brain called the reticular activating system (RAS). This RAS is the brain's focal center; it is the "tuner" for our internal television screen. The RAS doesn't take in the negative, it just paints pictures; it does not pick up the word "don't." If I were to tell you to close your eyes and visualize anything you want, but *don't* visualize the Statue of Liberty. Notice what happens—you will see in your mind the Statue of Liberty. The brain moves six times faster than we can talk. If you were backing up a vehicle and you did not want to hit the tree behind you, what would you need to keep in your field of vision? Right—the tree! That is how our brain works. In order for it not to do something, it must picture that same thing.

The good Lord put our eyes in the front of our faces. There is a simple reason for this—we look in the direction we are moving and we move in the direction we are looking. Aristotle said, "We are what we repeatedly do. Excellence, then, is not an act, but a habit." Let me suggest that everything we do or don't do comes from our thoughts and our belief systems. What we do in our head dictates what we do in our lives. If a picture is worth a thousand words, then the pictures we have in our mind's eye dictate the words that are demonstrated through our actions. I love the saying, "What you are doing speaks so loudly I can't hear what you are saying!" Your focus dictates your activity. The activity that comes from your focus on what you want is much different than the activity that comes from focusing on what you don't want! They are different directions.

It's very important for people to know what they want. True success has a starting point—you need to know what you want.

WRIGHT

So how does someone go about creating success or happiness or misery or anything for that matter?

BLACK

Well, believe it or not, it's much simpler than we want to make it, and here's the key: begin with the end in mind. In other words, act "as if"—pretend as if you already have what you want. Think about this: if you wanted to build a dream home, you would probably need a blueprint. You would probably go to an architect and he or she would take your dream home out of your head and put it into a picture. He or she would do this either by some CAD program or a sketch. It's the same with the other dreams too; you have to be the architect.

Dr. Covey talks about beginning with the end in mind. I work with a lot of people and organizations on goal getting. The reason why many people don't accomplish goals (of those who actually set them) usually comes down to one problem—location, location, location. The reason why most people don't accomplish bigger dreams and goals is because of their location—their starting point. They start in the here and now, and they start moving forward toward some goal they set. Along the journey, they hit normal problems and struggles. They run into fear and doubt, and start listening to all the reasons why they can't do what they set as a goal. This is usually followed by a good excuse as to why it didn't happen. They drop their shoulders, turn around, and say, "What was I thinking?" It is not that the person wasn't committed, or that he or she couldn't accomplish the goal. It's really a location, location, location issue—the person started in the wrong place. How do you get to a place you have never been to before? Why would you attempt to get to a place that you are not sure exists?

There is a great book called *Mozart's Brain and the Fighter Pilot: Unleashing Your Brain's Potential* by Richard Restak, MD. It is a great book on *how* the brain works. In essence, the mind does not know the difference between Hollywood and reality. When you mentally create in your mind's eye, you add your neurology. The mind reacts as if it is real and the neural pathways light up in your brain, just as if you had actually done that thing that you pictured. When you act *"as if,"* you create potential and an emotional response to your goal. We need to make it real—when we accomplish this goal, what will it look like, feel like, and sound like? A picture is worth a thousand words! We talk at a rate of roughly one hundred and twenty to one hundred and forty words per minute. So one picture is worth six to eight minutes of non-stop dialogue!

Project yourself into the future; when you accomplish this goal, this dream, this mission, and you know what it looks, sounds, and feels like you make it real. You are almost finished with the "Create it" part.

Once you have that blueprint laid out, then you just do an about face and you work yourself back to the beginning—to the *now.* All those steps looking backward are steps you took to get you to your prize. By doing this creating piece, you get your neurology involved, you know what it looks like, you know what it sounds like, you know what it feels like, you might even know what it smells like and what it tastes like! It now becomes real. You yearn for it; you want to get back to that place where it is real. Once you've been to a place that you love, you want to get back there again and again and again. So it actually pulls you, stirs you, and somewhat compels you to move in the direction of that dream. If you really want it, then you have to create it!

WRIGHT

So what's the most difficult part of the pattern of success?

BLACK

The most challenging part of the Pattern of Success is to *live* it—to walk your talk and to work the plan. Unfortunately, the world is full of hypocrites! In my intensive trainings, when I say the world is full of hypocrites, my hand goes up. A hypocrite is somebody who knows one thing but does it a little bit different. As a leader "Under Construction," one of my commitments is to be a little less of a hypocrite today than I was yesterday and a little less of a hypocrite tomorrow, than I am today.

There are many people with a blueprint in their attic for a home they're never going to build. Many people go to a financial planner and build a financial plan that they're never going to fund. You can have all the dreams in the world; you can fill out all the goal sheets, you can listen to the best speakers and read the best books, but if you are not taking action, they die! Bob Moawad said, "You can't leave footprints in the sands of time if you are sitting on your butt." And who wants to leave butt prints in the sands of time? There are so many quotes and sayings that are tied to taking action.

We live in a time where there is more information available than at any time. One can go on the Internet to learn how to do surgery, build a home, a business, or a bomb. Yet with all that information, we still have so many problems—more people today are helpless and hopeless. Depression kills more people every year in this country than the AIDS virus. Depression is basically a simple equation—helpless and hopeless.

People want and need power. There is a simple definition I like for Power: Action! You can't steal second base with your foot on first. The journey of a thousand miles begins with a step. We have all heard sayings like these. We've said them and know they are true. You can have all the dreams in the world, but if you don't take action—if you don't *live* it—then it is for naught. Don't cheat yourself by dreaming without action. You have to Live it and Live it with Passion—Heart, Body, and Soul—because when you live your life like it matters, it does!

WRIGHT

You say that there are tools along this journey called success. What are those tools?

BLACK

This is critical—we have tools available to all of us. We were born with these tools inside of us and around us. So many people don't even start the process of creating their dreams because they don't think they have what it takes. I believe that we all have the ability to live a life that matters. History books are full of people with lowly beginnings or with adversities and challenges, but they still accomplished great things. We all have tools that are inherent, they are God-given; they're with us all, we just have to get acquainted or reacquainted with them.

These are not the only tools—there are other gifts and talents that come into play. However, after studying and working with successful people and organizations, I believe that there are six foundational tools along this journey to realizing our dreams. These foundational tools are: Passion, Focus, Commitment, Purpose, Vision, and Team.

It is amazing that successful people come into our training knowing and using these six words. When they leave, two and a half days later, these words take on a new meaning. When you live these words, they become redefined. Properly using these six tools, we can accomplish more than most people think is possible, practical, or probable. Each one of these becomes like a "Power Up," on our journey toward our mission. They enable the passion and focus that allow us to commit to our purpose with a clear vision, utilizing them as team members in our lives to live our lives as if they matter!

WRIGHT

One of the tools you talk about for living your dreams is passion. Would you tell our readers why that is so important?

BLACK

The fuel that allows us to be more than most people think is realistic is passion. There are so many people going through life just numb, dead, just checking boxes off a list. Just like the little boy in the movie, *The Sixth Sense,* who saw dead people. Passion is an all-encompassing, powerful energy that makes it possible for anybody to want it, create it, and live it.

You may know the name Guy Kawasaki. Guy worked with Apple computers and in a book called *Selling the Dream,* he explained the power of passion in creating success. He wrote, "To the luckiest of people, a time comes when they join or launch a cause that forever changes their lives, and the lives of others. Losing yourself in a cause is delicious; it's intoxicating. The best word to describe the sensation is crusade. The first thing you need to believe about a crusade is this: never underestimate its power, it can transform ordinary people, products, and companies into devastating flame-throwers. You have to have a passionate desire to make a difference and fearlessly believe in your dreams." Passion is fuel, its emotional energy, and it's what stirs you up.

If you look back at history, it was passion that freed the slaves, it was passion that gave women the right to vote, it was passion that walked through the streets of Jerusalem and split time in two! Without passion—without that fuel, without that energy—it's easy to give up, it's easy to listen to the naysayers, it's easy to shrug your shoulders and shrink back when things go against you.

We need fuel to propel us into greater things. When we stumble, we need fuel to pick ourselves up, dust ourselves off, and hit it again. Passion is your fuel. It's like jumping in your car and wondering why you're not going anywhere and the reason is that your car is out of fuel. If you don't have passion, you won't accomplish anything great in life. Passion is the internal combustion that can propel you to live a life that matters. Without passion, we are just existing, accomplishing tasks. What stirs you? What keeps you going when others tell you to stop? That is Passion! Passion—it's what leaders have!

WRIGHT

In the age of information overload, how can people keep their focus on reaching their goals?

BLACK

That's a big one. The number one cause for accidents on the job site is lack of focus. We have a major focus issue in this world, and the sad part is we're in the Information Age. As I said earlier, we have more information available to us today than at any other time. The blessing and the problem is that no matter where we are, we can be working and we are accessible. We have e-mail, cell phones, BlackBerries, PCs, and laptops. As a general rule, I would say that's a good thing. However, any overuse of a strength can become a weakness.

The ability to be always connected can also be a negative thing. Being a single father of three children and a CEO of my company, a devout Christian, and a public speaker, there is always something that needs to be done. I know there are many people out there who want to take care of their families, themselves, their business, their spiritual life, and who are struggling to do any one of those items successfully. We tend to get scattered all over the place. Focus is critical to living a life of value.

Dr. Tiller at Stanford University took a forty-watt bulb, focused that energy, and created the laser beam, ten times more powerful than the sun. As little kids we took a magnifying glass, and we let sunlight through it. When that sunlight got to a fine point, it caused paper or leaves or whatever we focused the light on to catch fire. It's that type of focus in our lives that allows us to truly reach our potential. Unfortunately, there is a big problem in relation to focus. The problem is this lack of focus that seems to be so rampant in our world. Let's be honest—how many times have we been at work physically, but our focus is somewhere else? In my book that's called stealing because we make a commitment to our team, to our employer, that we will be the best possible employee, and they agree to give us a paycheck.

More importantly David, how many times have we physically been at home, but we've been working our BlackBerry, working on the computer, doing something else instead of truly being with our loved ones? It would hurt less if you just reach out and slap that kid, or slap that spouse. I am not advocating violence—I am making a point. The pain that they will feel from that physical slap will go away fairly quickly, but they will carry the pain they experience from your lack of focus for years. Kids who grow up thinking that everything is more important to Mom or Dad than they are will be emotionally scarred. Your spouse will question whether you still love him or her anymore. Those hurts stay with people for years and unfortunately, sometimes for a lifetime.

Here is the simple rule with focus: wherever you are, be there. If you're at work, be there 100 percent—heart, body, and soul. When at home, be there 100 percent—heart, body and soul. Focus—it's what leaders do!

WRIGHT

You know, some people comment that commitment seems to be lacking for many people in our culture. What effect does this have on goal setting?

BLACK

I would have to agree with that statement. There is a serious commitment problem in this world. It is not the problem of making commitments—most have that part down. The problem is to *be* committed. Shakespeare had it half right. To be or not to be is correct, but it is not a question, it is a commitment—a choice. We have to choose *to be* committed, *to be* passionate, *to be* a person of our word. The number one cause for divorce in this country is marriage. Everybody says, "I do," but what most people really mean is, "I'll try." They might mean, "I'll give it a test drive and see how it works out."

We don't have a problem making commitments; the problem is keeping those commitments that we do make. I think Margaret Meade got it right when she said, "Never doubt that a group of committed people can change the world, indeed, it is the only thing that ever has."

I love the fact that in my line of work I get to work with successful people. I hear people say all the time that they are giving 100 percent or they say, "I am giving 110 percent." I like to believe that most are not liars; they think they are giving their all. The problem is that it is hard to quantify effort unless you have an experience of what it really feels like to give everything you have. Most people have nothing to compare it to, so they assume they are giving their all. Commitment—100 percent can be hard to quantify.

One of the guarantees I make to every person who has the desire to better themselves through my leadership experiences is this: they will learn a brand new definition of 100 percent. I figured out what 100 percent is years ago. One hundred percent is Heart, Body, and Soul. I can prove my point. If I take away your heart and I take away your body and I take away your soul, what's left? Nothing is left—you give it your all: your heart, body, and soul. That is 100 percent and that is commitment.

It is hard to get to a place that you have never been to before. Once people have an experience, then they have a frame of reference. They know what it looks like, what it sounds like, what it feels like. In our Leadership Awakening course, people experience what it is like to be 100 percent committed to something. When they go home, they can then use that frame of reference to be committed to those things in their life that really matter. When you live your life as though it matters—it does! Commitment—it's what leaders live!

WRIGHT

Why is team-building crucial for achieving success? Does one need a team to succeed?

BLACK

No, I don't believe one needs a team to succeed. However, the power of synergy allows for greater impact from many, versus the output of just one. Depending on your definition of success, I believe anyone can succeed in life, but how many people are you taking with you? Anyone can cross the finish line.

I heard just recently that there are more than nine million millionaires in the United States alone! Anyone can succeed, but I believe we will be judged by how many people we take with us. A party of one is not much of a party!

In June I was the keynote speaker for APICS, the Association for Product and Inventory Control personnel. The Chapter president worked for a large tech company in San Diego. In our conversation he said that 80 percent of the employees who work for his company, who have been there for ten years, are millionaires. Now, *that* is a team most would love to be on.

I love to challenge the saying, "There is no 'I' in team." As someone who has built incredible teams throughout the last sixteen years, I challenge people to consider this non-truth. If there is no "I" in team then there is no "U" in team, and if there is no "You" in team, then there is no team, unless you are talking about someone else's team. On a regular basis, we take individuals from all over the world and in two and a half days they create the most powerful team most have ever been a part of. They start as a class and once each one of them commit—when each one adds their "I"—they go from being a class to being a powerful team!

The key here is to understand the power of the team, and the best way I've understood that is through the Spanish word for team, *equipo* (pronounced "a-kee-po"). The base of the word is "equip," and if you think about it, a team allows everybody to achieve more, like equipment. Think about what equipment means to a football player—the pads, helmets, balls, and other physical training equipment. The equipment allows them to do their job better. When you are properly equipped, you can run faster, hit harder, jump higher. Being a part of and using a team allows us to function on a higher level. Being part of a team allows all to accomplish more. You know the power of synergy, $1 + 1 = 3$ or 4 or maybe 5. By building and being a part of a successful team, everybody can accomplish so much more than one person alone. Team—it's what leaders build!

WRIGHT

We often hear about visualizing success. What can you tell us about the importance of vision and how to achieve a clear vision for the future?

BLACK

That's a great question. Vision is like faith. As the Bible says in the eleventh chapter of the book of Hebrews, "Faith is the substance of things hoped for, the evidence of things not seen." Vision is the ability to see what others can't see without your leadership.

When illustrating vision, I always go to one of the most famous speeches ever delivered, Martin Luther King's, "I have a dream" speech. No matter what country I go to, people have heard that speech and those famous lines. Dr. King had a dream—he had a vision. His words painted a picture; they were fuel that fed an entire movement. There is a good Book out there that tells us the importance of vision—without a vision people perish!

Over the years, I have come to believe that all true leaders ask themselves three questions:

Where am I now?

Where am I going?

What will it take to get there and how long?

We must be honest enough to identify properly our starting point. Whether you are using MapQuest or a GPS, you need to know your true starting point. No matter the navigation system that one chooses to use, you need a starting point to secure a route. Without that starting point, you can't get there from here.

You also need to know where you are going. This is another way of asking the question, "What do I want?" It is important to know where you are going so you can readjust along the journey. Again, if you don't know where you are going, then any road will take you there.

Then you need to figure out what you need to accomplish your goal—your outcome. What resources do you need to get you from point A to point B? It would also be nice to know when you can expect to be there. These are standard pieces of information for any well-organized traveler. Vision—it's what leaders see.

WRIGHT

Proof for any idea is in its results. Can you guarantee that this pattern works?

BLACK

Whenever I hear the "Guarantee" word, I always think of that saying about death and taxes! I can tell you, based on history and testimonies from classes over the years and in my personal life, when used, this pattern and these tools work! I've been doing this for over sixteen years now and the old saying that "the proof is in the puddin' " is true I can supply you with literally a thousand testimonials from individuals, corporations, and past graduates about the incredible changes that have been accomplished through this process.

I am reminded of a story about an elderly man who lived in a poor village in China. He was considered to be wealthy and successful because he had a son and he had a horse. One day his only horse ran away. Upon hearing this, the people of the village approached him said, "You poor man, your only horse ran away." The old Chinese man just looked at them and said, "Maybe." A couple of days later the horse comes back and with him came three wild horses, so now he has four horses. Upon hearing this, the people of the village approached him said, "You lucky man, your only horse came back and brought three more horses with him." The old Chinese man just looked at them and said, "Maybe." One day his son was breaking in one of the horses, getting him ready to ride and function as a workhorse and the son was thrown off his horse and broke his leg. Upon hearing this, the people of the village approached him and said, "You poor man, your only son has broken his leg and can't work the fields." The old Chinese man just looked at them and said, "Maybe." Not too long after this, the Huns invaded China. The military sent soldiers around to all the villages. They were to take all the young boys who were healthy enough to fight. The old man's son couldn't be taken because his leg was broken.

Everybody in the village came up to that old man and said, "You lucky man," and he said, "Maybe."

Will it work for you? Maybe. I know it has worked for thousands of people who I have been blessed to train and coach over the years. I love the old saying, "Shoot for the moon, because even if you fall short, you'll land on a star." This simple pattern and these God-given tools will work if you work them! It has worked for many. I just have one question for you: what do you want?

WRIGHT

What a great interview. I really appreciate all this time you've spent to answer all these questions for me, Scott. I've learned a lot and you've given me a lot to think about, which I definitely am going to do.

BLACK

Well, thank you for your time, David. I appreciate everything that you're doing.

WRIGHT

Today we've been talking with Scott V. Black, CEO and Founder of Empower U International. He has been described as one of today's greatest inspirational influencers for those in search of their optimum self. As a certified behavior specialist, Black has the ability to get straight to the inner core by reawakening others, helping them identify what's really important. His methodologies for helping identify one's true passion are powerful and proven, and often separate him from other life coaches and masters of NeuroLinguistic Programming (NLP). Scott has the dual gift of energy and experience, which empowers him to elevate others to excellence. His invigorating and move-to-action spirit is commonly evidenced at Empower U International's Leadership Awakening and Leadership Adventure Workshops, where participants find their purpose and inner strength in a passionate way. You may contact him at mrblack@empoweruinternational.com.

Scott, thank you so much for being with us on *Discover Your Inner Strength*.

BLACK

Thank you and remember, when you live your life as though it matters—it does!

CHAPTER Thirteen

Build Resilience
Yes You CAN: Coach Approach Now™

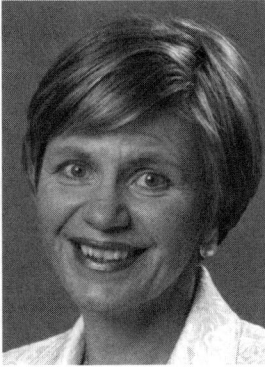

AN INTERVIEW WITH...

Arty Coppes, MA ACC

2149 North Courthouse Road
Arlington, VA
703.589.3608
arty@aeoluscoaching.com
www.aeoluscoaching.com

ABOUT THE AUTHOR

Arty R. Coppes practices as a certified executive/leadership coach improving individual and business performance and facilitates workshops with a focus on leadership and personal development.

Her coaching method CAN: Coach Approach Now™ invites you to discover your strengths and reflect on them after challenging assumptions, resulting in the execution of an action plan.

Ms. Coppes has held leadership positions with various volunteer organizations on local, national, and international levels.

Currently she is Chair of the Prism Award for the International Coaching Federation Metro D.C. Chapter, celebrating the excellence of coaching in organizations.

Arty is a peer-reviewed author who has published articles on the history of medicine and coaching, and has coauthored a book.

She holds a Master of Arts degree from the University of Leiden, the Netherlands, and a coaching degree from Royal Roads University in Victoria.

DAVID WRIGHT (WRIGHT)

Today we are talking with Arty Coppes, founder of Aeolus Coaching and Consulting. Arty is an internationally recognized speaker and facilitator. For more than five years, she has also coached executives and teams at some of the world's most recognized corporations and leading medical centers. Arty uses a unique combination of facilitation and coaching skills to help individuals and teams address barriers to growth, understand their potential, and succeed. Mrs. Coppes holds a Master of Arts degree from the University of Leiden in the Netherlands and obtained a graduate certificate in Executive Coaching from the Royal Roads University in Victoria, Canada. She is a certified professional behavioral analyst and a certified professional values/attitude analyst. In addition, Mrs. Coppes has authored books and articles on issues ranging from leadership to the history of medicine. Arty brings to her practice a broad understanding of individuals and groups shaped by having lived, taught, and coached throughout Europe and North America. She is an active member of the International Coaching Federation and presently on the Board of its Metro (Washington) D.C. Chapter.

Let's get straight to the point. Will you share with us why you think that coaching is such a great way to discover your inner strength?

ARTY COPPES (COPPES)

If I can put this in a simple way, there are theoretically two ways to discover your inner strengths. Either somebody points them out to you or, alternatively, you discover them for yourself. While the first way of discovering them is very practical and maybe provides instant gratification, the path of self-discovery affects an individual much more profoundly because the path itself is elevating, inspirational, and adds value to someone seeking his or her inner strengths.

The beauty of coaching is that good coaches will not so much point out your inner strengths and weaknesses but, rather, embark with you on a path of self-discovery. A good coach helps you access what is already there, but what you may be unable to identify and consequently use. In this process, a coach will focus on helping you identify what barriers prevented you from recognizing, strengthening, and implementing the inner strengths that you possessed all along. In this sense, coaching helps you to get in touch with your inner strengths in a highly interactive manner.

WRIGHT

How do you define coaching?

COPPES

There are many definitions of coaching. Personally, I like the description used by the International Coaching Federation (ICF). The ICF describes coaching as a partnering with clients in a thought-provoking and creative process that inspires to really maximize personal and professional potential[1].

Several words are striking. First, coaching is about a partnership, not about teaching, treating, caring, or managing. In a partnership, both parties are mutually responsible for achieving certain goals. So in coaching, the client is not a passive recipient but an active participant.

Secondly, in coaching, the partners are engaged in thought-provoking and creative processes. In other words, the client will be invited to think outside the box, to consider how he or she can use known personal tools and situations in different ways. Coaching clearly is not an excuse to validate the status quo.

Finally, coaching is about maximizing one's potential. Taken together, the definition suggests that coaching is not for the fainthearted. Some pretty lofty goals are set out, but in a good coaching engagement, they will be reached.

One of my clients recently pointed out why she was so delighted with the shift of thinking she had achieved through several months of coaching. The resulting action steps that she had formulated for herself were going to stretch her, and at the same time, in a strange way, they weren't really completely new. It felt more like an extension of things that were already part of who she was and what she stood for. Because of this, she did not feel overwhelmed; rather, inspired to have discovered what she felt was coming from inside—from her inner strength.

I felt that her ability to connect her renewed energy and refocused goals to her inner strengths was a great coaching success. The better we really know, understand, and accept our inner strengths, the more resilient we will be when life throws us a curve ball.

WRIGHT

Will you expand on the connection between inner strength and resilience?

---

[1] www.coachfederation.org/ICF/For+Coaching+Clients/What+is+a+Coach/ (accessed January 28, 2009).

COPPES

For me to do so, I would like to first expand a little on the term resilience. Merriam-Webster's online definition of resilience is *the ability to recover from or adjust easily to misfortune or change.*[2]

I like this definition for several reasons. First, it talks about ability. The word "ability" points to what one can do, not necessarily what one does or thinks one can do. Ability infers potential—talents that have yet to be discovered or developed. Often these hidden gems within ourselves are found in our inner strengths. Coaching that allows clients to discover or better define their inner strengths leads to greater ability and greater flexibility in good times and bad ones.

Secondly, the definition suggests recovery or adjustment. Resilience does not mean that you are immune from adversities, failures, or hardships. It means that you have the tools to either recoup from or adjust to hard times.

My husband is a pediatric oncologist in D.C., and in his profession meets parents who overnight face one of the most dreaded experiences a parent can have—a child with cancer. Over the years, he has been amazed at how some parents and families have been able to draw from previously untapped inner strengths and in doing so displayed resilience to adversity in a manner that becomes inspirational to others, including the medical staff. My husband would argue that such families don't just recover from misfortune—they grow to a much higher level. The same applies to the many people who have faced other hardships such as hurricanes (most notably Katrina) and of course the 9/11 disasters.

However, the definition of resilience that I have used is not restricted to *misfortune,* but includes *change* in a more general sense. Resilience is not something that will help you get through extreme negative events, but it will help you adjust to change. And whether we like it or not, change is part of our daily lives.

Because coaching really helps you discover and explore your inner strengths, it is a great tool for everybody, not just for those fighting to recover from misfortune. In fact, some of my most powerful coaching engagements have been with successful leaders who were not seeking to recover from anything; they were looking to explore their inner strengths so that they could keep growing and be innovative and transform their environments.

WRIGHT

Does this mean that coaching can improve resilience?

---

[2] www.merriam-webster.com/dictionary/resilience (accessed January 28, 2009).

COPPES

Absolutely. To better help understand the enormous value that coaching can have to improve resilience, let me use another definition of resilience, one used for physical materials that will help illustrate my contention. In this context, Wikipedia defines resilience as *the property of a material to absorb energy when it is deformed elastically and then, upon unloading, to have this energy recovered*[3]. As an executive coach I love that definition because it suggests an insertion (or investment) of energy that can be recovered after a change occurs.

This is exactly what many of my clients are looking for—an investment in themselves that will provide them with the energy to deal with change in the future. In other words, the gains obtained through coaching provide them with the ability to recover from or adjust easily to change.

My experience as an executive coach confirms that exploring (occasionally discovering) and nurturing your inner strengths in so-called "good times" increases resilience. As a consequence, the ability to respond to adversity is also increased. The importance of building resilience upfront lays with the fact that misfortune or acute changes usually are accompanied by stress. And while a little bit of stress can often help us achieve great performances, too much stress can greatly reduce our ability to respond creatively; sometimes it can even immobilize us. Trying to discover your inner strengths in the midst of truly stressful situations is not easy.

WRIGHT

Will you tell me more about the different behaviors you have seen in people when dealing with stress and how this affects their ability to respond to change?

COPPES

For me, one of the best tools to look at behaviors under stress is the DISC[4]. This assessment was developed in the early 1930s based on the work of Dr. William Moulton Marston[5] and examines the behavior of individuals in their environment. The DISC determines how one tends to behave in day-to-day situations and identifies how much of each of four basic behavioral styles we use.

It is good to remember that we all tend to use a combination of the four styles, and that it is exactly each individual's unique combination that allows a coach to help a client better understand his or her inner "natural" behavioral strengths.

---

[3] http://en.wikipedia.org/wiki/Resilience (accessed January 28, 2009).
[4] The DISC is an acronym for Dominance, *I*nfluence, *S*teadiness, and *C*onscientious.
[5] W. M. Marston, *Emotions of Normal People* (Routledge, 2002).

Briefly, the four behavioral styles reflect our tendency to achieve our goals through control and assertiveness (Dominance), through influence or persuasion (Influence), through patience, persistence, and/or submission (Steadiness), or through caution and compliance (Conscientious).

In the context of resilience (our ability to recover from or adjust easily to misfortune or change), we know that many people lose the capability to adapt when under great stress. Therefore, under those circumstances, people tend to fall back to a default behavioral style because it takes less energy, focus, and it feels familiar and safe.

However, the real question is what behaviors do you need to address the challenges you are facing? Recognizing your default styles, in particular their limitations can become a great asset for individuals expected to lead through times of change, challenge, and stress.

What I have been able to do for many of my clients is to help them analyze the strengths and weaknesses of their personal behavioral profile. While each aspect of a profile has clear strengths (e.g., somebody with a high Influence score is perceived by others as persuasive, warm, and charismatic), each profile aspect also carries drawbacks. These become very clear when things are not going well, when high stress makes us retreat to the safety of our "natural" behavioral style profile. Under those circumstances, many of us lose the flexibility necessary to overcome whatever challenge we face and "get stuck."

Stressing again that we all exhibit some of the four behavior styles measured in the DISC, let me bring up some concrete challenges around each profile when faced with stress.

Individuals who score high for Dominance are great at achieving results. They tend to be very direct, pioneering, and goal oriented. This of course is very positive. However, under stress, their behavior becomes more and more demanding and aggressive and those same strengths become liabilities. Others now view them as egocentric, as "bulls in a china shop." Under high stress, Ds will find it hard to take the time to reflect, listen, and gain the benefit from other people's perspective. They want to decide *now!*

The high I, by contrast, love to talk and are great at motivating people. These people are very optimistic and trusting. However, under stress it is hard for them to distinguish between friend and foe, as they assume that everybody will do what they say. The high I can also come across as fairly glib and self-promoting.

A third category is the group of people who primarily are process oriented and prefer focusing on one task at a time. More than any other group, the high S does not like change and under stress these people tend to dig in their heels in an attempt to avert change.

The final behavioral style is characterized by a preference for rules and regulations. Rather than goal oriented, the high C is task and fact oriented. Even under normal circumstances, this group worries about having enough information. Under stress, this need is amplified to the extent that decisions are postponed almost indefinitely based on the need for more information. These people will find it very hard to see the forest and often are seen as standoffish or exhibiting passive-aggressive behavior.

An important starting point is to create self-awareness, both around normal behavior and under stress. Coaching provides people the chance to hone their resilience skills when not under stress.

WRIGHT

What is a good method of honing our inner strengths—especially resilience—while at the same time dealing with how stress is affecting our productive behavior?

COPPES

Over the years, I have used the so-called CAN: Coach Approach Now™ quite successfully. CAN™ is a coaching process that includes the following eight elements:

1. Step back and observe.
2. Be curious and non-judgmental toward other people and yourself.
3. Ask powerful questions.
4. Re-frame the perspective.
5. Identify your barriers for success.
6. Create an action plan.
7. Execute the action plan.
8. Evaluate the process.

First, and often the most difficult step, is to step back and observe what is happening around you. This is not easy, as you have to let go of the behavior you automatically use when under stress. However, stepping back and carefully assessing the external environment as well as your own reactions to it is very powerful. It puts you back in the center, in control of whatever is happening. As such, you are much better able to manage your own, often strong, feelings and biases. Once in the center and grounded you have the real power to make constructive changes and tapping those powerful "hidden" inner resources.

Step number 2: Once you have centered yourself, I recommend opening your mind and actively becoming curious. Here some of us also may need to work on being sure that our thoughts and assessments will be non-judgmental. Simply wonder about the situation that you are dealing with. Sometimes it helps to consider how a child would approach the issue. Children tend to wonder more than adults do about how things work. So ask yourself:

- What skills could I use for his?
- What options do I have to resolve this?
- Who could help me or provide me with a different perspective?
- Do I really need to resolve it now or can it wait?

This approach is sometimes difficult; it is about getting out of your comfort zone and beyond your first, maybe intuitive, reaction. Some will have to let go of thinking, "Oh, this will not work," or "This is a bad situation," or "I do not have enough evidence," or "I need to resolve it now." Those instinctive responses often are an open door toward falling in the trap of your default stress behavior.

Once you have actively tried to open your mind and wonder, the next step, number three, is to ask questions to challenge and possibly broaden the problem and the situations that you are dealing with:

- How could I use this?
- What exactly is my goal? Is it the right one?
- Do I have a similar situation or activity in my business?
- Is there any way I could envision this being successful for me?
- What is appealing about this for me?
- What evidence is there that I have *no* control?
- What do I actually have control over?
- What is within my control and what is not?
- If it is not within my control, what will I do with it?
- What can I do to gain even some form of control over this situation?

As you go through this part of CAN™, make sure to question your own assumptions:

- Why do you think there is no way out?
- Why do you think no one cares about you?

- What is the basis for this?
- If I were at my best, what would I do right now?

If done well, this part allows you to discover the barriers that you may unconsciously be putting up to resolve the issue. This step is focused on ensuring that you take responsibility for your own actions. I like to think that each of us is the CEO of our own life.

Next, with the insights and gains achieved in the first three steps, you are now ready to reframe the issue at hand (step number four). A way of reframing is:

- Am I too judgmental?
- Is there another way of looking at this?
- What could I do/use/think that I have not yet done/thought of?
- How could I look at this differently?
- Can I see anything good/ or maybe even comic in this?

Reframing situations and questions is an art. In fact, some argue that modern technology has made it more and more difficult for us to reframe issues. The July/August 2008 edition of *The Atlantic* featured an article titled "Is Google making us stupid?"[6]. Nicholas Carr suggests that we increasingly accept information without verification or contemplation. What he proposes is that our way of thinking seems to be changing. I would argue it already has. We don't spent time reflecting or contemplating what we see, hear, or read. Many seem to accept information at face value and instantaneously move along to the next song, movie, paragraph, Web page, or person. We are losing our ability to thoroughly read, question, and understand. So this step does not come easy to some people but is vital; contemplate so that the issue can be reframed.

For some leaders it is hard to provide (constructive) feedback to their team members or employees. What if giving feedback was not about you feeling bad about having to provide negative comments on performance, but more about the possibility of being a mentor for the person? This gives you the opportunity to guide someone and help him or her be poised for the next level or simply to support the person to do his or her job in the best way possible. If you see the issue in that light (reframe it) it might be a much easier step for you to take.

---

[6] http://www.theatlantic.com/doc/200807/google (accessed January 28, 2009).

Before going into action, we have one more step to go. We need to identify barriers (step number five). We have been able to reframe the issue but need to delineate the limitations—the dangers of inaction. Here are some ways of getting to your barriers:

- Where am I resisting?
- Where is the exciting part, the scary part?
- Where do I drop the ball?
- What would keep me from moving forward?
- Which assumptions are tenuous?
- Where will I depend on others for success?
- Where do I need to make sure to involve others?
- What still keeps me worried or keeps me up at night?

Once you have identified barriers and limitations, you can take action. But make sure you do not let the whole initiative fail because you can think of barriers. Rather, deal with the barrier(s) and keep moving forward.

There are of course ways to get around the barriers. Graphically, you can go over barriers, under them, or around them. Actually visualizing barriers and ways to address them provides you with a different view of the issue.

One of my clients experienced difficulties with making important decisions. After some coaching, he was able to understand that the barrier for making decisions was related to the fear of dealing with the unknown consequences down the road. How can one know what affects certain decisions would have in the long-term or even the short-term for example? During our coaching engagement, I took him on a walk through the city and advised him that he would make each and every decision as to where we would go. Initially it was fun. He decided ad hoc without thinking, but within half an hour he realized that he had not paid attention to where we were going. Since I was not going to make any suggestions or decisions, all of a sudden his stress level increased as he realized that every decision became important.

As we went from street corner to street corner, he started "seeing" the streets and paying attention to patterns he had previously been oblivious to. As we proceeded, he gained confidence, realizing that as he came to new decision points, he had the knowledge and wisdom to make the right decisions. Debriefing the "walking coaching experience," the barrier of fear for unknown consequences was uncovered, made visible, and tackled in such a way that he could move forward.

The next step (number six) and important for success, is the creation of a concrete action plan. You have identified the problem, you have reframed it, and you have acknowledged the existence of some barriers and dealt with them, now you are ready to move. Brainstorming time!

- What are the solutions?
- What are the advantages and disadvantages of each potential solution?
- On a scale of one to ten, which one has the best chance of being successful?
- What are the alternatives?

Specify your next steps and determine how you will be accountable for achieving the SMART goals. (SMART is an acronym that stands for: Specific, Measurable, Attainable, Realistic, and Timely.) At this stage, it is time to focus on the desired solutions and outcomes and forget the problem.

A good question to ask would be: what is one thing that I can accomplish today that will help me move in the direction I want to go?

Then comes execution (step number seven). Many business leaders will argue that execution is what makes or breaks success and companies. An excellent book that describes the importance of focused execution was written by the acclaimed CEO Larry Bossidy and the equally talented Ram Charam[7]. They describe execution as the *missing link between aspirations and results.* That is great food for thought. Execution includes accepting feedback on your actions so that you make sure you stay the course. Coaching can be of great help during execution. This is where working with a coach supports reaching results. While the accountability for executing the plan is completely the client's, a coach will support you by providing honest feedback on where you are going compared to where you intended to go.

The final step (number eight) in the Coach Approach Now™ is evaluation. Make sure you appraise how things went—how things worked for you. Reflect and ask for feedback. This process of self-discovery and contemplation contains powerful stepping-stones toward building resilience.

---

[7] Larry Bossidy, Ram Charam, and Charles Burck, *Execution: The Discipline of Getting Things Done*, (Crown Business; 1 edition, June 15, 2002).

WRIGHT

Will you give me a concrete example of how this worked for somebody?

COPPES

Not that long ago I coached a well-respected physician who felt that many of his ideas were credited to others. This made him angry and frustrated because he felt that this lack of credit resulted in his not being promoted within the hospital hierarchy. During our coaching sessions it became clear that he really had great ideas, but during meetings he would disengage because the meetings took forever. Everybody had to have the opportunity to have a say and the Chair made sure that due process was followed during the meetings. My client was way too impatient for this. When late in the meeting others came up with ideas that my client already had considered an hour ago (but had not expressed because of his disengagement), credit went to his colleagues.

When we discussed this together, he came to realize that his unrecognized inner strength was his ability to quickly come up with out-of-the-box ideas and solutions. However, he was stuck in a stress behavior of disengagement. His barrier for meaningful contributions (and subsequent credit) was disengagement from the process.

We worked hard together for him to recognize these moments. He learned to respond to these moments by stepping back, refraining from being judgmental, asking powerful questions, and recognizing that disengagement was his barrier to providing an important contribution. Within a few months, be became recognized for his brilliant and creative ideas, and his team has started to rally around him. Recently he was asked to represent his boss when away and he now speaks up when interacting with high-level visitors to his medical research facility in Washington, D.C.

WRIGHT

Do you need to practice CAN™?

COPPES

Yes, certainly. It is like learning to drive a car. You build up skills so you can do them without any conscious thoughts. Compare it to playing professional tennis or driving racecars. Once you are engaged at a high level and you're under pressure, it is very difficult to focus on the individual steps that you need to take. In order for things to go smooth and give you the competitive advantage, some of the actions have to come automatically, even when the unexpected occurs. How do top players achieve this? It is called practice and at the highest level, champions practice day in and day out. Similarly, practicing CAN™ on small issues when you are not under stress will pay off when something big occurs—something that is accompanied by stress.

WRIGHT

I would like to finish by looking at resilience at an organizational level. Would you say it could be adapted at that level as well?

COPPES

Totally. Look at companies like Capital One, Goldman Sachs, Coca Cola, and Toyota—all very resilient businesses. Coca Cola, for example, reinvented itself in the late nineties from a specialty carbonated soft drink company with its own bottling business to a beverage company, selling a variety of "competing drinks."

Goldman Sachs, founded in 1869, started as a private trading company, and then morphed into a private investment bank. In the early seventies, trading was reintroduced. While the company underwrote many significant Initial Public Offerings or IPOs (Sears, Ford Motor Company, Microsoft, Yahoo), its own IPO in 1999 occurred after decades of debate among the company's partners. The original question posed to the Board was whether or not they should consider going public. Twice the partners voted against this. The third time, however, the question was posed differently (reframed!) to "What will the strategy of Goldman Sachs be at the end of the twentieth century?" A number of issues floated to the top and it quickly became clear that in order for the company to compete and succeed, it required access to considerable financial resources. Going partly public was not that difficult of a decision anymore. Most recently, Goldman Sachs reframed its business yet again, following the global financial distress. This time they have evolved into a traditional bank holding company, bringing to an end the era of investment banking on Wall Street.

Several people, including Albert Camus and Robert F Bennett, have said, "Life is the sum of all our choices." I would add that those choices would be so much better if we really know who we are, what inner strengths we can draw on, and especially, where we want to go. Grounded in our inner strength, we can then draw on our resilience whenever the need arises.

WRIGHT

Today we've been talking with Arty Coppes. She is the founder of Aeolus Coaching and Consulting Company. She is known internationally and recognized as a speaker and facilitator. Arty uses her unique combination of facilitative and coaching skills to help individuals and teams address their barriers to growth and understand their potential so they can succeed both personally and corporately in their lives.

CHAPTER Fourteen

Simplify, Then Serve

AN INTERVIEW WITH...

Alice Fulton-Osborne & Patty Liston

740 E. Alpine Blvd.
Alpine, UT 84004
801.636.1793
alice@frontporchconferences.com
patty@frontporchconferences.com
www.frontporchconferences.com

ABOUT THE AUTHORS

Patty Liston is Managing Director of Partnerships for WoogiWorld.com, a former schoolteacher, and serves as Director of Women's Initiatives for Reach the Children, a non-profit in Africa. She served as a delegate to the International Forum on the Family, Mexico City.

Alice Fulton-Osborne is Managing Director of Public Relations for WoogiWorld.com, a former school and college teacher, and hospital commissioner. She coauthored the best-selling organization book, *It's Here . . . Somewhere*, and was a television spokesperson for the bathroom product 2000 Flushes. Both are former newspaper columnists and radio talk show hostesses. They're popular public speakers, e-newsletter columnists, and founders of the national women's conference, The Front Porch.

THE INTERVIEW

DAVID WRIGHT (WRIGHT)

Today we're talking with Patty Liston and Alice Fulton-Osborne. Patty is Managing Director of Partnerships for WoogiWorld.com, a former schoolteacher, and serves as Director of Women's Initiatives for Reach the Children, a non-profit in Africa. She served as a delegate to the International Forum on the Family, Mexico City.

Alice Fulton-Osborne is Managing Director of Public Relations for WoogiWorld.com, a former school and college teacher, and hospital commissioner. She coauthored the best-selling organization book, *It's Here . . . Somewhere*, and was a television spokesperson for the bathroom product 2000 Flushes. Both are former newspaper columnists and radio talk show hostesses. They're popular public speakers, e-newsletter columnists, and founders of the national women's conference, The Front Porch.

Patty, Alice, welcome to *Discover Your Inner Strength.*

PATTY LISTON (LISTON)

Thank you.

ALICE FULTON-OSBORNE (FULTON-OSBORNE)

Good to be here.

WRIGHT

So when we think of clutter we obviously think of stuff, but can clutter be defined as something else as well?

FULTON-OSBORNE

Yes, clutter *is* stuff—anything we don't like, use, need, want, or have room for. And it's *more* than stuff. It can be the clutter of busyness, too much activity, too much audio stimulation, too much visual stimulation, too much scheduling, and too much expectation. All of this disrupts our balance, sidetracks us from what matters most, and buries our inner strengths.

LISTON

Which then get in the way of our being able to serve and nurture others—whether this is within our own family, community, or the broader, larger world.

FULTON-OSBORNE

In fact, it doesn't matter how much inner strength a person has. If people are buried under mental, emotional, and physical clutter, they'll struggle to access those strengths. And even if they *can* access them, the execution of them will be hampered. Clutter is a barrier to reaching our fullest potential and discovering and using our inner strengths.

WRIGHT

So let's start with the stuff then. Aside from looking messy and making it difficult to find things, what are other problems with keeping things we don't like, use, need, want, or have room for?

FULTON-OSBORNE

You just defined clutter! It is anything we don't like, use, need, want, or have room for. We say it's the fish food on the kitchen windowsill for the fish that have been dead for six months. Clutter—we all have it, and it's no respecter of persons, income, or education level. It's confusing, nerve-wracking, and exhausting. It obscures, overwhelms, and distances.

As a society we're buried in things, and as physical things take up space in our lives, it crowds out what matters most. With the removal of clutter we'll find more space, more time, and more energy. Then we can put this energy into what matters most—serving others.

LISTON

We're always inspired by those we know who are spending their lives on what matters most—who are living what we call an abundant life. Through the practice of living simply and giving daily they've accessed their inner strengths—the strengths of generosity, thoughtfulness, and kindness. They are not *self*-centered, but are *others*-centered and available for meeting the needs of others.

Besides understanding what clutter is and how it can hurt us, we need to understand that we're *not* talking about organizing things. Organizing is what you would do after you've gotten rid of your clutter—you organize what's left. But the process we'll be discussing should always come *before* any organizing, and we call it streamlining—deciding what to keep and what to toss.

WRIGHT

Makes sense! Then what are your suggestions for getting rid of this physical clutter—for streamlining?

FULTON-OSBORNE

Well, David, first let's look at the three reasons why people hang onto things that they don't like, use, need, want, or have room for. First: *Sentiment.* We keep clutter because of who gave it to us or because of memories attached to it. Second: We keep clutter because we paid "good money" for it. "Those glasses cost us $230—I can't toss those!" (Never mind that they haven't been worn for twenty years.) And the third reason, and this is a real killer (and your readers are already thinking it): "I might need it someday." When Patty and I speak to audiences, we say, "Yes it's true, you absolutely will need it someday, but that's not the point. There *is* somebody who *does* need it today, so let's get past the mental barriers to being clutter free and pass things along to who can use them now."

With the barriers gone we can now take the eight specific steps to getting rid of clutter:

Step one: *Prepare yourself and your family.* This is a gruesome and exhausting experience initially, but so worth the pain and effort. Prepare by having your meals planned ahead of time. Let family members know what you'll be doing and assure them you won't touch their things. You'll only toss your things. Then set aside some unbroken blocks of time for the project.

LISTON

This isn't just some little reorganizing of a drawer or closet—this is a major blowout. Streamlining is the process of touching every physical thing in the room and asking yourself some specific questions about each thing. This takes *time.*

Step two: *Get some containers.* The idea is to haul away lots of stuff. If the average home (between 1,800 and 2,200 square feet) were streamlined down to the bare bones, thirty-five to forty-five *full* thirty-gallon-size trash bags of stuff would be eliminated—80 percent would go to charity and 20 percent would go to trash. So you need containers to put things for somewhere else, things for trash, things to be filed, and things that will go off to charity.

FULTON-OSBORNE

Step three: *Start in the master bedroom.* People ask, "Why start there? That's not a place anybody really sees." We start in the master bedroom because that's the first room *you* see, and the last room you see, every day. Our self-esteem is either nurtured or hurt in the master bedroom. So we start there, with the objective of creating an absolute little spot of heaven by getting the clutter out. In fact, we always do the bedrooms (of those who want this help) before we ever move to the more public areas of the home.

Step four: *Use keeper questions.* Do I like it? Do I use it? Do I need it? Do I want it? Do I have room for it? The answers to these questions determine which container an item goes into or if it stays in the room. These questions help you know what to keep and what to get rid of.

LISTON

Step five: *Evaluate and assign.* Once we find the things that we call keepers we're going to evaluate where they need to be put, and we're going to give every physical space its own assignment. Consciously decide what you want in every space in the room you're working in and make sure that those spaces fulfill that function and none other. This stops the "chucking and stuffing" of things.

Next, Step six: *Group and store like items together.* This approach stops the "wandering and pondering." We spend two years of our lives looking for things, but if we grouped and stored like items together, there would be far less wandering and pondering.

FULTON-OSBORNE

Step seven: *Use memory boxes.* Every member of the family should have one. This is where treasures go. You might not need them, you might not even use them anymore, but you want them. They are part of our personality and character, in that they build our past and create part of who we are. They need and deserve their own special safe place.

Finally, the last step, Step eight: *Enjoy the empty space*—the spaces that you end up with as you get rid of your clutter. Empty space is soothing and calming, easy to maintain, and it opens you up to what matters most.

LISTON

We like to tell our audiences as an aside: there is nothing wrong with opening up a drawer and seeing *nothing* in it. We don't have to fill every nook and cranny of our house. There's nothing more liberating than to open up a drawer and say, "Oh my goodness, there's nothing there! Isn't that wonderful?"

FULTON-OSBORNE

And David, we talk a lot about how "big isn't better"—it's just big. In America we subscribe to the idea that we have to have all this space, but all it does is beckon us to fill it up. We also talk about "quality over quantity"—a good benchmark to use when deciding what to do with our spaces. And then, "less is always best." If we can keep these ideas in mind, then we're going to be able to get rid of our clutter.

WRIGHT

You mentioned earlier that too much activity can also be clutter. What can we do to eliminate or minimize this?

FULTON-OSBORNE

Be clear on your life's vision and mission—a concept Stephen Covey speaks so eloquently to. With this approach, you eliminate anything that doesn't serve your mission or your vision, including the physical things that you bring into your spaces. Once you're clear on your vision and mission, it is your criteria for the rest of your life—a guide to how you fill up your spaces and how you fill up your time.

LISTON

As everyone knows, McDonalds does hamburgers, French fries, and drinks. They don't do tacos; they don't do burritos. Their parameters are set as far as what they do, and they consciously work on that. It's the same thing with us—we're miniature McDonalds, or we're miniature little businesses, so we want to focus on what we want to accomplish in our lives.

When we're bogged down with too much activity, there is no time to just meander, whether that's a physical or mental meandering. "Meandering" leads us to places where we can really find out who we are and what our mission in this life is, and what we should be doing with this free time that we now have because we're no longer taking care of all our clutter.

I've worked in Africa for over ten years, and one of the things I have noticed is that the women there meander. When they walk they are not in a hurry, they take their time to just walk and visit with friends. And whenever I am there, I can take a deep breath because there is no hurry. The importance is in the moment, not something out in the future. They really live in the moment, and I think we as a society are missing those moments because of all the activities that are in our BlackBerries, on our calendars, or in our day planners.

WRIGHT

Besides being overrun with busyness, it's a noisy world. How can we tune some of it out?

FULTON-OSBORNE

Well again, we think we should set aside some time—some quiet time that Patty alluded to here—for pondering and mediation every day. This quiet gives us the chance to evaluate and be sure we're engaging only in what serves our mission and our vision. We want to be really clear on that. We don't just sit and listen or watch, think, and meditate anymore.

When a Kenyan exchange student was asked what was one of the major differences between Americans and Kenyans, he answered, "You are a nation of human *doings;* we are a nation of human *beings."*

So to quiet the world down, we're going to have to be pretty assertive about it. Let's not just mindlessly allow the cacophony of the world to butt in. Make sure the music you're listening to pleases you. Make sure the people you're listening to are people you care about listening to. Make sure the media you're watching is worthy of your time. And finally, let's take some time to quietly sit and think and assertively—even aggressively—decide what we want in life, and how it will fill our mission and vision. Anything else, we eliminate.

LISTON

Alice and I believe people are afraid to be still for fear of what it is they may hear in those quiet moments. This quiet voice—call it spirit, consciousness, or impressions—yearns to be heard and acted upon. If you read the histories of great scientists, authors, or musicians, their "ah-ha moments" came when they were pondering.

As Mozart was sitting at his table thinking and hearing the sounds of nature coming in through his window, he would hear entire concertos in his head. He would quickly write it all down on paper, napkins, or the tablecloth—anything he could find. After his death, dozens of partial compositions were discovered throughout his home—things that he had heard just during his moments of quiet contemplation. Why not follow Mozart's lead and at least once a day put our hands up and say, *"Stop!* This five minute time period [ten minutes, fifteen minutes, or more] is for me to get in tune with myself so I can hear what I need to hear."

FULTON-OSBORNE

We'd also like to suggest some other ideas to eliminate some noise: Have a "no television night," and a "no computer night," and turn the cell phone off. Try a "no cell phone evening" where you deliberately create some silence in your world. You'll have to be aggressive about it, but we know this is an effective way to bring quiet into one's life.

WRIGHT

Aside from moving to the deep woods and turning into a hermit, what do you suggest for the visual stimulation overload mentioned earlier?

FULTON-OSBORNE

The above suggestions apply here as well. Consider the no television night and no computer night idea. Your readers may go into delirium tremors over this, but the benefit of just sitting and gazing out a window, quietly reading a book, or just sitting with your own thoughts can be expansive and liberating—opening up a whole new world. People discover who they are when they're quiet. The bottom line: assertively turn things off and shut out the world for a while.

In our home we refuse to answer the phones during dinner; we shut them off. On Sunday afternoons, we engage the family in quiet time. Phones, computers, televisions, and radios are shut off. Whether we snooze, read a book, or just lie in the sun and watch the clouds, we deliberately schedule in "stillness." We can then connect with that inner self—that place where our inner strengths reside. Our unique strengths have an easier chance of being discovered if they don't have to compete for our attention.

LISTON

And although a Herculean task in this very technological era, we need to remember that we are not the servants of technology, we are the masters of technology. We need to develop the fortitude to say *No!* to all the clamoring outside noise.

When Mother Teresa visited the United States, she viewed what she called the emotional poverty of America—that we have a lot of stuff but we are not fulfilled. We don't take the time to develop character or intellect.

There are many ways of living in poverty. A speaker once said of those living in developing countries that the trouble with being poor is that it takes up all of their time. Even in a developed country there is "poverty"—poverty in the inability to connect with other people, to do that which is essential and not just what is necessary. Eating, drinking, and working for a living are all necessary to sustaining us as individuals. But it is in what we give outside of ourselves—our time, talents, compassion, comfort, financial resources—that are essential to sustaining our humanity.

WRIGHT

We can all relate to these twenty-first century technological intrusions, but how do we know what to pay attention to, what to stay involved in, and what to eliminate?

FULTON-OSBORNE

That's the $64,000 question! The answer hearkens back to our earlier advice: create a personal vision and personal mission. With these in place, you will more easily be able to evaluate all activity in terms of that vision and mission. If activities don't serve them, you don't get involved.

We like to tell our audiences that it's okay to say, "No thank you." In fact, this is a response that we have our audiences write down, memorize, and repeat: "Thank you for asking me to be part of your project. I appreciate the confidence you have in me. However, I won't be able to participate, as I have another commitment. Please think of me another time."

Now that's never a lie. We always have a commitment to be true to our personal vision and mission—*always.* If we don't keep ourselves true to it, the whole world is going to be grabbing for pieces of us, and then that's when we get fragmented, frustrated, and frenzied. And that's when our inner strengths don't get used to their maximum.

LISTON

And this is the foundation that stress builds. We're a stressed-out society, living on Prozac, taking sleep aids to go to sleep, and amphetamines to wake up. To get ourselves percolating, we drink two to three cups of coffee even before we get to work. I once heard someone say that stress is when the mind says "no," but the mouth says "yes." As Alice said, when we have our own personal mission and vision, it's easier to be able to define what it is we will and won't do, what it is we will and won't get involved in, and how we will and won't spend our free time.

WRIGHT

Streamlining—removing the physical clutter, excess busyness, intrusive noise, and uninvited visual stimulation does imply a change in expectations. But how do we adjust our expectations and still maintain a balance between simplicity and twenty-first century demands? Seems nearly impossible given the expectations of today's plugged-in society.

FULTON-OSBORNE

It's a paradigm shift for sure. It calls for valuing the simple, and seeing the beauty and the glory in the simple. We live in such a razzle-dazzle world that the first place to start this shift would be to change our perspective as to what matters most. For instance, time spent with others and creating ways to spend more time together could be the start of this paradigm shift. We are concerned when we see families running themselves ragged because they feel the need to be involved in everything that comes along—over-scheduling negatively affects everyone. Simplifying schedules may be one of the easiest steps to take in achieving the balance between simplicity and the demands of the twenty-first century world.

LISTON

We're not suggesting dropping out or giving up. We're suggesting whittling away and monitoring intrusions. We won't give up our computers or using the Internet, for instance. But we *will* consciously decide when we'll have it on and for how long. We won't give up extracurricular after-school activities for our children, but we will, as a family, agree to scale back on the number of activities we participate in. By taking control of what will and what won't infringe on our space and time, we make room for what matters most: relationships and the needs of others. And by eliminating some or at least minimizing distractions, we now have the quiet needed to ponder what we can do for others.

True happiness comes from simple acts of daily kindness—those things that identify us as human beings and not human doings. Steve Robinson reminds us that we are the arsonists of our own happiness. It takes tremendous discipline to implement these suggestions, but research shows there are not only emotional but physical benefits also to simplifying and connecting with others.

FULTON-OSBORNE

One other thought: as we get rid of things and adjust our expectations, we need to know what's "enough." If a little isn't enough, a lot will never be enough. We hope this chapter will be a clarion call to pare back the expectations and look to more sustainable living. Let's become content with less of the physical and the material that passes away, and devote more energy and time to what matters most. As Patty mentioned, that's relationships, that's people, and that's the service aspect of this chapter.

WRIGHT

You both made a good case for why too much gets in the way of what matters most, which you believe is serving others. Why do you believe service is such an important aspect of life? And, can anyone give service?

LISTON

That's the beauty of service—anyone can participate. Marian Wright Edelman, the founder of the Children's Defense League, has said, "Service is the rent we all pay to be living. It is the very purpose of life; not something that you do in your spare time." Service is a gift we not only give to others but to ourselves because it stretches us into better human beings and gives us opportunities to discover and use our inner strengths. It is a source of peace and contentment and gives life meaning.

Also, there is a rippling affect from service—by helping one we help all. Communities, for instance, are strengthened by the compound efforts of individuals within those communities.

WRIGHT

What then, are your suggestions for ways to serve?

LISTON

There is a woman who every Wednesday gathers people together from her church and neighborhood to sew, knit, and quilt. All of the items they complete are given to women's shelters, orphanages, and developing countries. Here you will see people of all ages and demographics, from women in wheelchairs who thread needles, to a blind man who knits stocking caps, to young people who lift and move heavy boxes. For every person out there, there is a service that can be rendered.

To mothers we say, "The greatest service you can give is to your own family— your children, your husband, your elderly parents." There is much that we can give that requires no monetary outlay, such as a phone call, an offer to take someone shopping, or sitting and listening. Life is constructed of times and seasons—let's not be afraid to do a little, because we may not be in a place where we can do a lot.

FULTON-OSBORNE

Service can really be broken down into three efforts: Service Effort Number Three calls for more intensive physical involvement on our part—shoveling a neighbor's snow, helping a neighbor lay some sod, bringing in a meal, or organizing your neighborhood children to collect pet food for your local animal shelter, for instance.

Service Effort Number Two doesn't require quite as much physical time or involvement. Maybe you're going to keep an eye on a vacationing neighbor's property or you might donate to a humanitarian fund or you might share some extra garden produce.

LISTON

You might donate blood to the Red Cross.

FULTON-OSBORNE

Or make a cheer-up phone call. Finally, there's Service Effort Number One, and this is what Patty was talking about when she said that everyone can serve. Everyone can smile as they pass others on the sidewalk, everyone can pay a genuine heartfelt compliment, everyone can listen when others are speaking, everyone can pass on to others the good things heard about them. And everyone can be cheerful and positive and remember names (and actually call a person by his or her name). We don't think of these things as service, but they truly are. Anything we do to uplift, encourage, and inspire others to be better is service.

LISTON

It goes back to what we talked about earlier regarding having our mission and vision in place. Using that as a reference, we can ask ourselves, "What do I want to do that sings to my heart?" Now that we're living in greater simplicity, we feel freer to take the time to be still and listen to what rises to the top. We promise you that ideas will come—follow up on those impressions because they are important.

WRIGHT

I can see that there are tremendous benefits to everyone involved.

FULTON-OSBORNE

Yes, let's get specific. There are five things those who are served generally experience: 1) they enjoy a lightened load when someone pinch-hits for them, 2) they have an encouraged heart from knowing that someone cares and they're not alone, 3) their mind is calmed, again because someone is sharing their burden, 4) their soul is soothed and their sadness is lifted. When other people share our heartache, cry with us, and hold us, it lifts that sadness and, 5) we experience healing—whether physical or emotional or both.

LISTON

Medical and scientific research proves that a real physical healing takes place for *everyone* involved. We've talked about the benefits to the "served," but there are also some specific benefits to the person who does the serving.

When we are able to serve another person, we bond with him or her in ways that we wouldn't normally. This bonding is an effective antidote to the disconnection and loneliness many women tell us they feel. This is one of the reasons we started our Front Porch Conferences—so women could rub shoulders with and learn from one another.

WRIGHT

If you had one final thought for those who want to find their inner strengths in terms of simplifying and serving, what would it be?

FULTON-OSBORNE

We look to Helen Keller—a benchmark in a sense. She said, "All states have their wonders, even darkness and silence. And no matter what state I'm in, therein I learn to be content." If we could have, as part of our personal vision and mission, a simpler, quieter, yet richer life, therein we too could find contentment. Contentment is an amazing inner strength that draws on the other strengths that lead us to making a difference with our lives. This leads us to pursuing what matters most.

LISTON

Let's close with a story. Several years ago, I went with a couple of women to Ghana for research. We visited several little clinics in outlying villages that were incredibly poor—there were no medicines and no sheets on the beds; women were giving birth on black plastic. There was nothing to wrap their newborns in. We asked the head nurse what it was we could bring when we came back that would be most helpful to the clinic. She suggested we bring bed sheets so the women would have something comfortable and sanitary to give birth on.

Six months later, we returned with duffle bags full of sheets that communities and neighbors had donated. The nurse was thrilled with this donation and invited us to visit some women who had just given birth in very dark and sweltering rooms. As we were leaving, we almost tripped over two women who were kneeling by the door. They talked to the nurse with tears rolling down their cheeks. We looked at the nurse hoping for an explanation. We thought perhaps we'd done or said something wrong. It was explained to us that the women were kneeling in gratitude to us for the sheets we shared.

Ponder this scene. Let's understand that we all have "sheets," literally or figuratively, that we can give during our lifetime. If we are still, if we have clear purpose and mission, and if we have been able to get the stuff that is not essential out of our lives, we will be able to discover what "sheets" we can give. Every morning when we wake up, let's ask ourselves, "What are the 'sheets' I can give today?" If we listen, we will know what to do, we will take the time, and we will have the confidence and the inner strength to go and do that which is essential.

FULTON-OSBORNE

In summary, what we've talked about echoes the title of our chapter, "Simplify, Then Serve." In so doing, you'll find not only your inner strengths, but yourself as well!

WRIGHT

What a great conversation and important reminders. We have much to think about. I don't know why I haven't done some of the things you're suggesting. They're very simple, aren't they?

LISTON

They really are. It doesn't require a college degree or a fat wallet. All that is required is a willingness to do "something" to use your inner strengths to uplift those around you. In so doing, you'll bring purpose and meaning to their life and yours.

FULTON-OSBORNE

In fact, the most profound inner strength anybody could possibly possess is the ability to be other-oriented. Really, that's the bottom line for meaningful and joyful living—using the strengths we've been blessed with to bless the lives of others!

WRIGHT

Ladies, this is a wonderful message. If we simplify and then serve, we'll find not only our inner strengths, but also ourselves. We appreciate your bringing it to our attention and this chapter is going to influence many!

LISTON

We have loved being able to visit with you, David. It's just been the highlight of our morning. Thank you so much for giving us a call.

FULTON-OSBORNE

Yes thank you. We're excited to be involved with your program and your project. We appreciate this lovely opportunity.

WRIGHT

Today, we've been talking with Patty Liston, Managing Director of Partnerships for WoogiWorld.com, and Alice Fulton-Osborne, Managing Director of Public Relations for WoogiWorld.com. Both are public speakers, e-newsletter columnists, and founders of the national women's conference, The Front Porch.

Patty, Alice, thank you so much for being with us today on *Discover Your Inner Strength.*

LISTON

Thank you, David.

FULTON-OSBORNE

Our pleasure. Thank you, David.

CHAPTER Fifteen

Only with Moxie is Success Inevitable

AN INTERVIEW WITH…

Ann Tardy

27 Madison Ave.
Red Bank, NJ 07701
1.888.Ms.Moxie
ann@lifemoxie.com
www.lifemoxie.com

ABOUT THE AUTHOR

Ann Tardy is a professional motivator. As the Founder and Chief Catalyst of The LifeMoxie ™ Company, Ann is a motivational speaker, author and advisor, helping companies everywhere increase the engagement and effectiveness of their individual contributors. Ann and The LifeMoxie Company impart their moxie strategies to people, teams, and organizations that crave to be extraordinary in an otherwise mediocre, complacent, and ordinary world.

Prior to launching The LifeMoxie Company, Ann was an attorney for fourteen years, practicing corporate securities law at two of Silicon Valley's largest law firms. Subsequently, she managed the legal departments of a start-up that fell to the dotcom bust and a start-up that squeaked by to IPO, before launching her own law firm representing moxie entrepreneurs of all shapes and sizes.

During her tenure as in-house counsel, Ann also served for five years as co-director of the Entrepreneurial Education program at a girls' middle school, training twelve-year-olds how to use their moxie to start and run businesses.

Ann earned an accounting degree from the University of Illinois, a law degree from Chicago-Kent College of Law, a CPA from the State of Illinois, and licenses to practice law in Illinois and California.

Ann was honored by The McGraw Hill Companies with the prestigious Vanguard Award and as an Outstanding Business Woman of the Year by the American Business Women's Association.

Her first book, *LifeMoxie! Ambition on a Mission—9 Strategies for Taking Life by the Horns,* was published in 2007. She is a featured author in *Best of the Best* published by Insight Publishing in 2008. Her next book, *The Moxie Mindset*, is scheduled for release in the fall of 2009.

DAVID WRIGHT (WRIGHT)

Today we're talking with the woman that Sally Jesse Raphael calls "energetic!" Ann Tardy is Founder and Chief Catalyst of The LifeMoxie Company and a professional motivator. She is the praise-winning author of *LifeMoxie! Ambition on a Mission*™*—9 Strategies for Taking Life by the Horns* and the forthcoming book, *The Moxie Mindset*™, as well as a featured author in *Best of the Best*.

As a professional motivator, Ann teaches people how to use moxie to self-motivate in order to triumph at work and in their life. She equips people with the skills and strategies they need to create relentless, uncompromised attitudes, behaviors, and actions, resulting in people exceeding their potential. Her motivational keynotes have inspired audiences of all sizes, ages, and professions to discover their own inner strength and then act on it.

Ann's unique approach has helped thousands discover the difference between ordinary and extraordinary.

Ann, welcome to Discover Your Inner Strength.

I am eager to learn about moxie! I'm sure you've heard many definitions for the word, but how do *you* define moxie?

TARDY

Moxie is my favorite word! It is composed of so many different elements that it requires many words to explain what it means. The dictionary describes *moxie* as courage, nerve, vigor, verve, pep, skill, know-how, and initiative.

But I say it's even more than this. It's the determination required to not settle for mediocrity, the guts to risk failure or embarrassment, the perseverance to move forward on your goals in spite of setbacks and failures, and the chutzpah that makes others say, *"Who do you think you are?"* When people take action based upon their commitment to achieve something, they discover that they care more about that commitment than they do about what other people think of them. That's moxie.

Some people suggest that moxie is being free of failure, but it's the failure that defines moxie. People who move forward in the face of their circumstances—failures, mistakes, obstacles, setbacks—have moxie. Most people use excuses for why they didn't follow through on a commitment or fell short of their goal. It is much easier to provide an excuse than to pick yourself up and move forward.

In psychology there is a fun word for this: "confabulation." Simply put, confabulation is making up reasons for why something happened or didn't happen. It rears its ugly head when we are trying to reduce cognitive dissonance. Cognitive dissonance occurs whenever we make a commitment but don't follow through. Cognitive dissonance is just brain conflict. Our brain (the cognitive part) is in conflict (the dissonance part). It tells us that we are smart, successful and accomplished. When we fail at something or make a mistake, our brain is in conflict because that failure or mistake does not fit with who our brain tells us we are—smart, successful and accomplished.

When brain conflict occurs, our heads hurt, and the "aspirin" we apply is called "excuses." The excuses we confabulate relieve the brain conflict. We tell ourselves that we would have been successful but because of X, Y, or Z, we could not succeed, and therefore, because it's not our fault, we are still smart, successful, and accomplished. This self-victimization is a disservice to our personal and professional growth. If we did nothing else but recognize when we engage in it, we would discover many opportunities to learn about ourselves. Instead, we relieve the brain conflict and miss the opportunity to grow.

Other people suggest that moxie is being fearless, but it's the presence of fear that summons moxie. It is acting in the face of that fear that creates moxie. Moxie is all about action. It's not about positive thinking or the law of attraction. It's about taking action.

There are three components to every act of moxie: a passionate commitment, an out-of-the-box attitude, and persistent actions. A passionate commitment occurs whenever you are so passionate about something that you're ready to make a commitment to it. I'm very passionate about dark chocolate and red wine, but I don't have any commitment to them. On the other hand, I'm very passionate about being the best motivational keynote speaker my clients have ever hired, and I'm so passionate about it that I continue to make commitments around this passion.

An out-of-the-box attitude occurs when you approach a challenge with the attitude of *"Why not?"* when most people think *"Why?"* Most people will create reasons for why something can't be done. The glass is half-full is an example of this out-of-the-box attitude.

Babe Ruth's success is attributable to his out-of-the-box attitude. In one history-making game, Babe Ruth was playing for the Yankees during a World Series game against Chicago when he was up at bat after already hitting a home run. With the score tied and the count at two balls and two strikes, Babe Ruth took a dramatic pause. He walked around home plate, kicked the dirt, and pounded his bat on home plate. He then pointed his bat to the centerfield bleachers indicating where he was going to hit the next pitch. This infuriated the pitcher, inciting him to throw the ball with all the speed, power, and sizzle he could muster. Babe Ruth swung and hit the ball in a line shot right into the centerfield bleachers—exactly where he had pointed. A sports writer later asked Babe Ruth about his bold move at home plate—what if Babe Ruth had not hit the ball to the spot where he had pointed? The great batter responded, "I never thought of that." That's an out-of-the-box attitude.

Persistent action is taking action again and again and again. It's not giving up after one "No" and declaring the goal unachievable. When you apply for a job, you submit your resume or complete an application. If one employer says "No," you don't throw up your hands and say, "Well, I guess work is not for me!" Instead, you send out more resumes, complete more applications, and apply for more jobs. That's persistent action.

When you combine these three elements, you are using your moxie and you may not even realize it. Ultimately, these essential components define the line between ordinary and extraordinary.

WRIGHT

Do you think moxie is more based on nature or nurture? In other words, are people born with moxie?

TARDY

People are not born with moxie. People create moxie, just like they create health or happiness. We take actions to become healthy and happy; similarly, we take actions to create moxie. And just like we're never done creating health or happiness, we're never done creating moxie—we're always working on it.

Most people are busy making excuses for why they didn't accomplish something, and they inevitably include an excuse as to why some people are so successful—they must have been born with that courage, chutzpah, determination, passion, and vigor. It is easier for most people to chalk it up to successful people being born with it than to admit that these extraordinary people just work harder and are more committed to their goals than ordinary people are.

If you stop to think about it, there was a day that Paul McCartney did not know how to play a guitar. He picked up his first guitar and had a first lesson just like every other guitar player. There was a day when author Hans Christian Anderson's fairy tales were not immediately recognized and as a result sold poorly. And there was a day when Mark Twain began his lifetime writing career authoring articles for local newspapers. Even Katherine Hepburn started her Oscar-winning journey by acting in school plays at Bryn Mawr College. Jack Welch started at GE as a junior engineer making an annual salary of $10,500. Former President of Ireland Mary Robinson (1990–1997) was the first woman president of Ireland and began her political career by first serving on the Dublin City Council. And German-U.S.

psychiatrist, author, and lecturer, Ruth Westheimer began her career as the notorious "Dr. Ruth" as a guest on a New York City radio program, from which the producer gave her a thirty-minute show on Sunday nights to answer listeners' questions about sex. These successful people generated their own moxie with their actions – they were not born with it.

This is great news for us! That means we all have a shot at creating the one factor that differentiates the ordinary from the extraordinary, the average from the outstanding, and the mediocre from the magnificent—moxie.

WRIGHT

You espouse nine moxie strategies for taking life by the horns. What are these moxie strategies and how do they work?

TARDY

I developed nine strategies to help people with the "how" behind moxie. Many personal performance gurus like to tell people what they need to do to succeed, but not the *how*. The nine strategies are the how to create moxie. Consider them the blueprint for taking the three components—passionate commitment, out-of-the-box attitude, and persistent actions—and grounding them into the reality of our lives.

The nine strategies are as follows:

Strategy Number 1: Beat the Alarm Clock. Before your head hits the pillow, create some reason to get out of bed early—your beat-the-alarm goals for the next day, week, month, and year. Get excited about something in your life, even if you have to make it up.

Strategy Number 2: Celebrate Your Wins. Take an accomplishments inventory of your past successes. Focus on all the times when you've won before so your brain will work with you to win again.

Strategy Number 3: Choose Your Channel. Surround yourself with Yaysayers—people who will say "yes!" to you, your goals, and your dreams. Just like you change the channel on your television when the programming is distasteful, change the channel on the Naysayers, and stop listening to their distaste.

Strategy Number 4: Say Yes First, Figure Out the How Later. Stop trying to figure everything out. Jump first and you'll force yourself to come up with a plan on the way down.

Strategy Number 5: Act As If. Act as if you are the perfect person to take on whatever challenge your beat-the-alarm goal presents. This will force you to manufacture the confidence you need to step forward. Soon you will start to feel as confident as you act.

Strategy Number 6: Respond, Don't Just React. This is the bounce-back rule. When something in your life or work does not go as planned, stop and learn a lesson first, and then respond accordingly, instead of make excuses.

Strategy Number 7: Ask. Start asking for what you need to move you closer to your beat-the-alarm goal. Care more about your goals than you do about what other people think of your asking.

Strategy Number 8: Be Uncomfortable. Nothing great ever happens in the comfort zone. If you're ready to pursue your beat-the-alarm goal, get ready to be uncomfortable!

Strategy Number 9: Keep Moving. This is the Forrest Gump rule. Just keep running. Without movement, there is no moxie. Take the mountain of your goal, break it into a bunch of small molehills, and start hopping over them. A law of physics says that it takes force to put a body in motion, but once a body is in motion, it stays in motion. Essentially, your life in motion stays in motion.

WRIGHT

You talk about a moxie moment. What is this?

TARDY

A moxie moment occurs when you create moxie in the moment. For example, it's the moment you raise your hand in a crowded auditorium to make a comment about a passionate topic of yours, and you have never done this before in your whole life. Your heart is pounding through your chest, but you do it anyway without worrying about what other people think of you. That's a moxie moment.

Creating moxie moments is the best way to begin creating moxie because after the moment, we realize that we did it, we didn't melt, and regardless of the outcome, we moved something forward. It's the moment you ask for the job or the business. It's the moment you express a dissenting opinion in the face of rejection. It's the moment you get down on one knee and ask your future spouse to marry you. It's the moment you talk to a stranger or decide to travel by yourself. It's the moment you take any action that is atypical—out of the ordinary—for you.

We usually create moxie moments when we are so focused on our goal and passionate commitment that we lose sight of the risks. It's at those times when we are caught up in the moment and we ignore our fears altogether. Psychologist Mihaly Csikszentmihalyi identified this state as "the flow." When you're in the flow, you naturally create moxie moments.

Moxie is defined by you—it's not defined in relevance to anyone else. For example, you may be scared to death to manage a group of people, whereas your boss manages people on a daily basis. A moxie moment for you may be saying "Yes!" to a new project that requires you to lead a team of people, while the same "Yes" would not be a moxie moment for your boss.

The moxie moment was beautifully illustrated by Sue, a wife and mother of three who grew up in South Africa with dreams of moving her family to America. At the age of forty-three, Sue's chances of moving were growing slim when she underwent surgery to have a tumor removed from her brain while her husband recovered from skin cancer. On top of which, the country's browbeaten real estate market was making it nearly impossible for them to sell their house for the money they needed for the big move. Then one day a man came to the school where Sue worked and inquired about enrolling his children in the school. He didn't live in the area and was looking for a home. In a moxie moment, Sue drove this man to her house and sold it to him. In spite of her circumstances, Sue moved forward in the direction of her beat-the-alarm goals.

WRIGHT

Can you give us a few more examples of people who exhibit moxie?

TARDY

Wildly famous people are fascinating to study when we talk about moxie because it's their moxie that made them, and keeps them, so successful. They exude so much moxie every day that they wouldn't recognize life without it. They have turned up the volume on their life extra loud. They are creating moxie on a regular basis, as opposed to only once in a while, and they are often very controversial characters. Why? Because they care more about their passionate commitments than they do about what you think of them. As a result, they have a tendency to ruffle a few feathers along the way.

An example of people who exhibit moxie is the Clintons. Regardless of your political views, Bill and Hillary Clinton demonstrate unfailingly their unwavering passions and their commitment to those passions. Neither of them is failure-free, and in the face of mistakes, judgments, obstacles, setbacks, and harsh, personal attacks and criticisms, they are undeterred. They both keep moving forward in pursuit of their passionate commitments.

Another example is Carly Fiorina, former CEO of Hewlett-Packard Company. In her commitment to save HP during the burst of the dotcom bubble in Silicon Valley, Carly proposed and fought for merging HP and archrival, Compaq. Amid a public clash with board members and the families of HP's founders, the merger was successful. Carly then shouldered the blame for the company's struggling stock price in the following years and was eventually fired. In the face of controversy, criticism, and angry shareholders, Carly continued to move forward in her determination to save HP.

WRIGHT

What would you say is the biggest advantage of using moxie to create personal and professional success? In other words, why is having moxie important to one's everyday work and career?

TARDY

The business world reeks of ordinary people armed with a slew of excuses. According to a Gallup poll, a staggering 76 percent of employees in corporate America are not engaged in their jobs. And when you're not engaged in your job, you will sling an excuse before making an effort. You will likely tell a sob story about how you are stuck or in a rut. Stuck is just a mindset. Consider moxie the anti-rut and the cure for being stuck. When you approach your work with moxie, there isn't room for any excuses or stories about being in a rut. Creating moxie demands that you take action again and again and again; when you're so busy taking persistent actions, there is no room for being stuck.

So while everyone is making excuses, you're making motion. This alone will set you apart from everyone else. And your personal and professional success requires that you set yourself apart from all of the ordinary and average walking zombies in corporate America.

In addition, all of this motion will drive you in the direction of success, even if you meet some failure and obstacles along the way. Those failures and obstacles will help you uncover your path to success.

Moxie is the difference between mediocrity and magnificence, and since the world is overflowing with complacency and mediocrity, it is starved for magnificence. The guaranteed route to magnificence? Moxie.

WRIGHT

How can you use moxie to impact your work, life, and relationships?

TARDY

Moxie prevents self-sabotage. We are the sole reason for our success or failure, but too often we are so busy being stuck that we don't realize the role we play in feeling stuck. The magic of moxie is that you can't create moxie and feel stuck at the same time. So while you're busy creating moxie, it's busy creating you. When you intentionally work to identify and pursue your passionate commitments, cultivate an out-of-the-box attitude, take persistent actions, and employ the nine strategies, you will notice inevitably that it feels like someone has turned up the volume on your life. Suddenly, whatever hesitations, concerns, or fears you once focused on will be overshadowed and drowned out by the loudness of your moxie. And when you start creating moxie in one area of your life, it will naturally flow over into all areas of your life.

WRIGHT

How does someone use moxie to make changes in their life?

TARDY

It takes an aircraft carrier twenty-two miles to turn around. I always ask our clients how many miles they need to turn around their lives, their team, or a situation.

Change requires resilience—spirit, hardiness, and toughness—the essence of moxie. And ultimately, any successful change in our professional and personal lives demands passion, perseverance, and an out-of-the-box attitude—the key components of moxie. When we apply the nine strategies for creating moxie to our goal called "make a change," we force ourselves to stop resisting the change and instead, to embrace it with determination, vigor, and excitement. No one likes to change, no matter how bad the current situation is; we usually find a way to justify not changing because of our fear of the unknown. When we approach the change with moxie, we take it on like an adventure. Consequently, we are able to turn around faster than an aircraft carrier.

WRIGHT

If moxie is something that differentiates all triumphant, extraordinary people from the ordinary, then why don't more people work on creating their own moxie?

TARDY

The challenge, David, is that we are human, and as such, we face a huge obstacle in trying to take on our professional and personal lives—our brain. We are in constant struggle with the games that our brain plays on us. In fact, we are run by these games and they start and end with our thoughts. Thoughts have so much control over us that they actually impact our mood, our actions, even our physical energy.

Psychologist Albert Bandura concluded from his research that when we think of a time when we have been successful, neurons in our brain are triggered to remember other times when we have succeeded. Similarly, if we ruminate over a recent failure, then the neurons in our brain conjure up all the other times we have failed, and soon we are in a downward spiral, unable to remember a single time when we succeeded. This mind game is a recipe for disaster.

In addition to this potential downward spiral, our thoughts are also responsible for the dissonance reduction that I mentioned earlier that is working so hard to relieve our brain conflict.

And finally, our thoughts are even responsible for triggering our fears as well as triggering the automatic reactions to such fears—fight, flight, or freeze.

So mastering your thoughts seems to be key, but it begs the question, how do you master your thoughts? Through actions—passionate, committed, persistent, conscious actions.

WRIGHT

Would you say that when someone creates moxie, and continues to create it, then does the moxie bring the success or does the success bring the moxie?

TARDY

A little of both. Undoubtedly, we need moxie to create success, but then the success tastes great and that gives us the confidence and strength to repeat the actions that just produced the success, that is, create more moxie.

WRIGHT

What drives you to live your life with moxie?

TARDY

I've tried it both ways and I always have a lot more fun with moxie. I'm far more successful when I'm creating moxie because I'm in action and moving forward. With each little success, I feel stronger too. I also notice that when I'm feeling stuck, it just takes creating a moxie moment to get myself unstuck.

When I first met my husband, I was in a rut, commuting two to three hours a day to a job that hated me. I felt stuck. As the dating ritual requires, I shared with him stories from my life, and each time I replayed for him one of my gutsy moves, I became re-energized from my own life! Born and raised in New York City, he declared, "Wow. You've got moxie!" and I remember thinking, "What's that?" I immediately ran home and researched the word "moxie." I saw the words: courage, vigor, and guts, and thought, "I want more of *that* in my life!"

Cognizant today of what it takes to create moxie, I intentionally set really big, juicy, drive-me-out-of-bed-early goals, and as a result, I fall in love with my life on a regular basis. I have more energy, more experiences, and far more fun than I ever did before.

I was never a morning person. I used to hate getting up early. I had no reason to get up. My mom will tell you what a struggle it was for seventeen years to drag me out of bed for school each morning. This reluctance to wake up continued throughout college and law school and into my first job. The times I did jump out of bed with excitement were few and far between. When I reflect on those times, I now see that they were moxie moments that gave me those spurts of energy. Now I wake up early every morning with a renewed excitement about taking on my day. This is a result of creating moxie.

WRIGHT

How did you conclude that moxie is your passion?

TARDY

I am passionate about moxie because it is grounded in behavioral motivation— an understanding of human behavior combined with the motivation to use that understanding and take action.

When I became excited about speaking in public, I said, in a moxie moment, "Yes!" to delivering a motivational speech to a room filled with unemployed individuals. In preparing for that speaking invitation, I was committed to bringing these people more than just a rah-rah. I was committed to educating them about themselves. I outlined nine strategies that I thought might reignite the fire while giving them the tools they needed to take action. I then incorporated my personal stories based on these strategies.

This group of downtrodden men and women were suddenly lit up, excited, and primed to take the next step in their journey. Many attendees came running up afterward to share with me their forgotten experiences, which were clearly their moxie in action! They had forgotten that they had tasted moxie once and loved who they were in their memories. Other people called and e-mailed me for weeks afterward with their stories of how they had put moxie into their lives and made major shifts in their lives. How could I not be passionate about moxie when it is clearly the differentiating factor between settling for mediocrity and craving magnificence for all these people?

WRIGHT

So, what makes your perspective unique?

TARDY

It is impossible to be successful without moxie. Moxie is the one ingredient that can be identified in every successful person, regardless of his or her story, struggle, race, or gender. If people are successful, they used moxie to succeed. They may not have known it at the time or may not have been intentionally creating their moxie, but they used moxie.

Success is not dependent on any other quality, idea, habit, or mindset. Other qualities and ideas certainly contribute to people's success in different ways, but success is not dependent on any one of these in particular. All successful people use different qualities and ideas in various ways to create their own success. But no one has ever been successful without moxie. Success is dependent on the moxie formula.

Other perspectives on success and inner strength provide suggestions for how to become successful, but those suggestions will not guarantee your success. Moxie guarantees your success.

WRIGHT

What about luck or fate? Isn't there some element of luck or fate in people's success?

TARDY

Not at all. In fact, luck and fate supply the foundation for excuses. Isn't it easier to say, "I didn't succeed because it wasn't meant to be," or, "If I had had better luck, I would have gotten the job"? Instead of using moxie to push through any obstacles, failures, or setbacks, people toss up their hands and blame it on their bad luck or fate. They let themselves off the hook.

Just as it has no tolerance for excuses and victims, moxie has no tolerance for luck or fate. Moxie demands that you take 100 percent accountability for your actions, regardless of the outcome. If the outcome isn't what you wanted, Moxie Strategy Number 6 requires that you pick yourself up and respond.

My husband always laughs because I say "Good moxie" instead of "Good luck." He'll say, "Wish me luck!" And I'll say, "There is no such thing as luck. You just need to use your moxie. Good moxie, Sweetie!"

There is no luck or fate in moxie. Sometimes people like to point to a successful person and say that he or she must be lucky to be so successful, which is just an excuse as to why the successful people made it and the ordinary people didn't. Ordinary people don't acknowledge that extraordinary people worked hard, used their moxie, and earned their success. They chalk it up to luck or fate.

When I say that there is no such thing as luck or fate, then I force myself to keep all of the control over my life. My choices become mine. I don't sit back like a sufferer and wait to see what luck and fate will deliver. I take action and am responsible for creating the journey I want.

WRIGHT

Who are the people who have served as your role models for moxie?

TARDY

My mom is the person who first introduced me to what living a life of moxie looks like long before I had any idea of its meaning or impact. My mom became a stay-at-home mom before she had a chance to attend college. For fifteen years she cooked and cleaned, raised three children, and fed the farm animals every morning and night, while my dad, the traveling salesman, supported the family financially. She had no money of her own, no job, and no means to support herself. My dad's ambitions became her ambitions. Along the way, I never heard my mom complain about her life or her situation. Instead, she taught us to take responsibility each day for our outlook, our choices, and our lives. She always had a solution for any obstacle. She never had a bad mood to share. Finally, after fifteen years of supporting everyone else's ambitions, my mom began supporting her own. She went to school, earned her Real Estate license, and launched her Real Estate business. Almost twenty-five years later, my mom makes her own money, pursues her own goals, and takes care of herself. That's moxie.

I'm confident my mom acquired her moxie mindset from my other model for moxie, her dad, my grandfather. As an alcoholic, Gramps (as we called him) had created a mess of his life. He spent years drinking any money he made at his job while my grandmother, a Ma Bell operator, raised four children essentially by herself. Gramps took on his life when his first grandchild was born. He joined

Alcoholics Anonymous and became sober. After retirement, he went back to school, earned a degree in counseling, and became a counselor for others dealing with alcoholism. He began cycling and, at the age of seventy, completed a hundred-mile bike ride—a beat-the-alarm goal for him. He volunteered as a crossing guard at a local school to help children get to and from school safely. With his long white beard, thick white hair, big nose, big belly, and hearty laugh, he also volunteered as Santa Claus during each Christmas holiday. By the time he passed away, he was thirty-eight years sober, happily married to my grandmother, had enjoyed five doting grandchildren, created a lifetime of experiences, and left a town full of adoring fans. That's moxie.

Finally, Madonna is my third favorite model for moxie. Madonna was working on her passions in high school long before American Band Stand discovered her. She pursued her passions in college and dance school, moved to New York City to dance and sing, and became a star with her first big and somewhat controversial album in the early '80s. Since then, Madonna has reinvented herself over and over in the pursuit of her passionate commitments. Along the way, she has lost a few fans, but she never seems to care what people think of her. That's moxie.

CHAPTER Sixteen

Step Into Your Greatness with Passion & Perseverance

AN INTERVIEW WITH...

Joy Klepac

916.746.7878
joyklepac@surewest.net
www.joyklepac.com
www.klepaccoaching.com
www.freeprospectingreport.com
www.squidoo.com/joyklepaccoaching
www.saleschampioncoaching.com

ABOUT THE AUTHOR

Joy Klepac specializes in working with entrepreneurs and sales professionals. Joy speaks to them on many different topics to motivate them to achieve their desired lifestyle. She brings a wealth of knowledge and life experience to her clients. She has had twenty-four years of experience in the sales industry, starting her own company in 1992

Joy is a speaker, a coach, and a successful author. One of the books she has written is called "The Diamond Mind"—Transforming Your Dreams into Lifelong Success.

Joy has spoken to women's groups, motivating them on passion and perseverance. Joy's purpose in life is to encourage and positively influence her clients to better their life and their business.

Joy is a coach with Eric Lofholm International, Inc. an international sales training company.

DAVID WRIGHT (WRIGHT)

Today we're talking with Joy Klepac. Joy specializes in working with entrepreneurs and sales professionals. Joy speaks to them on many different topics to motivate them to achieve their desired lifestyle. She brings a wealth of knowledge and life experience to her clients. She has had twenty-four years of experience in the sales industry, starting her own company in 1992

Joy is a speaker, a coach, and a successful author. One of the books she has written is called *"The Diamond Mind"—Transforming Your Dreams into Lifelong Success.*

Joy has spoken to women's groups, motivating them on passion and perseverance. Joy's purpose in life is to encourage and positively influence her clients to better their life and their business.

Joy, welcome to *Discover Your Inner Strength.*

JOY KLEPAC

Thank you, David. I am honored to speak with you and share with your readers.

WRIGHT

How did you discover your inner strength?

KLEPAC

I suppose I would have to attribute that to times of adversity. I believe you can use those experiences to make you or break you. I think we all have trials to go through and some of us will choose to become angry, bitter, or depressed. I decided long ago that I wanted to have meaning for all the challenges life would bring. I could not believe that challenges, problems, trials, or whatever you call them are meaningless. I had to believe the emotional or physical pain was meant for something. I believe you can use them to grow or choose to allow your spirit to die inside of you.

With those two choices, I decided I wanted to be an optimist. I wanted to find the good in each situation. I wanted to see the glass half full instead of half empty. I have encountered many life experiences that can cause any person to pick which road he or she will choose. At each moment, I would do soul-searching.

This process wasn't always easy. Because I am just like everyone else, my human emotions would get the best of me and I could see myself getting angry or fearful. I don't like those feelings and it is very stressful to carry those emotions. So at those moments I needed to decide will I let this get me down or will I overcome this challenge? We all are faced with these situations. I discovered I wanted to be a person people are attracted to. I want to be engaging and fun to talk with.

I wanted to be an inspiration to others. So I believed that in order to become that person, I needed to pull myself out of the mindset of a pity party or depression. I needed to find the good in each situation. This would allow me to recognize the purpose of my life's challenges.

I guess you could equate it to great athletes. They practice and practice until they are great at their sport. They get better and better over time, but not without pain. Perhaps they have setbacks and hurdles to overcome. But they don't stop improving their game.

I believe we all have that choice. I am choosing to continue to "turn my lemons into lemonade," as they say.

One day I learned about the process of how a diamond becomes a diamond. A lump of coal is put under tremendous pressure and becomes a diamond. This crystallization process requires tremendous heat and pressure. Diamonds are so strong they cut glass, yet they can be beautiful, delicate, and one of our precious wonders. I thought this is a great way to look at our life's journey. Then it came to me, I have those rare gems awaiting me!

I used to tell my daughter about the diamond process when she was going through a trying time. This crystallization process requires tremendous heat and pressure (one thousand to twelve hundred 1000 degrees centigrade or eighteen hundred to twenty-two hundred degrees Fahrenheit and fifty kilo bars of pressure). I would tell her that even though the stress or problem seems like too much, it was a process to make her a beautiful diamond. In other words, she knew I meant that all these experiences, if she allowed them to, would transform her in to a beautiful person.

We can choose to use allow our tough times to mold us in two different ways—we can either learn from them or become bitter by them. I choose to learn from them.

I have written another inspirational book titled *"The Diamond Mind"—Transforming Your Dreams into Lifelong Success.* I hope the books I write will be thought provoking and maybe encourage readers to expand their opportunities and discover some talents that they have. They can find all my books on my Web site www.klepaccoaching.com.

WRIGHT

What caused you to tap in to your inner strength?

KLEPAC

It is interesting that I have been able to tap in to my inner strength due to my childhood experiences. I was born the baby of the family and also a twin. I can remember always feeling like the baby. Many times I felt I was struggling to be heard. Maybe all last-born kids feel this way. I guess it made me try harder to be me. I wanted people to know who I was, especially being a twin. We would hear at school "Oh, you are one of the twins." I wanted to scream, *"No! I am Joy! Not one half of a pair! I am me!"*

All in all, it probably made me stronger as it pushed me to be separate and find my own friends, take separate classes, and develop separate relationships other than my twin. My mom always encouraged us to have our own independence. I appreciate that she wanted us to have the best of both worlds. We had each other and we had our own friends.

One of the challenges I experienced growing up was that my father was quite strict. He also was not one to give out compliments. He was quick to point out things I did wrong, which was not helpful to my self-esteem. I grew up following the rules and was careful what I said or did. I grew up with believing I was just normal. I had to follow the rules. I would always have to listen to people in authority and not challenge them with my position. I did not know at that time how this would suppress my ability to be all I could be.

That is when I decided that I wanted to be more. I did not want to be just normal. With some positive self-improvement in the years to follow, it would help me transform into who I am today.

I believe your inner strength is both a mental and an emotional decision. It is not just enough to emotionally want something, it also requires a mindset of belief. I believe that with the mindset, passion, and perseverance, you can accomplish all you want to become. Those are components of your inner strength. We all have characteristics inside of us, we just need to choose to use them. Along with that for me, I have a strong faith in God and I use prayer and faith to give me the courage to change the outcomes of my life.

Sometimes we don't realize that there are others people in our life who can be truly inspirations to us. Encouragement and inspiration can come from anybody.

WRIGHT

Why is telling the readers about discovering your inner strength important to you?

KLEPAC

I have a few pieces of my personality that I believe were God-given talents. I love to give and I love to encourage people.

Sharing my thoughts through this book is my way of encouraging the readers to go for it, whatever "it" is to them. I believe we have too many people who will unknowingly hold us back.

Our friends and loved ones want what is best for us but some of them don't have the ability to dream and encourage us to greatness. I had those in my life too. While they were all well-intentioned caring people, I called them my "dream-stealers." I often had people who would tell me why I could not achieve something. I know they meant well and loved me, but they were holding me back and not allowing me to unleash the inner strength within me.

At times I would meet people who had great success stories. By "success" I mean a great story about overcoming odds. For example, I have a friend, Janie, who was born in New York City to parents who were addicted to alcohol and drugs. All of her siblings were addicted to drugs like her parents. She grew up living in twenty-two different foster homes and had very little opportunity to pull herself out of that lifestyle. At fifteen she was adopted and within three years, her adoptive mother taught her how to be a successful woman. Janie found out what real love was from a parent. Because of her stepmother's faith in God and spiritual influence, Janie was taught how to love and be loved for the first time.

Janie then wanted to repay her mom for all she had done for her, but her mom just said to pay if forward. She told Janie to give to others as she had given to her. Due to Janie's perseverance, faith in God, and her inner strength, she is now the founder of a non-profit organization called Future Leaders Now. She helps kids who live in circumstances like hers was to stay off the streets and to learn a better way of life. Wow, this is just a miracle of the spirit and shows us how people can truly be anyone they want to be. You can find her at www.futureleadersnow.com. People like her inspire me. In turn, I hope my story will inspire many others out there.

I truly want all of the readers to believe in themselves and know that they have what it takes to passionately pursue whatever they want.

WRIGHT

What experiences has your inner strength brought to you?

KLEPAC

I remember one experience I had when I was young—about nineteen. I had one friend who said something surprising to me. He said, "Joy you are always so pessimistic." I was surprised by his statement because I had never seen myself that way. I think I had started to allow some of my experiences to create bitterness in me.

What I decided to do was make every effort to change those negative thoughts. I guess I would call it looking at the glass half full instead of half empty. We can all find things wrong with situations and I believe we can also find good in all situations. Some situations are harder than others; but it became my mission to learn from all experiences and look for the good. I took this philosophy and used it as I pursued my growth as an adult.

Another experience have been through is a divorce. I spent twelve years being a single mom. I spent many years with a verbally abusive man, which continued to destroy my self-esteem. Once we split up, I was faced with being a sole provider of this beautiful little angel God had given me. I was born to be a mom and wanted to be the best ever.

Being a single parent challenges every part of who you are. A single parent is forced to be two parents in one, to be the provider, be nurturing when needed, fun when needed, a disciplinarian when needed—everything wrapped up in one person. When this happened, I knew that to be true to who I was and be the best Mom I could be, I needed more strength. I would, of course, turn to God and pray but I also needed to step up and make it happen. I couldn't depend on anyone except me. I prioritized each and every day the best way I could and used my time wisely to create a better situation for our future. This was exactly one of those times where I could either feel sorry for myself and become bitter or turn it around to use my inner strength and my faith to make things better.

When my daughter was eight years old, she knew I was struggling to build my business to support a new lifestyle that allowed me the flexibility to be home when she was not in school. She wanted me to be home with her more and she would keep telling me I could do it. What a wonderful gift—childlike faith. She knew nothing of the financial worries, business challenges, or lack of self-esteem, she just wanted the lifestyle I was creating and having more of my time. That was enough to keep me on track to achieve my goal.

I will never forget the time when my sweet angel came to me one day when I was feeling down. I was just not good at the "stay strong for your kids" game that day. I was depressed and very worried. My daughter, in her wisdom of only eight, knew exactly what I needed to hear. She said, "Mommy, I have something I want you to hear." She took me to her room and put on a new song that she loved by Mariah Carey. The song was called "Hero." She played it and when the song came to the part where it says, ". . . and then a hero comes along with the strength to carry on, when you feel like hope is gone, look inside you and be strong, you will finally see the truth that a hero lies in you." My daughter was singing it to me. She then pointed to me and said, "Mommy, you're my hero." What a precious gift God had given me—this little angel telling me I am her hero when I felt like I was falling apart.

This became "our song" because she was my hero for keeping me going when times were so hard. She was my hero and still is. I can't hear that song without floods of tears streaming down my face. Probably because she was so strong for me then and it really helped me keep going. I will always cherish these times.

Since then I don't sit and wait for life to happen. I take steps to create my destiny. I do have things that I cannot control, just like everyone else, however, I have decided to take those areas of my life that I want to change, and change them. I remember all those people who supported me and continued to tap into my inner strength to push to make the changes I wanted to make.

WRIGHT

How are things different for you now than they were before you discovered your inner strength?

KLEPAC

I choose to be careful about decisions that discount what I want or need and I don't mean in a selfish way. Let me explain. I am more likely to find solutions to a situation in the best win-win scenario I can. I believe that if you help enough people get what they want you will get what you want. With that said, we can't always deny what we need or want.

Often, if there is something I would like to achieve, I make a plan. I decide how much of a priority it is to me first. Then I either sacrifice in another area or I work with others to communicate what I would like to have happen. I then see if we can create a win-win. For example, participating in this book was very important to me. However, I am extremely busy at my business. I had to choose to either pay someone to take some things off my desk or I would have to work on the weekends or perhaps both. I decided that this was important to me and I would sacrifice some of my weekend time to write this chapter.

My inner strength allows me to believe in me and gives me the desire to accomplish those things that I find important in my life.

Before tapping into my inner strength, I did not believe in myself. I had to go through a personal growth process to move me from where I was. There are several success principles I learned along the way. Only those who risk going too far can know how far they can go. Many times before, I would stop myself from dreaming because I had limiting beliefs. Many people struggle with this, which is why I am excited about sharing how I got where I am today. I know now that if I can, all people can discover their inner strength and achieve what they truly want in their life.

WRIGHT

How did you come to be an author and motivational speaker?

KLEPAC

I grew up very poor and as a single mom; I could barely rub two nickels together. When I was thirty-five I was tired of struggling and decided to start a business. I realized then that there were so many beliefs in my head I had to fight. For example, when I was growing up my parents were good parents but very poor. I would hear them say things like, "Money doesn't grow on trees" or "We can't afford that." These statements, while true, were teaching me to limit my potential. I was taught that you grow up and got a job. I never had encouragement that I could break out of the typical mold of just working a job.

As I started my business I knew I needed to change my mindset and change what I was taught as a child. My parents did the best they could do but I wanted to believe I could achieve my dreams instead of always denying what I had hoped for. I decided to surround myself with other business owners and people who shared those kinds of visions. That was one of the best things I have ever done to move me from a mindset of feeling that I am not special and I cannot be different.

Over the last sixteen years I have been an entrepreneur and now I own and operate several businesses. Along with this professional experience I have continued educating myself for constant self-improvement.

I am now on the other side and living what most people would call a desired lifestyle. I live in a very nice house in California, I drive a very nice new luxury car, I have a husband most people would dream about, a great family, and my income is in the six-figure range. I only say these things with the hope that I can encourage readers. Because of the road I travelled to where I am now, I can relate to where most people are or have been. One thing I never forget is that people don't care about how much you know until they know how much you care. I truly care about the people I speak to.

I believe everyone has a special purpose. We all have special gifts. I have found through my experience that people are drawn to me. I have a gift of making people feel better and helping them look at things from a different perspective. Because of the path I have been on, I believe that being a motivational speaker is my purpose in life. I was born to share, encourage, and motivate people to reach their full potential. If I can achieve what I have achieved, so can any of my readers—they just need to believe it.

I love speaking to audiences to inspire them to dream and believe. I know that most people are fighting the same mindset I had to fight and I love being able to move people to step in to their greatness. When we know better we do better.

Writing my books has been one of those desires I put off for so many years because I just could not find the time. I now believe there was a reason and now is the time for my voice to be heard through speaking and my books. It is my greatest desire to touch people in a way that changes their life for the better. I want to leave this Earth knowing I made a difference in the people I touched while I was here. I am blessed to be able to have this gift and share it with others.

WRIGHT

Have you read any books that have helped you to be where you are today?

KLEPAC

Oh, yes. Here is a list of some of those books:

1. *One Minute Millionaire* by Mark Victor Hansen and Robert G. Allen
2. *The Automatic Millionaire* by David Bach
3. *Value Based Selling* by Bill Bachrach
4. *The 7 Habits of Highly Effective People* by Stephen R. Covey
5. *One Minute Manger* by Ken Blanchard
6. *The E Myth* by Michael Gerber
7. *The Power of Positive Thinking* by Norman Vincent Peale
8. *Think and Grow Rich* by Napoleon Hill
9. *The Greatest Salesman in the World* by Og Mandino
10. *Rich Dad Poor Dad* by Robert Kiyosaki
11. *The Richest Man In Babylon* by George S. Clason
12. *Self Matters* by Dr. Phil McGraw
13. *The Proper Care and Feeding of Husbands* by Dr. Laura Schlessinger
14. *Rescued* by John Bevere
15. The Holy Bible by God

WRIGHT

Is there one mistake that you think keeps many of us from using our inner strength?

KLEPAC

Yes absolutely, I believe many people allow self-doubt to creep in and they don't believe in themselves. Therefore, they never get to tap in to their inner strength. Too many people don't recognize their individual specialness. Each person has special gifts and talents. We allow others to decide for us too often because we care about what they think, which is the biggest way we get our dreams stolen. We don't use our inner strength to persevere to greatness.

I believe that when we are faced with a decision, most of us will consult others. Usually we will talk to our friends and relatives. We want to get advice or perhaps some reassurance. This is a mistake because most people don't step outside of their comfort zone. So why are we soliciting advice from people who have never stepped out of that box or used their inner strength? They will most probably advise us against what we want to do because they themselves would not do it. As I mentioned earlier, have fondly referred to these people as dream-stealers. They mean well and the probably care, but most people are not comfortable with doing what is required to step outside of what they know and what is familiar.

Some would think it is crazy to create a situation and march into the unknown! What is truly the key to becoming an entrepreneur is going it alone and carving out your own path. This is one of the hardest things anyone can do. However, where there is risk there is reward and the rewards are great. You will gain so much from personal development, not to mention probably a greater lifestyle than you have ever had. Of course, if it was easy, everyone would do it and we wouldn't be here talking about it today. It is okay to be a bit frightened. Just don't let those who are in the box prevent you from stepping out of the box!

WRIGHT

What can someone do to overcome that?

KLEPAC

Many times I have counseled people who are down or don't see their special gifts. I tell them I wish they could see what I see. Many times we look in the mirror and we start judging ourselves about our physical appearance or external characteristics. Things like, I am too fat, I am too thin, my butt is too big, my hair is too flat, etc. Other times we judge ourselves and think things like, I don't make enough money or I have an old car. We attach our worth to physical or monetary things.

At the end of the day, our bodies will change, our financial situations will change, but who you are inside is where our focus should be. I am always encouraging people to see their internal characteristics. For example, they are kind, they are understanding, they care about others, they are funny, they are easy to be around, they don't judge others, and they are giving. I do believe beauty truly comes from within.

Many years ago, I did some soul-searching. I asked myself what I really wanted in life. Many of the things I wrote down were income goals because I wanted more for both my daughter and me. It wasn't really the income as much as what the money could buy. Creating this kind of list can be such a great way to grow into the person you want to be. It is a great way to encourage us all to strive for greatness. God has given us so many talents that they become gifts to others when we use them properly.

Many people are not able to look at themselves in this way. I have suggested to many people I have counseled to get a real good friend—someone who is their biggest fan. I asked them to have their friend make a written list of all the things they loved about them. And they should do the same for their friend. Trade lists. Your keep the list that your friend wrote about you and read it daily. This is a good way to give yourself positive self-talk. You read what they think of you often enough and eventually you will believe it. This little exercise is very helpful in overcoming self-doubt and helping you tap into your inner strength.

Another thing I did was to take a big piece of colored poster board. I looked through magazines and cut out pictures of things I wanted to achieve—a paradise in my backyard, a new car, more money, a new office, a happy family, a healthy family. Then I attached my words to what the pictures represented. I keep it in a place where I can look at it every day. Some of those things have been achieved and some have not. I will keep striving until my dream board is completed. If we stop dreaming, stop learning, and stop striving, we will stop hoping and start dying. I want to live each day to the fullest because it is a limited precious gift.

WRIGHT

Will you tell our readers what continues to drive your inner strength?

KLEPAC

My dream list or my "why" keeps on evolving. By this I mean that when I first started really tapping into my inner strength it was to make more money and to be a better mom. I wanted to provide a better environment for my daughter and myself. As time went on, I would add things to that list. I called that list "my why." Not all of the items on the list are monetary in nature, although money does open up other doors to achieve things on my list. For example, I wanted to start my own business when I was a single mom so I could have the freedom and time I needed to be the kind of mom I wanted to be. Even though I needed more money, it was the time and freedom that kept pushing me to use my inner strength and create that lifestyle. There are so many things I want for my family and me, and quality of life is at the top of the list.

I keep my written list on paper and on a dream board that includes pictures. This reminds me all the time about why I need to keep going and tap into my inner strength.

Here are several items from my "why" list. These are the reasons why I would work hard and stay on task:

- I want to have time and freedom with passive income for life.
- I want to make a difference if people's lives.
- I want to live as healthy as I can while I am here on this Earth.
- I want to eventually travel the world helping others and training others.
- I want to work a lot less but have more money.
- I don't ever want my daughter to worry about taking care of us financially.
- I don't ever want my daughter to worry about taking care of us as we get older and as our health declines.
- I want to really live each day.
- I don't want to "have" to work each day but "choose" to work the days I want.
- I want to be able to work anywhere I am—beach, mountains, vacation, etc.
- I want to always have enough savings for those emergency car repairs, etc.
- I want to take more vacations.
- I want to be able to have more time for my family.
- I want to work side by side with my husband.

Most people don't just happen to achieve their dreams—they achieve them through passion and perseverance with planning. Those who dream more, risk more, and do more will be successful. Being successful is not just dreaming about it. You must take risks, work hard, and work toward your dream. We get no more than we are willing to risk. Some people will make it happen. Some people will watch it happen and some people will wonder what happened. The reason most people don't go after their dreams is because it is really hard work and many people are not willing to sacrifice what is needed to obtain what they want. I decided long ago that I am a make-it-happen kind of gal. I want to achieve my dreams more than I like being in my comfort zone.

Those things on my list and on my dream board are the priorities in my life. I hope that as I continue to live this life, I positively affect the people I am fortunate to have in my life.